DIETRICH BONHOEFFER: PERSPECTIVES ON COSTLY LEADERSHIP

Dr. Jay Harley, Editor

PREFACE

Dr. Jay Harley

Dietrich Bonhoeffer is regularly mentioned by Christian leaders and American politicians as an example to follow. United States President George W. Bush invoked the memory of Dietrich Bonhoeffer on May 23, 2002, when he said in a speech in Berlin:

> One of the greatest Germans of the 20th century was Pastor Dietrich Bonhoeffer who left the security of America to stand against Nazi rule. In a dark hour, he gave witness to the Gospel of life, and paid the cost of his discipleship, being put to death only days before his camp was liberated.[1]

President Bush reflected upon the courageous leadership of this German academic theologian and received rousing applause from his German audience. Dietrich Bonhoeffer, again, at the forefront of political encouragement considered a prominent leader and influencer during Germany's darkest time.

President Bush's comments reflect a typical approach to Dietrich Bonhoeffer. Bonhoeffer's life, heroism, courage, and leadership are lauded while his academic work and theology remain relatively unknown. Even after reading the popular contemporary biographies on Bonhoeffer by Eric Metaxas and Charles Marsh, a reader would likely not get a full sense of Bonhoeffer's theological thought. Dietrich Bonhoeffer served as an unlikely hero during the reign of the Nazis and days of World War II, but a hero that has interested many. The goal of this work will continue in that vein of interest and give an overview of the leadership behaviors and characteristics of Dietrich Bonhoeffer. We should be encouraged by Bonhoeffer's leadership as his life and influence demonstrate that leaders are not always the most physically impressive or strongest, but influence can be wielded using the gifts and abilities one possesses. Bonhoeffer certainly influenced in unique ways and exhibited how Christian thought and speech combined with courageous action made this man a memorable figure in Germany during a very difficult time. While certainly involved in saving lives, he did not turn the tide of the Nazi regime or completely stop their vile actions. However, his legacy of leadership and influence through speech, writing, sermons, and courageous involvement encourages people years later.

This book developed over time due to this collection of authors' interests in leadership, along with the relevance, and popularity of Dietrich Bonhoeffer. While Bonhoeffer's leadership is commended as one who should be emulated, this work aims to explore his leadership behaviors and analyze how he influenced not only his contemporaries but also the enduring memory of his leadership actions. In 2014, I developed a travel study program that focused on Dietrich Bonhoeffer where students traveled to Europe to learn while seeing sites connected to World War II, the Nazi regime, and Dietrich Bonhoeffer. Students that participate in this program visit the Bonhoeffer family home in Berlin, reflect at the site of the illegal Confessing Church seminary at Finkenwalde in Poland, contemplate the terror of the places where he was imprisoned, and stand at the site of his execution. For university students, this in-person and hands-on interaction with Dietrich Bonhoeffer undoubtedly challenges their understanding of leadership and influence while providing a distinctive view of events surrounding the twelve years of the Nazi regime and World War II.

Dietrich Bonhoeffer's Theology

While this book is not a treatment of his theology and beliefs, we would remiss not to give a brief mention of this topic. It is important for anyone who studies Dietrich Bonhoeffer to always have in mind that he was a mid-twentieth-century German Lutheran. He was not a twenty-first-century American evangelical, and it is easy to paint him in this light and forget his upbringing and background. This book will discuss his family life along with how he was raised which impacted his development as a leader. We must resist the temptation to view Bonhoeffer as someone who is aligned with modern American evangelical thought and belief while appreciating him for who he was even at our points of disagreement. A study of Bonhoeffer by an American evangelical Christian should not diminish what can be gleaned from his academic theological writing and thought nor should we disregard his leadership actions.

Most American Christians who are familiar with Bonhoeffer's theological thought have read or discussed his most popular work, *The Cost of Discipleship.* This book has wide appeal as at its heart, Bonhoeffer challenges the reader to take Christ seriously and actively live what Christ has said specifically in the Sermon on the Mount from the Gospel of Matthew chapters 5-7. However, within *The Cost of Discipleship,* challenging parts exist where his understanding of doctrine should cause serious thought and contemplation before categorical acceptance.

Richard Weikart discussed his journey with Bonhoeffer. His introduction and involvement with Bonhoeffer followed a typical path, and he describes how this is similar for many evangelical Christians who encounter Bonhoeffer. His summary of this path of study is appropriate for one who is specifically studying Bonhoeffer's leadership behaviors and actions:

> First, most evangelicals read *The Cost of Discipleship* and maybe *Life Together,* works where Bonhoeffer's theological problems are not so obvious. Second, Bonhoeffer was a courageous individual who uniquely combined a powerful intellect with compassion for the disadvantaged. Third, most evangelicals do not understand Bonhoeffer's intellectual context. He was a sophisticated thinker completely conversant in—and heavily influenced by—Continental philosophy, including Kant, Hegel, Kierkegaard, Nietzsche, Heidegger, and others. Fourth, many evangelicals applaud Bonhoeffer for rejecting liberal theology, not realizing that the neo-orthodox theology he embraced is still far from evangelical theology. Even if it rejects nineteenth-century-style liberal theology, neo-orthodox theology is on the liberal side of the theological spectrum, since it rejects biblical inerrancy and other doctrines central to genuine Christianity.[2]

So, Bonhoeffer held some challenging theological beliefs and interpretations of Scripture which would be divergent from contemporary evangelical doctrine. It is helpful for readers and students to be aware of this and not assume him to be an American evangelical who just happened to be a German Lutheran.

Bonhoeffer's Prison Theology

A major area of Bonhoeffer's theological thought that is often discussed and critiqued is the time when he was imprisoned and wrote many letters on various subjects. Much of this correspondence can be read in *Letters and Papers From Prison* which was originally compiled by his close friend, Eberhard Bethge. In some of the letters, poems, and other writings while imprisoned by the Nazis, he explored a wide variety of theological, practical, and spiritual topics. A reader of these writings should be aware that when he authored these writings, he is disconnected from his family, colleagues, and friends and often is exploring ideas and subjects as though he is in conversation with the letter's recipients. Bonhoeffer thrived on academic discussion and debate and lacking this dynamic while in prison could result in correspondence to family and friends which explore topics that drift from orthodoxy almost as though he was discussing thoughts and ideas in a conversation. Since he could not have the conversation, he was forced to have discussion through written letters. It is also wise of us to recognize that we have not experienced Nazi imprisonment and eventual death like he did, and certainly, this fact impacted his thinking and writing.

Not all of Bonhoeffer's writings survived from the time of his death until the present day which also creates challenges to gaining a full understanding. In an excellent collection of essays on Bonhoeffer's theological thought entitled *Engaging Bonhoeffer: The Impact and Influence of Bonhoeffer's Life and Thought,* Kirkpatrick cautions the reader in regard to lost and missing aspects of Bonhoeffer's writing:

> Some of Bonhoeffer's work has been lost, left incomplete, or we only have it indirectly. In terms of Bonhoeffer's provocative prison theology, for instance, we know that a wide variety of letters have gone missing and that Bethge destroyed a whole batch before his arrest in October 1944 – letters which have were written during one of Bonhoeffer's perhaps most provocative and creative periods.[3]

Therefore, the case of missing writings is certainly an issue and must be recognized when exploring this period of his life and thought.

While the reader should be aware of Bonhoeffer's theological positions and differences from typical evangelical doctrine, he remains a fascinating thinker and theologian. Even in areas of disagreement he can be helpful to our learning and understanding. Bonhoeffer will challenge our thinking and stretch our minds, and while we may disagree, he will force us to think and consider things from different perspectives. His writings will likely benefit our theological thinking.

Additional Resources to Explore Bonhoeffer's Theology

For the reader who desires to explore Bonhoeffer's theological thought further, the following works are recommended among the many others cited and reference in this book:

Bonhoeffer's Seminary Vision: A Case for Costly Discipleship and Life Together by Paul R. House.

Bonhoeffer the Assassin? Challenging the Myth, Discovering His Call for Peacemaking.

The Bonhoeffer Reader edited by Clifford Green and Michael P. DeJonge.

Bonhoeffer, a Treasure

Complex and complicated theological thought combined with coura-geous leadership from this well-trained, brilliant academic produces an appealing character. His leadership, the focus of this book, is worthy of our time and study. He was certainly complex, he lived in a precarious time, he wrestled with the events of his day, and we can say more than seventy-five years later that he led well.

Endnotes

[1] Bush, George W. Speech in Berlin on May 23, 2002. Retrieved from: https://www.theguardian.com/world/2002/may/23/usa.georgebush.

[2] Weikart, R. "The Troubling Truth about Bonhoeffer's Theology." *Christian Research Journal*, 35(6), 2012.

[3] Kirkpatrick, 2016. *Engaging Bonhoeffer: The Impact and Influence of Bonhoeffer's Life and Thought*, xi.

TABLE OF CONTENTS

Chapter 1

INTRODUCTION: WHY DOES BONHOEFFER MATTER TODAY?

Dr. Jay Harley

Dietrich Bonhoeffer's courageous leadership caused him to become one of the most influential Christian thinkers and writers of the twentieth century. He is praised for his brave resistance to the Nazi government and held as an example for modern Christians and others who desire to see radical change. In the first two decades of the twenty-first century, interest in Dietrich Bonhoeffer increased dramatically with many American evangelical Christians and academic scholars taking a renewed interest in the life and writing of this German Lutheran theologian and pastor known for his different aspects of belief, depth, and nature within his involvement in the resistance against the Third Reich. In the introduction to one of the many printings of Bonhoeffer's *Cost of Discipleship,* Gerhard Leibholz provided an introductory biography of the life of Bonhoeffer and referenced the importance of Bonhoeffer's legacy: "Thus Bonhoeffer's life and death have given us great hope for the future. He has set a model for a new type of true leadership inspired by the gospel, daily ready for martyrdom and death, and imbued by a new spirit of Christian humanism and a creative sense of civic duty. The victory which he has won was a victory for us all, a conquest never to be undone, of love, light, and liberty."[1] Therefore, the purpose of this book will not be another biography, but an examination of his leadership behaviors. He was not the conventionally thought of World War II leader, because he was not a soldier, military leader, or politician.

Leadership should never be too narrowly defined to a specific set of behaviors and actions which disregard others' opportunity to lead and influence. Thus, a discussion of Bonhoeffer's leadership and actions that led to influence is important, as Bonhoeffer will show that leadership can occur and influence can be profound through actions such as speaking, writing, and teaching. Leadership during the time of World War II is not relegated to the soldiers and politicians, but through Bonhoeffer, evidence was shown that an academic pacifist could make an impact. Since Bonhoeffer was a skeptic of any leadership other than the leadership of Christ, this work will explore his rejection of leadership.[2]

Although the popularity of Dietrich Bonhoeffer increased dramatically in the United States, during travel study trips, students would often be asked by local Germans about the reason for their travel. After mentioning their studies of Dietrich Bonhoeffer, most locals seemed to be entirely unfamiliar with him and his work. However, in the United States, Dietrich Bonhoeffer appeared to increase in popularity with many individuals, especially Christians, interested in his life and work. Popular biographies such as Eric Metaxas' work *Bonhoeffer: Pastor, Martyr, Prophet, Spy* brought the story of this German pastor and theologian to more people. Charles Marsh's *A Strange Glory: A Life of Dietrich Bonhoeffer* was also a popular biography that offered a slightly different perspective from Metaxas. Collections of Bonhoeffer writings organized as daily devotions became more numerous, and Bonhoeffer was viewed as an important theological and spiritual growth voice for Christians. The 75th anniversary of the end of the European theater of World War II and the death of Bonhoeffer also increased the interest in his writing and action.

An overview of Bonhoeffer's costly leadership actions will give the reader preparation for the remainder of the book exploring specific types of leadership behaviors.[3] In order to orient the readers to the story of Bonhoeffer, the book will provide a brief biography of Dietrich Bonhoeffer.[4] The biography gives the background on the life of Bonhoeffer, so the reader will interpret the leadership behaviors through the lens of his life, imprisonment, and death. After the biographical chapter, an exploration of his development as a leader will be explored, tracing crucial life events from a psycho-social development perspective.[5] The role of the leader as a prophet is rooted in the biblical story. Prophetic leaders are key influencers within the Christian faith, and Bonhoeffer operated as a prophetic leader through his preaching and writing.[6] Bonhoeffer's *Ethics* gave glimpses into his struggle to understand appropriate Christian ethics, and while connected to the German resistance against Hitler, his leadership efforts focused upon challenging the German church to change course and follow Christ, not Hitler.[7]

During his time of ministry in the church, Bonhoeffer expressed that some of his most meaningful moments were working with children and youth. He embraced the teaching of confirmation classes to children with great vigor and excellence, and this book will survey his time as a student and as a teacher and leader of students.[8] Bonhoeffer is now most well-known for his teaching, preaching, and writing, and his preaching was a call for political, cultural, and spiritual reform.[9] The curriculum of the seminary of the Confessing Church was intentionally designed by Bonhoeffer to create spiritually competent pastors ready to lead the true church.[10] Bonhoeffer was the curriculum designer and the primary teacher of the Confessing Church seminary. He also capitalized on the leadership potential uniquely available through written language, and the impact of his writing must be considered to fully evaluate Bonhoeffer's leadership.[11] Leadership often manifests itself through personal crisis, and oftentimes the crisis is in the life of the leader and is brought on by external forces. The final chapter aims to show Bonhoeffer's courageous leadership amid persecution. Viewing Bonhoeffer's leadership behavior from the perspective of his willing choices, placing him on the path to imprisonment and eventual death, is significant in grasping his legacy as a leader.[12] This thorough exploration of Bonhoeffer's leadership behavior will provide an analysis of how he influenced his country and why his legacy has been maintained for the last 75 years.

Why Does Bonhoeffer Matter Today?

It is a working supposition of this book that Bonhoeffer can be an important voice and influence on American culture and the American Christian church. Bonhoeffer was a pastor and theologian who spoke and wrote critically to his country and culture when most people, including many Christians of the day, agreed with, or docilely went along with the message and practices of the Nazi government. He spoke boldly and directly to the German church to challenge the individual members of the church to resist and reject these popular views. The German Christians (the commonly accepted term for the churches that accepted Nazi ideology and allowed it into the church) were deeply connected to the Nazi movement and even allowed Nazi control of the church. The condition of the German church during the time of the Third Reich was horrific, as they merged the purposes of the German nation with the purposes of the German church. Mary Solberg compiled and translated many documents from the German church during the time of the Nazi regime and said this about the combining of national ideals and church mission: "The German Christians were quite sincere in identifying the Nazi cause with the cause of Jesus Christ."[13] The most well-known departure from orthodox Christian doctrine was the Aryan paragraph barring Jews from the German Christian churches, which Bonhoeffer wrote against in 1933. His writing affirmed that the Aryan paragraph of the German Christians could not align with the historical and correct Christian faith. He even went as far as to assert that he would withdraw from the church if it implemented the Aryan paragraph.[14] Opposition such as this made Bonhoeffer an enemy of both the German Christians and the Nazis, and attempts were made to silence him to stop his influence.

This book was written during the late spring/early summer of 2020 when the world is amid a pandemic due to the COVID-19 virus. The American political landscape is polarized fervently, and it seems that agreement or working together across political ideologies are not allowed. Even the government response to the pandemic is now a point of contention and disagreement among Americans. The Bonhoeffer legacy can be invoked on all sides of these debates, all while more pressing issues exist where the legacy of Bonhoeffer can be beneficial. These issues exist within American society and cause great concern for some people. Thankfully, concentration camps like those that existed during the Third Reich do not exist in the year 2020 in the United States of America, but major societal and cultural issues exist and cause alarm among Christian leaders.

A poignant question for the reader:

As you read this examination of Bonhoeffer's leadership, where would his voice and action land on these and the many other issues of today?

Memorial to the Murdered Members of the Reichstag

In 1992, a small monument was constructed at the front of the German parliament building. If you face the impressive facility, the small monument is to the right side of the front of the building. The memorial monument remembers the 96 members of the parliament either sent to concentration camps or murdered by the Nazis between 1933-1945. The pursuit and torment of these individuals began after the Reichstag fire of 1933, as these were the individual Parliament members who spoke against Hitler after the decree which gave him complete authority over Germany. These parliament members were some of his first victims of political oppression.[15] When we travel with students to Germany to study Bonhoeffer, we always visit this memorial and ask the students if they would have resisted and been counted among these 96 challengers to Hitler.

A poignant question to the reader:

Would you resist like Bonhoeffer and the 96 German Parliament members?

Endnotes

[1] Gerhard Leibholz, "Memoir," in *The Cost of Discipleship* (New York, NY: Touchstone, 1995), 33.

[2] See Jack Goodyear's chapter in this volume, "Bonhoeffer and the Fuhrer Principle" (ch. 5).

[3] See Michael Whiting's chapter in this volume, "'When Christ Calls a Man': The Cost of Bonhoeffer's Leadership" (ch. 2).

[4] See Mike Williams' chapter in this volume, "A Life and Death to 'Give Us Great Hope for the Future': A Brief Biography of Dietrich Bonhoeffer" (ch. 3).

[5] See Jordan Davis' chapter in this volume, "The Phenomenology of a Leader" (ch. 4).

[6] See David Cook's chapter in this volume, "Bonhoeffer as a Prophetic Leader" (ch. 6).

[7] See Mark Bloom's chapter in this volume, "The Leader's Responsibility to Act" (ch. 7).

[8] See Dale Meinecke's chapter in this volume, "Bonhoeffer as a Leader of Students: His Development Into a Relational Leader" (ch. 8).

[9] See Brent Thomason's chapter in this volume, "Bonhoeffer's Leadership Through Preaching" (ch. 9).

[10] See Mark Cook's chapter in this volume, "Bonhoeffer as a Teaching Leader" (ch. 10).

[11] See Mary Nelson's chapter in this volume, "Bonhoeffer's Literary Leadership" (ch. 11).

[12] See Jay Harley's chapter in this volume, "The Leadership Path to Flossenbürg" (ch. 12).

[13] Mary M. Solberg, ed. & trans., *A Church Undone: Documents from the German Christian Faith Movement, 1932-1940* (Minneapolis, MN: Augsburg Fortress Publishers, 2015), 43.

[14] Ibid., 75.

[15] Uwe Seemann, "Memorial to the Murdered Members of the Reichstag," Information Portal to European Sites of Remembrance, accessed, https://www.memorialmuseums.org/eng/denkmaeler/view/1421/Memorial-to-the-Murdered-Members-of-the-Reichstag.

Chapter 2

"WHEN CHRIST CALLS A MAN": THE COST OF BONHOEFFER'S LEADERSHIP

Dr. Michael Whiting

"People who lead frequently bear scars from their efforts to bring about adaptive change. Often, they are silenced. On occasion, they are killed."[1] Many aspire to lead. Few aspire to suffer. Whether one desires to lead with vanity for power and glory or from a sincere desire to lead a transformational movement, few would choose the suffering that inevitably comes with leadership. As Jesus warned disciples James and John in Mark 10:35-45, to aspire to lead requires counting the cost and accepting the burden of the cross that comes with the prize of the crown. J. Oswald Sanders in *Spiritual Leadership* says, "To aspire to leadership in God's kingdom requires us to be willing to pay a price higher than others are willing to pay. The toll of true leadership is heavy, and the more effective the leadership, the greater the cost."[2]

All forms of leadership that seek to create an alternative movement or perhaps even to reform against change, even when not from a so-called position of authority, involve a level of personal suffering. Confrontation, conflict, and great personal sacrifice inevitably come with the territory of being a leader. Sanders describes self-sacrifice, loneliness, fatigue, criticism, rejection, and other sufferings as "scars" of leadership.[3] Even when a decision is morally neutral, such as envisioning new paths or forms for an organization, the exercise of leadership will almost always include some amount of personal sacrifice along with the endurance of conflict, opposition, and sometimes even misunderstanding of popular opinion and the established status quo. Leaders of social movements or those who live prophetically in contrast to established norms are an open target for accusation, judgment, and criticism—for their intentions as much as for their actions.

The Lutheran pastor Dietrich Bonhoeffer exercised leadership "without authority" in standing with a persecuted Jewish minority against the prevailing tide of German national opinion during the dark days of the Nazi Third Reich. Following in the example of other great moral heroes of history, Bonhoeffer accepted the realities of suffering and hardship that came with leading movements that challenged popular opinion and the status quo.[4] Much like Martin Luther King, Jr., Bonhoeffer did not lead from the very top, as such positions of authority were denied both of them in their respective cultural contexts, but each nonetheless inspired and led movements of resistance against injustices and suffered as a result. Unlike King and his context in the racially charged and segregated American South, Bonhoeffer under the circumstances of the Nazi Reich became less involved in public efforts to change the mind of a whole nation to follow him in foregoing personal safety and comfort. Bonhoeffer chose to focus on leading a small pastoral remnant of underground resistance in a movement that defiantly and dangerously chose the narrow path—not in hopes that they could change their culture—but simply because it was the right choice.[5]

Bonhoeffer did not live long enough to witness the actual fall of the Nazi regime in 1945. He was executed in the Flossenbürg work camp just weeks before its liberation by invading Allied forces. To his own German nation and government, he had appeared powerless and foolish, executed in weakness by the apparent triumph of naked power. However, his execution with few witnesses would, paradoxically, become the very trophy of his public glory that continues to inspire moral courage for generations since the Holocaust. In the words of Craig Slane, his "martyr's death accentuates his *life*."[6] Bonhoeffer was executed in weakness by the Nazi regime, but in the end, emerged vindicated—a martyr for the cause of moral righteousness in a culture of unrighteousness. Though seemingly powerless in defiance against an evil empire that at one time had spread its might over much of the European continent, the victory of righteousness to which Bonhoeffer was committed eventually prevailed, such that history now exalts his courageous leadership on behalf of the oppressed Jews while scorning and vilifying the memory of the leaders of the Nazi Empire.

The purpose of this chapter is to narrate specifically the many sufferings that Bonhoeffer increasingly experienced in leading a movement of resistance to the Nazi takeover of the German Church and the oppression of the Jewish people. It also discusses his theological reflections on discipleship and suffering in a few select writings, followed by some concluding thoughts on the relationship between leadership and suffering.

As Mark Devine states in his book, "Suffering never becomes, for Bonhoeffer, a thing good in itself. Suffering remains suffering." However, because of Jesus Christ, God who suffered with and for us, the evil of suffering is seen as overcome by redemption. "We now live in the midst of suffering but with the demonstration of its limit behind us and with the promise of its end before us."[7] Bonhoeffer's story gives leaders hope that suffering for a noble cause, especially a moral one in obedience and imitation of Christ, will ultimately be rewarded. As Bonhoeffer himself states in his most famous work, *Discipleship*, "Suffering willingly endured is stronger than evil, it spells death to evil."[8]

The Cost of Bonhoeffer's Leadership, 1933-1945 [9]

Two days after Hitler became the reigning Führer of Germany, with the Weimar Republic and democratic constitution of Germany in jeopardy, the almost twenty-seven-year-old ordained Lutheran pastor and university professor, Dietrich Bonhoeffer, delivered a radio address criticizing the ending of civil liberties and the movement of Germany's government toward a fascist dictatorship (*Führerprinzip*). Bonhoeffer astutely recognized that Hitler's rise to absolute power came at a vulnerable time when Germany was looking for a deliverer following its humiliation in World War I. Hitler had seized upon Germany's national pride and the hope of economic restoration and national glory, offering many promises the German people could not refuse. But Bonhoeffer wisely discerned that the ascendency of Germany in Hitler's vision would come at a cost, a cost to Germans' civil liberties, a cost to the allegiance of the churches to Christ alone, and soon, by the passing of the Aryan paragraph in April 1933, the cost of oppressing a particular ethnic people—the Jews. (Within two weeks, Bonhoeffer penned his reply in the "The Church and the Jewish Question."). In essence, it was the promise that Germany would gain the world at the cost of losing its soul.

Not surprisingly, Bonhoeffer's live broadcast was cut off only ten minutes into the address. This would be but the harbinger of many conflicts to come between Bonhoeffer and the Nazi regime, including his ethical divergence from most of his pro-nationalist Berlin University colleagues (as well as faculty at other German universities) and the new united German Protestant Church,[10] ultimately culminating in his execution by hanging on April 9, 1945.

In the years that followed that radio address, Bonhoeffer continued to resist the regime and participated in the formation of the Confessing Church, which in May 1934 adopted its reactionary confession (co-authored by Karl Barth) that stated emphatically its affirmation of supreme obedience to the Lordship of Christ and the authority of the Word of God rather than the Führer or the Nazi Party. At the same time, following his drafting of the Bethel Confession denouncing the Aryan anti-Jewish exclusionary measures in the churches, Bonhoeffer would later criticize Barth and other leaders of the Confessing Church for not being as explicit and bold on the Jewish question as it was in its call for the independence of the churches from the state. In September of 1933, he was warned in a letter from the Foreign Ministry to cease his treasonous pastoral opposition to Nationalist Socialist political policies. Bonhoeffer, frustrated for a lack of support on the part of other Protestant pastors and theologian friends, left his beloved homeland to accept pastorates in London where he preached vociferously against the fall of the German Church for becoming willingly co-opted by the Nazi regime to the neglect of a genuine Christian faith lived out in love for the oppressed. At one point, Theodor Heckel, an emissary of the German Evangelical Church and its national bishop, Ludwig Müller, met with Bonhoeffer at the Savoy Hotel in London to threaten his criticism of the Nazis as tantamount to criminal activity against the state.

Bonhoeffer remained undaunted, however, and returned to Germany in 1935 to lead a rural seminary of the Confessing Church. First located in Zingst on the Baltic but transferred within just a few months to better facilities in Finkenwalde, Bonhoeffer hoped to train ministers free of Nazi propaganda as well as to form an alternative, semi-monastic Christian community based on a Benedictine model of *ora et labora* (prayer and work) and instruction in the theology of Jesus' Sermon on the Mount. It was in the context of lectures given at the seminary in Finkenwalde and flowing out of Bonhoeffer's vision to recover real pastoral discipleship in imitation of Christ that he would publish his most beloved work, *Follow Me* (*Nachfolge*, 1937)—known later in English as *Cost of Discipleship (1948)*—as well as *Life Together* (1939). This subversive and unique experiment in Protestant monasticism would be closed down forcefully by the Gestapo in 1937 in more aggressive efforts to eliminate religious resistance to the state. Before this, arrests of other dissenting Confessing Church pastors had occurred in 1936, and in that same year, Bonhoeffer lost his faculty affiliation at Berlin University. No longer a part of a legally recognized church or university, Bonhoeffer, in the eyes of his beloved fatherland, had forfeited his recognized credentials and calling as a pastor and teacher of German Christians. The profound psychological impact of this public disowning on Bonhoeffer's personal identity cannot be lost on anyone who understands the value of social recognition in professional life. Yet Bonhoeffer continued to meet clandestinely to train collectives of dissenting pastoral apprentices in a Christ-centered theology shielded from Nazism. It was becoming much more difficult and dangerous to continue such ministry activities under increasingly tightened restrictions against the Confessing Church, and Bonhoeffer was even prohibited from entering the city of Berlin itself in 1938.

Through his family connections to a secret pocket of resistance in the office of German military intelligence, or *Abwehr*, Bonhoeffer began to wrestle with the moral implications of a more active conspiracy against the absolute power of Hitler. Indeed, 1938 witnessed increasing pressure and persecution against dissenting pastors as well as the acquiescence of the majority remaining in the Confessing Church to swear the oath to Hitler. Also, on November 9-10, the *Kristallnacht* (Night of Broken Glass) brought violence against Jews, their synagogues, and their businesses in the beginnings of Hitler's stronger effort to once and for all cleanse Nazi Germany and its occupied territories from the so-called "Jewish infection" in the Final Solution. With Hitler's eyes bent on expansion through war and territorial conquest, as well as Bonhoeffer's certain conscription into the German army and the criminality of his conscientious objections, his friendship with Reinhold Niebuhr at Union Theological Seminary in New York secured a way for him to make his second and last visit to America in 1939. However, after barely a month, feeling homesick and shamefully convicted for fleeing his beloved homeland, Bonhoeffer made the historic decision to return home to face whatever would befall him. He felt compelled, if necessary, to choose suffering and death in Germany as a light and witness for righteousness then to leave Germany in darkness even if staying in America guaranteed his own personal safety. He knew his life counted for something bigger than himself. He knew war against Germany was looming and inevitable and, regardless of the outcome, he could not in good conscience remain distant and passive from participating with God's incarnate immanence in the sufferings of his homeland, with the Jews, or with his fellow Confessing Church brothers.

Upon his return, Bonhoeffer continued to minister to what was left of the Confessing Church's dissident pastors and students but was under stricter surveillance by the Gestapo, was banned from preaching throughout the Reich, and was forbidden to publish anything. (His book *Ethics* written during this period was later published posthumously by his friend Eberhard Bethge.) At the same time, to avoid being called to fight on the frontlines for Germany, he took a position with the *Abwehr.* It would utilize him for his contacts in England and America to gather Intel, while Bonhoeffer would use those same contacts to work secretly as a co-conspirator of a planned coup against Hitler's regime and in the hopes of garnering Allied support for a new, non-Nazi government in Germany. Bonhoeffer struggled far more, however, with the ethics of plotting a direct assassination attempt on Hitler's life. After all, in his own *Cost of Discipleship* years earlier, he had written of the call for believers to be in fellowship with Christ who did not take vengeance on His enemies but willingly and peacefully endured evil patiently. Regardless of his actual personal involvement in the hundreds of such attempts, which is historically doubtful, Bonhoeffer actively ministered to the conspirators and ultimately reassured them that such moral evils were, if not justifiable, forgivable in the grace of Christ.

Bonhoeffer was arrested on the evening of April 4, 1943, at his parents' home in Berlin. At this point, Bonhoeffer was mainly charged with his continued illegal activity with the Confessing Church and encouraging the avoidance of military service, not for any involvement with conspirators in assassination attempts, including the most recent failed attempt on March 13. Bonhoeffer was placed in solitary confinement in Tegel Prison for almost two weeks before being moved to a larger cell with somewhat improved living conditions, spending eighteen months there before being transferred to a Gestapo prison in Berlin where he received much harsher treatment, his connections to the circle of coup conspirators and assassination plotters having been discovered. After that, in February of 1945, he was moved to Buchenwald concentration camp, then Regensburg, and finally Flossenbürg work camp where he was court-martialed on April 8 and hung the next morning along with six others. Bonhoeffer had believed his initial charges could be acquitted and, once his relationship to the conspirators in the *Abwehr* was uncovered, he had even launched a plan to escape Tegel prison that never materialized due to the potential of endangering his family. Once it was clear his death was sealed, it is said by witnesses that he prepared for his execution at Flossenbürg with prayerful repose and faith in God.

Bonhoeffer was murdered (and perhaps cremated) as a treasonous conspirator and enemy of the Nazi government in Germany, but from the perspective of morality and history, he was martyred as a champion for the innocent and a voice for the moral right against a grave injustice.[11] This was the kind of suffering and persecution, according to Bonhoeffer, that Jesus blesses in Matthew 5:10: "Blessed are they which are persecuted for righteousness' sake." It may not have been explicitly for his confession of Christ's name that he was killed, but as Bonhoeffer had written in what was later published as his book *Ethics*, "Jesus gives His support to those who suffer for the sake of a just cause."[12] For Bonhoeffer, this would even include those who resisted Nazism who were without an explicit faith in Jesus Christ.

Just a few weeks later, the Allies liberated the camp, the war ended, and the might of a powerful evil empire fell. In November, the war crimes tribunals would commence in Nuremberg at the Palace of Justice to pass sentence against Hitler's leading associates in the Nazi Party. Although Bonhoeffer suffered with and for the oppressed in the midst of an evil age, in the end, it was he who was left standing in history's memory on the winning side, the victory of the righteous inheriting the earth.

Passio Passiva: Bearing the Cross of Leadership

Many years before that solemn April morning in 1945, Bonhoeffer wrote about the sacrificial costs of Christian discipleship, acknowledging that following the Lord "may even lead to martyrdom" and that "some God deems worthy of the highest form of suffering, and gives them the grace of martyrdom."[13] Lectures given at Finkenwalde to the seminary students and emerging pastoral leaders of the Confessing Church spoke of the need to apply the doctrine of salvation by grace to a life lived in conformity and imitation to Christ in costly obedience. It was the characteristic and bold Lutheran emphasis of justification *sola fide* (by faith alone) paired with the calling of Jesus' Sermon on the Mount. It is the gift of God's *costly grace* in Christ Jesus, not cheap grace, which compels obedience to suffer for righteousness. Jesus was the leader of a counter-cultural movement, and the disciples were chosen and prepared to carry on that leadership in obedience to Christ. Their leadership of this movement would not come without a cost and without much suffering, which they were to count and weigh carefully, choosing self-denial, love of Christ, and service to His kingdom over their own personal comfort and welfare.

Bonhoeffer states that "Christianity without discipleship is always Christianity without Christ."[14] In Germany, to be Christian had come to mean, as exploited by Hitler, being a good German citizen who supported the Nazi state and who was a committed member of the established national Church. Cultural Christianity in Germany became associated with patriotic support of the glory, power, and prosperity of the German nation even at the expense of injustice against others. Yet Bonhoeffer saw in the life of Christ, the very cornerstone of the Christian Church, a radical challenge to this association and the "false Protestant ethic which diluted Christian love into patriotism."[15] It was not love for a particular nation that defined Christian commitment, although Bonhoeffer did often express love for his homeland, but identification and compassion for those socially excluded. Christ did not come wielding His way in coercive power nor in praising Jewish ancestral pride but with humility and willingness to suffer with and for the suffering. His own life was marked by obedience to God for the sake of righteousness in an unrighteous land. The cultural Christianity of Nazi Germany, however, taught Christians to seek the avoidance of suffering by conforming rather than embracing suffering in imitation of Jesus whose righteous life challenged existing norms and expectations. It was for Germans to "proclaim their pride in being disciples of Christ" while denying the "utter poverty it may require."[16] In the words of Bonhoeffer:

...that the 'must' of suffering applies to his disciples no less than to himself. Just as Christ is Christ only in virtue of his suffering and rejection, so the disciple is a disciple only in so far as he shares his Lord's suffering and rejection and crucifixion. Discipleship means adherence to the person of Jesus, and therefore submission to the law of Christ which is the law of the cross.

Suffering, then, is the badge of true discipleship. The disciple is not above his master. Following Christ means *passio passiva*, suffering because we have to suffer.[17]

To follow Christ is to die completely to self. "When Christ calls a man, he bids him come and die."[18] But the death of self that involves suffering is not to be thought of as a tragedy but a glory and a cause for honor and rejoicing for it embodies a new life lived in and for Christ alone. In fellowship with the suffering Christ, discipleship is a life lived with and for others, as Christ Himself demonstrated. "In Bonhoeffer's spirituality, Christian freedom must include utter devotion to those in need after the manner of Jesus, whose cross is the ultimate symbol of being for others."[19]

Bonhoeffer developed this emphasis in later letters to friend Eberhard Bethge while imprisoned at Tegel in 1944.[20] It was here that Bonhoeffer began to experiment with his underdeveloped concept of "religionless Christianity," that which is neither individualistic nor other-worldly but is focused precisely on living in and for the world, sharing in the sufferings of God who became incarnate and immanent in the world in weakness: "By this-worldliness I mean living unreservedly in life's duties, problems, successes and failures, experiences and perplexities. In so doing we throw ourselves completely into the arms of God, taking seriously, not our own sufferings, but those of God in the world—watching with Christ in Gethsemane."[21] True Christianity is not isolated from the world in a way that is indifferent to or detached from the sufferings of mankind that demand responsible action. A Church that enjoys privilege and power without suffering, much like the Reich Church, has not attained imitation, union, or fellowship with Christ whose life was not about power and glory but about humbly and sacrificially serving the needs of the unloved and oppressed, even suffering to the point of death for commitment to righteousness: "… the church is the church only when it exists for others. … The church must share in the secular problems of ordinary human life, not dominating, but helping and serving. It must tell people of every calling what it means to live in Christ, to exist for others."[22] Christ was both the one who suffered and the one who suffered for others. Similarly, the Church is called to suffer with and for others and to see in those oppressed, "in the alleyways of destitution and the shadowy recesses of poverty and despair, Christ's contemporaneous presence."[23] Christ, therefore, lives both in the one who is suffering and in those who choose to suffer with and for others through loving identification. This perspective radically challenged the alignment of patriotic values and a false Christian triumphalism in Nazi Germany.

To lead others to live in a way that runs counter to cultural norms, even cultural Christianity, invites persecution, criticism, and suffering. Leaders of movements without positions of authority who are critical and prophetic in word and deed can expect to be reviled by the established system in place. A Christian must determine when discipleship means defending that system or living counter to it. What was clear to Bonhoeffer was that any system that involved the mistreatment and death of the innocent could not be supported, actively or passively, by those who claimed to be followers of Jesus Christ. There could be no harmony between claiming fellowship with Christ and rejecting solidarity with the oppressed. And that precisely describes the moral failure of the German Christians who thought patriotism to their country and government, and the temptations and promises of their own worldly comfort could justify the exclusion of others. How foreign to the spirit of Christ who came not in power and self-protection but in suffering and weakness to serve others. How could the Church be deceived into desiring and expecting a crown on earth, when its own Savior and Lord carried a cross? This was the counterfeit kind of religion and cultural Christianity that Bonhoeffer openly challenged through simply looking again to the humble life of Christ and His ethical teachings, especially the Sermon on the Mount. Where the Church and the State have enjoyed a privileged relationship with each other, as it has in many Western nations, Christians have often demonstrated reluctance to forsake their comfort, position, and prosperity even in defense of unrighteousness against others, forgetting that the Lordship of Christ when it runs counter to culture calls for the disciples of Jesus to accept suffering in self-denial. Those who stand out to lead in such contexts must be willing to accept the cost of persecution and suffering in identification with others in obedience and imitation of Christ. The fruit of such obedience, as in the case of Bonhoeffer, may not be witnessed within a leader's lifetime, and it may seem that good has been triumphed by evil. But that is for the Lord of history to determine. Disciples of Jesus, as leaders of righteousness in cultures of unrighteousness, must see the victory of the resurrection of Christ as hope for the redemption of their pain and suffering for others, both with expectation in the future history of this world and the reward of the next and must simply be faithful and entrust themselves to the God who knows personally what it is to suffer and is compassionate toward suffering.[24]

Even when leaders face a morally neutral decision, as not everyone who is a leader will have to confront such social injustices, to move people in a new or different direction will require the acceptance of suffering in the form of opposition, criticism, or misunderstanding. As Heifetz says, "Leadership is dangerous."[25] Leaders run the risk of failure, unforeseen consequences, and, occasionally, admitting that they were wrong. Yet leadership cannot happen, and change can never occur without taking risks. The outcomes of leadership and change are never known until after taking steps into the unknown; and rarely, if ever, does any leadership and accompanying change occur without friction. Those who aspire to lead from motives of personal achievement or even a desire to affect transformational change, then, must count and accept the cost of suffering that leadership requires.

For Bonhoeffer, Jesus Christ was the leader *par excellence* who, at great cost to Himself, exemplified standing for the right in face of the so-called power wielders of His context—both Jewish and Roman. Yet, much like Nazi Germany, that power was only momentary and, from the vantage point of history, illusory. In the end, the land of Israel and its Temple were devastated by Roman armies, and the Roman Empire itself later crumbled and became the stuff of history books and television documentaries. The legacy of Jesus Christ, however, in the living institution of the Christian Church remains alive and well in millions of followers around the world who abide in His Spirit of sacrificial love and compassion for others. When Christ died that day, it seemed that evil had won—the cruel murder of a blameless one by naked power—but from the perspective of His resurrection and the spread of the preaching of His cross throughout the centuries, it was a triumph over the aggression of evil. The meek, as Christ had promised in the Sermon on the Mount, were indeed inheriting the earth.

Endnotes

[1] Ronald A. Heifetz, *Leadership Without Easy Answers* (Cambridge, MA; London, England: The Belknap Press of Harvard University Press, 1994), 235.

[2] J. Oswald Sanders, *Spiritual Leadership* (Chicago, IL: Moody Publishers, 2007), 115.

[3] Ibid., 116-123.

[4] On Bonhoeffer's spirituality and moral leadership, see Geffrey B. Kelly, F. Burton Nelson, and Renate Bethge, *The Cost of Moral Leadership: The Spirituality of Dietrich Bonhoeffer* (Grand Rapids, MI: William B. Eerdmans Publishing Company, 2002). See also Patrick Nullens, "Towards a Spirituality of Public Leadership: Engaging Dietrich Bonhoeffer," *International Journal of Public Theology* 7 (2013): 91-113.

[5] For a comparison and contrast of Bonhoeffer and King as moral leaders, see Reggie Williams, "Bonhoeffer and King: Christ the Moral Arc," *Black Theology* 9.3 (2011): 356-369; also "Christ-Centered Concreteness: The Christian Activism of Dietrich Bonhoeffer and Martin Luther King, Jr.," *Dialog: A Journal of Theology*, Vol. 53, Issue 3 (Sep 2014): 185-194.

[6] Craig J. Slane, *Bonhoeffer as Martyr: Social Responsibility and Modern Christian Commitment* (Ada, MI: Brazos Press, 2004)

[7] Mark Devine, *Bonhoeffer Speaks Today: Following Jesus at All Costs* (Nashville, TN: Broadman & Holman Publishers, 2005), 170-71.

[8] Dietrich Bonhoeffer, *The Cost of Discipleship*, Revised Edition (New York, NY: Collier Books, 1959), 159.

[9] This section on Bonhoeffer's biography relies on Charles Marsh, *Strange Glory: A Life of Dietrich Bonhoeffer* (New York, NY: Alfred A Knopf, 2014). For other accounts, see also Eberhard Bethge, *Dietrich Bonhoeffer: A Biography* (Minneapolis, MN: Fortress Press, 2000); Eric Metaxas, *Pastor, Martyr, Prophet, Spy* (Nashville, TN: Thomas Nelson, 2011).

[10] Karl Barth at Bonn, Paul Tillich at Frankfurt, and Helmut Thielicke at Heidelberg were all fired from their posts for opposition to Hitler.

[11] On defining Bonhoeffer as a "martyr" in light of his being executed for connections with those plotting an assassination attempt on Hitler, see Craig Slane, *Bonhoeffer as Martyr: Social Responsibility and Modern Christian Commitment*.

[12] Dietrich Bonhoeffer, *Ethics* (New York, NY: Macmillan Publishing Co., Inc., 1955), 60.

[13] Dietrich Bonhoeffer, *The Cost of Discipleship*, Revised Edition (New York, NY: Collier Books, 1959), 98-99.

[14] Ibid. 64.

[15] Ibid. 170.

[16] Geffrey B. Kelly and F. Burton Nelson, *The Cost of Moral Leadership: The Spirituality of Dietrich Bonhoeffer* (Grand Rapids, MI and Cambridge, MA: William B. Eerdmans Publishing Company, 2003), 135.

[17] Bonhoeffer, *The Cost of Discipleship*, 96, 100.

[18] Ibid. 99.

[19] Kelly and Nelson, *Cost of Moral Leadership*, 133.

[20] See Haein Park, "The Face of the Other: Suffering, *Kenosis*, and a Hermeneutics of Love in Dietrich Bonhoeffer's *Letters and Papers From Prison* and Marilynne Robinson's *Gilead*," *Renascence* Vol. 66, Issue 2 (Spring 2014): 103-118.

[21] Dietrich Bonhoeffer, *Letters and Papers From Prison* (New York, NY: Touchstone, 1971), 369-370.

[22] Ibid, 380-383.

[23] Kelly and Nelson, *The Cost of Moral Leadership*, 178.
[24] Devine, *Bonhoeffer Speaks Today*, 152-172.
[25] Heifetz, 235.

Chapter 3

A LIFE AND DEATH TO "GIVE US GREAT HOPE FOR THE FUTURE": A BRIEF BIOGRAPHY OF DIETRICH BONHOEFFER

Dr. Mike Williams

Early on the morning of April 9, 1945, Nazi guards summoned a brilliant thirty-nine-year-old pastor-theologian from his cell to join several other prisoners on the way to death in the Nazi extermination camp at Flossenbürg in Bavaria. Their crime—plotting to overthrow perhaps the most diabolical dictator in world history, Adolph Hitler—and now after months of imprisonment, as Allied forces closed in, the Nazi madman continued to lash out in vengeance against those who had opposed him. Though part of a conspiracy that reached back years in Nazi Germany, and a prisoner of the Third Reich since early April 1943, he and some of his co-conspirators had avoided execution for two years as the Gestapo tried to intimidate and torture information from them that might reveal other opponents of Hitler for the madman's revenge. But now the gallows waited. According to one account, before departing to meet the hangman's noose, the young man knelt in prayer and then again prayed as he mounted the gallows, proceeding to his death calmly and peacefully. Afterward, like so many of those murdered in those dark and dreadful years, Nazis burned his remains to ashes. His name was Dietrich Bonhoeffer.[1]

Both theological liberals and conservatives assert that he is one of their own. Even atheists have acknowledged his inspiration. Evangelicals and liberals, pacifists and advocates of just war all want to claim him. He received the finest formal German theological education possible but, in his twenties, discovered a voice for the oppressed in an African American Baptist congregation in New York City. He completed two doctoral dissertations yet found some of his greatest satisfaction teaching teenagers in a catechism class or mentoring young seminarians in an underground seminary. His courageous stand against Nazism and his calm response to his own execution, virtually within the sound of the guns of his Allied liberators, have intrigued Christians and non-Christians around the world, particularly those in Europe and the United States. As Geffrey Kelly and Burton Nelson write in the foreword to *The Cost of Moral Leadership*, there is a persistent "hunger for the kind of inspiration that Bonhoeffer's spiritual journey seemed to spark and an eagerness to discuss the creative force behind his life's decisions, his exemplary moral leadership, and his courageous struggle against Nazism."[2]

Undoubtedly contributing to this recent and current "hunger" for what is essentially Bonhoeffer's post-mortem endorsement also comes because of his brilliant intellect, searching spiritual nature, caring pastoral gifts, and heroic anti-Nazism. His brilliance is unquestioned. He dialogued, both in person and through his writing, with some of the premier theological and philosophical minds of his day. Both before the great cataclysm of war and the darkness of Nazism and after his imprisonment due to his role in the German resistance, he struggled with the great questions of life and spirituality. Yet, near the end of his life, he returned to the simplicity of his faith, and, finding community with other believers, he ministered to those facing brutal deaths for their opposition to an evil and failing regime.

Who was Dietrich Bonhoeffer and what influences made Bonhoeffer whom he became? It is the purpose of this short biographical essay to explore some of the people, ideas, and experiences that shaped him into the man, theologian, leader, or "Pastor, Martyr, Prophet, Spy" as Eric Metaxas defines Bonhoeffer in his biography.[3] It is not intended to be an all-inclusive list, summary, or comprehensive biography, but is written simply to suggest what elements contributed to his emergence as a great leader during a critical time in history. As the decades of the 1930s and 1940s unfolded, it became apparent that not only was western civilization on trial but also Christianity. Bonhoeffer recognized that how the leaders of

Christianity responded to trial would contribute to and perhaps define the future of Christianity in the western world.

Childhood, Adolescence, and Early Educational Experiences

Born into a German family a few minutes before his twin sister Sabine, Dietrich Bonhoeffer entered the world on February 4, 1906, as the fourth son and sixth child of eight children. The upper-middle-class Bonhoeffer family benefited from the academic prestige of their father Karl, a renowned medical doctor and professor of psychiatry at the University of Berlin, and the rich family, somewhat aristocratic lineage, and religious devotion of their mother Paula. By all accounts, Dr. Bonhoeffer did not openly discourage Paula's piety, but the family's participation in Lutheran church services remained sporadic throughout Dietrich's childhood, and Dr. Bonhoeffer himself remained disinterested in religious matters. Most of the family's spiritual development came from their mother's form of upper-middle-class German religion and her teaching within the home. As Bonhoeffer's best friend from his adulthood, Eberhard Bethge, writes, "She made sure…that the children knew the Bible and the hymns that she herself cherished… The principle aim of the upbringing as having a Christian value and her husband saw it as having a humanist one."[4] Dietrich's niece Renate Bethge writes, however, in the "Foreword" to Kelly and Nelson's *Cost of Moral Leadership,* that the Bonhoeffer family influence extended beyond this. She argued that his family fixed a deeply embedded "personal sense of ethical responsibility in the Bonhoeffer children from the very beginning." If this is true, it undoubtedly led further to Bonhoeffer's "embrace of the gospel, particularly the Sermon on the Mount…"[5]

Dietrich Bonhoeffer spent most of his childhood and early adolescence in a somewhat physically sheltered and idyllic upper-middle-class comfort. His parents and siblings surrounded him with good books, music, and strong family ties, including his mother Paula, a certified teacher, teaching all eight children in a home classroom that provided discipline and "free exploration and invention." His siblings challenged him with their intellectual gifts, and they all benefitted from visits by some of the premier intellects of early twentieth-century German academic life, including Adolf von Harnack, prominent liberal church historian and theologian, Ernst Troeltsch, classical liberal theologian and philosopher, and leading sociologist Max Weber. How much these childhood and teenage visits from family friends influenced him is debatable, but in his later studies and writings, he often interacted with their writings.[6]

Bonhoeffer's picturesque childhood continued after the family moved to Berlin when the family purchased a summer country house in Friedrichsbrunn. Thus, he benefitted from the intellectual stimulation of a highly competitive family in an academic home environment in Berlin, while also enjoying summer times in the country. Later in life, Bonhoeffer reflected often upon his "sheltered" childhood and regretted it. Indeed, Bethge insists that he carried this sensitivity to his comfortable upbringing even to his prison cell in 1943. Perhaps some of his sensitivity for the oppressed came from self-imposed guilt over his comfortable childhood and young adulthood. Even when war came in 1914, the family remained somewhat aloof from the catastrophe falling upon many other German and European families. Their serene existence crumbled in 1918, when two of Dietrich's beloved older brothers, Walter and Karl-Friedrich, volunteered for the German army in what became the last year of the war. Only a month later, the family received word that Allied artillery had badly wounded Walter, and a short time later he died from infection. The news shattered the family's tranquility and privileged existence and the comfortable reality they had known never fully reappeared. Karl-Friedrich further disrupted family harmony when he returned from the war with slight physical wounds but disillusioned, radicalized, and a confirmed agnostic. Indeed, Bethge surmises that Dietrich's adoption of theology as a vocational path came partially from his competitive nature and trying to distinguish himself from his intellectually gifted siblings. But he also suggests that his career choice became a way of clarifying himself to Karl-Friedrich's philosophical skepticism. An often-retold story about Dietrich's decision to pursue theology demonstrates this. When at the age of thirteen he shared his decision with the family about his vocational choice, older brothers Karl-Friedrich and Klaus sought to steer him to another career path and spoke critically of the church calling it "a poor, feeble, boring, petty bourgeois institution." Accordingly, Dietrich responded enthusiastically, "In that case, I shall reform it!" In this regard, he demonstrated his mother's continued influence upon his life rather than that of his father.[7] On another occasion when Karl-Friedrich argued against Christianity from the perspective of science, Dietrich responded, "You may knock my block off, but I shall still believe in God." Roark adds that only during his imprisonment did he reconcile with science "suggesting that this reconciliation led to his Letters from Prison taking the revolutionary tone that some recognize."

A significant element of Bonhoeffer's development, Bethge notes, came from the fact that his family read extensively. By his final year in high school, Bonhoeffer had read many of the classics of German literature as well as such weighty academic texts as those by Max Weber and Friedrich Schleiermacher. Throughout his school years, he also found himself academically challenged and surpassed by Maria Weigert, described as a "beautiful, brilliant, energetic" young scholar and daughter of a Jewish judge whose family moved in the same social circles as Bonhoeffer. Somewhat frustrated with his inability to outshine Weigert, Bonhoeffer remained friends with her following completion of high school as they went on their separate pathways.[8]

University and Travel Experiences

After completion of his high school education, Bonhoeffer studied for a year at the University in Tubingen. Despite the fact many in theology spent their time considering the early work of Karl Barth, Bonhoeffer seemed to have taken little notice of Barth's work at this point. He spent most of his time studying philosophy, the history of religion, and the current form of higher textual criticism for which the University was known, as well as participating in a Swabian fraternity known as the Hedgehog. Both his father and uncle had held membership in the Hedgehog as first-year university students. Largely due to his membership in the Hedgehog, he served for two weeks in a call-up of university students for military training. His particular group was labeled the Ulm Rifles. Though technically a violation of the Treaty of Versailles, the German government issued the activation because of many problems: unrest in Saxony, national tension from extreme hyperinflation and food riots in the Weimar Republic, the collapse of the German economy leading to the nation's default on WWI war reparations, French and Belgian armies' occupation of the rich Ruhr region in response to the default, and the revolt in Bavaria later labeled the "Beer Hall Putsch" and led by World War general Erich Ludendorff and a then-unknown Nazi agitator named Adolph Hitler. While many of the student units sympathized with Ludendorff, and Hitler, or other far right-wing German nationalist groups, Bonhoeffer and his fraternity brothers leaned to the left against the more reactionary Reichswehr units that Bonhoeffer observed elsewhere. The spirit exhibited by some of the radical right student military groups likely served as Bonhoeffer's first exposure to elements that would support Hitler and the Nazis in the years to come. Ultimately, he resigned from the fraternity in 1936 because of its "excessively nationalistic" leanings which he believed left it open to Nazism.[9]

Despite the problems in the German economy but demonstrating his family's essential financial security, after he completed his first year of university study, Dietrich Bonhoeffer vacationed in Rome, traveling for a time with his older brother Klaus to Sicily and North Africa. While Klaus remained less interested in spiritual and religious matters, Dietrich reveled in visits to churches and worship services and found himself captured by the immense aesthetic beauty of Roman Catholicism. He also delighted in theological debates with an equally young Roman Catholic seminarian who undoubtedly hoped that he might convert the German Lutheran to his ancient faith. He took every opportunity to experience Holy Week in all its pageantry in Rome in the spring of 1924, beginning with a Palm Sunday Mass at St. Peter's Basilica and concluding with Easter Sunday High Mass again at Saint Peter's.[10]

Bethge opines that this sojourn in Rome introduced Bonhoeffer to Roman Catholicism in a way that dramatically affected his view of the Church in the years to come and suggests that some of this exposure influenced his dissertation. In fact, Bethge states that Bonhoeffer regarded Catholic Rome as "a real temptation to him." Not only did he acquire a deep appreciation for the aesthetic beauty offered by Roman Catholicism but also for the long history and the catholicity or universality of Roman Catholicism. He saw these things transcended what he regarded as the provincial nature of the Lutheranism in which he had been educated. Marsh offers that when he left Rome he felt "supersaturated." In a somewhat similar but also different fashion, his introduction to North African culture and Islam left a distinct impression. He witnessed the tremendous cultural influence of Islam among the Arabs and compared their culture to his studies of the Old Testament. He also observed how religion and the Muslim lifestyle closely mixed, much as he understood ancient Jewish life. While Bonhoeffer never discussed ecumenism at this point, it is evident that the first stirrings of what he later called "religion-less Christianity."[11]

Later Education and Early Ministerial Experiences

When Bonhoeffer returned from Rome and North Africa, however, he did not return to studies at Tubingen. Instead, he enrolled at the Berlin University, the home of classical liberal theology and positivism. Founded by Friedrich Schleiermacher, an institution of the late Ernest Troeltsch, and home of Adolf von Harnack, as Marsh writes, "the university had assembled an unrivaled theological faculty" that included not only von Harnack but also Karl Holl and Reinhold Seeberg. All three men played significant roles in the development of Bonhoeffer's theology as he immersed himself deeply in classical liberal Protestantism. While ultimately, he rejected many aspects of his professors' approaches and became associated with "Neo-Orthodoxy" or "Neo-Reformation" ideals of Karl Barth, Emil Brunner, and others, as James Woelfel suggests, Bonhoeffer "never really neglected the influence of his Berlin mentors."[12]

In particular, Holl equipped Bonhoeffer with a thorough going understanding of Martin Luther that transcended Bonhoeffer's previous interpretation of Luther and Lutheranism. During Bonhoeffer's sojourn in Rome, he had come to criticize German Lutheranism as "provincial, nationalistic, and small-minded," but now sitting under Holl's teaching, he began to interpret Luther more broadly and deeply. Holl also exposed Bonhoeffer to the Genevan Reformer John Calvin, as well as Eastern Orthodoxy. He especially appreciated Holl's explanation "of Luther's faith as a religion of conscience," Holl's rejection of Germans' "vague cultural Protestantism" that Bonhoeffer already had reflected upon, and Holl's focus upon Luther's justification by faith. He found himself troubled, however, by Holl's failure to ground this doctrine deeply in Luther's Christology. He also rejected liberal Protestantism's understanding of sin as interpreted by Holl, as Green and DeJonge explain in their editorial comments on Bonhoeffer's *Act and Being,* his post-doctoral dissertation that German higher education required for university teaching. Holl's interpretation would have been consistent with the pervasive liberal Protestantism found at Berlin, and by the time that he published it in 1929, demonstrated his further reaction against Holl and others. Despite this, Bonhoeffer might have chosen Holl to direct his first doctoral dissertation had Holl not died prematurely in 1926, at the age of 60.[13]

Instead, since Bonhoeffer's primary locus of study was systematic theology, Reinhold Seeberg directed his initial doctoral dissertation at Berlin.

Seeberg did not always see eye-to-eye with his prize pupil. Despite this, Bonhoeffer thrived under the challenges of Seeberg's instruction, even though according to Bethge, he "rejected out of hand Seeberg's attempt to harmonize the Bible and the modern spirit, Luther and idealism, theology and philosophy" all consistent with the *zeitgeist* of Berlin's theological faculty at that time. Also, in spite of his disagreement with Seeberg, the theologian gave him the freedom to develop his own thought and eventually gave him a lukewarm endorsement of his dissertation while expressing limited concern over some of "Bonhoeffer's criticisms of Ernest Troeltsch [whose spirit still ruled at Berlin University] and German liberalism."[14]

Adolf von Harnack served as the final major academic influence on Bonhoeffer at Berlin. Even though semi-retired, Harnack still taught doctoral seminars and remained "Germany's grand old man of Protestantism." Woelfel suggests that Harnack most influenced Bonhoeffer through the elder professor's "passion for truth and intellectual honesty." Indeed, in his eulogy for Harnack's 1930 funeral, Bonhoeffer said, "He became our teacher; he became close to us the way true teachers become close to their students. He stood beside us with questions and across from us with superior judgment." Because of this, Bonhoeffer continued, "We knew that with him we were in good and solicitous hands, we saw him as the bulwark against all trivialization and stagnation, against all fossilization of intellectual life... Theology means speaking about God... In Harnack the theologian we saw the unity of the world of his intellect; here truth and freedom found unifying bonds..." He added, "It is here that we find Harnack's legacy to us. True freedom of research, of work, of life, and the most profound support by, and commitment to, the eternal ground of all thought and life."[15]

Under all three of these men, as well as other members of the faculty, Bonhoeffer excelled. He might well have alienated them, however, because he had begun to read the controversial Karl Barth who challenged the liberal Protestantism represented by Holl, Seeberg, and especially, Adolf von Harnack. As Marsh writes, "Barth wrote theology with the ferocity of a soul on fire." Marsh adds of Bonhoeffer, even though he was well aware of the Berlin faculty's "strong opposition... [to Barth's return to orthodox language, his immense focus upon Jesus, and Barth's rejection of the German nationalism pervasive in the German Lutheran church], "Bonhoeffer made no secret of his admiration of Barth." He especially appreciated the way that Barth re-focused theology upon Scripture in a way that liberal Protestantism ignored it in favor of the science of theology. Bonhoeffer embraced many of Barth's ideas and his neo-orthodoxy but did not lose his independence. He sought to stand between his liberal Protestant tradition and Barth, developing "new confessional energies to the liberal tradition" and hoping "to re-accommodate the liberal tradition to a greater one, the two-thousand-year tradition of Christian orthodoxy" while also drawing Barth's neo-orthodoxy back to "God's immanence in the concrete relationships of Christians in community, the patterns and practices of living faith." In fact, his dissertation, *Sanctorum Communio*, sought to be a mediating influence between the truth set forth by Barth's appeal to historical Christianity and Scripture and the existential Christian life. Regardless, James Woelfel insists that "The major theological influence on Bonhoeffer was Karl Barth. Bonhoeffer was a theological student during the period when Barth was shaking continental theology to its foundations, and he remained a lifelong friend of Barth. Although Bonhoeffer very early became keenly aware of what he considered to be inadequacies in Barth's theology, he nevertheless remained dominated by Barth's understanding of the nature and method of theology." He would spend the remainder of his life in dialogue with Barth's ideas and seeking to bridge this gap between two different schools of thought in one manner or another. As Bethge writes of his dissertation, *Sanctorum Communio*, he sought to reconcile Troeltsch and Barth even though "later critics regarded this as more bold than successful." [16]

Woelfel in *Bonhoeffer's Theology* offers that Bonhoeffer's discovery of Martin Luther contributed significantly to his development as a theologian. Woelfel writes, "Another formative influence in theological development was his adherence to Lutheran Christianity." Much as one finds in the Danish theologian Soren Kierkegaard, observes Woelfel, Bonhoeffer was also "profoundly molded by the personality and thought of Luther himself, as well as by the theological emphases and ethos of the Lutheran tradition... Many of the riddles and seeming antinomies in Bonhoeffer's prison writings can only be resolved only if he is seen to the very end as a Lutheran churchman." While his professors, "Holl and Seeberg had uncovered more of the richness in Luther's thought than earlier liberals ... they had failed to uncover the whole Luther of the Reformation, the Luther from beginning to end had his sights fixed firmly on the objective revelation of God in his Word, Jesus Christ." Correctly he argues that Bonhoeffer recognized that the key to understanding Luther could only be found in Luther's Christology, a Christology that his classical liberal professors largely rejected. He also adds that Bonhoeffer understood that "All the psychological depth and introspection in Luther is misunderstood if it is detached from its rooting in the non-subjective Word of God witnessed in the Scriptures. This was the discovery of Barth, Bonhoeffer, and the other Neo-Reformation [neo-orthodox] theologians."[17] This understanding further separated him from his Berlin professors.

Beyond his studies with Harnack, Holl, and Seeberg, and his discovery of Luther and Barth, the young German scholar located an unexpected treasure, a real friend. Bonhoeffer's friendship with Walter Dress during his Berlin days helped to define and influence the young theologian further. Dress, who eventually married Bonhoeffer's sister Suzanne, became Dietrich's first real friend outside his family. Slightly older and ahead of Bonhoeffer in his studies by about two years, Dress became a confidante, mentor, and sounding board. As some writers have observed, even in his youth, Bonhoeffer lacked closeness with others his age. Other than his twin, Sabine, he admired his siblings and competed against them lovingly but never truly drew close to them, maintaining a perpetual aloofness. Even he and Sabine grew somewhat apart as they moved into adolescence and young adulthood. Sometimes, his siblings even regarded his intentional separation and introspective manner as what Marsh describes as "snobbery." Throughout his life, Bonhoeffer appears to have been the type of person who, while loving and pastoral and so wonderfully brilliant, that he drew people to him, but could also be so contemplative that he often found himself alone in a crowd. Dress both understood and addressed this side of Bonhoeffer's personality and filled a huge void in his life and, in doing so set the stage for relationships that Bonhoeffer later forged with Eberhard Bethge and Bishop G. K. A. Bell. Perhaps some of the pastoral warmth that the young theologian demonstrated afterward might not have been possible had it not been for this friendship.[18] Bethge also speaks to this inherent loneliness in Bonhoeffer's life when he writes, "It might be said, with some exaggeration, that because he was lonely he became a theologian and because he became a theologian he was lonely."[19]

All these influences converged to help Bonhoeffer produce and publish his doctoral dissertation, *Sanctorum Communio*. While a discussion of his dissertation falls outside the scope of this chapter, suffice it to say that while it did have weaknesses, he produced a work of depth and academic soundness surprising for one so young, completing the work a few months after his twenty-first birthday. He successfully defended his work in December of 1927, just months before he turned twenty-two. As mentioned above, while his work later resulted in criticism—the same concerns that Bonhoeffer himself offered about the document—including nationalistic sentiments he later abhorred, his professors gave him high marks and Barth called it a "theological miracle" or "surprise," probably because it came from a university that had produced some of his strongest critics on the continent. He built its primary arguments around the statement found early in his thesis, "The concepts of person, community, and God are inseparably and essentially interrelated." As one reads through excerpts of the document, the reader can find glimpses of themes to which Bonhoeffer would return often. A longing for something more from the church in terms of relationship may also be sensed, and Barth commented on that in his observations on Bonhoeffer's work.[20]

Bonhoeffer did not only seek to be an academic professor and theologian but also hoped to become a minister. In Germany at that time, however, he could not be ordained before the age of twenty-five and thus he went to Barcelona, Spain to serve as an assistant to the pastor of the German-speaking congregation there. The sojourn, though brief, influenced Bonhoeffer in several ways. It further developed his speaking and preaching skills, and it demonstrated his rapport with younger people. This work also continued to develop his theology of the church and his determination to continue to make the church relevant. He found no mentors or role models there as the senior pastor came to resent the young Bonhoeffer's popularity with his parishioners and the superior attendance when they knew Bonhoeffer was preaching. However, Bonhoeffer enjoyed himself immensely and found his horizons further broadened. It deepened his appreciation for Roman Catholic tradition, pageantry, aesthetics, and what he described as a spring-summer theology as opposed to German "winter theology."[21]

Two lectures he delivered while in Barcelona shed considerable light on both how Bonhoeffer was transitioning away from the ideas of liberal German theology represented by von Harnack towards Karl Barth, his neo-orthodoxy, and Barth's Christological center but at the same time retaining a heavy nationalism that he would later regret. In a lecture entitled, "Jesus Christ and the Essence of Christianity," he makes broad evangelical statements very different from his University of Berlin professors and much more like Martin Luther or Karl Barth. For example, he writes,

"[Christianity] requires merely that we acknowledge the exclusive honor due the eternal God and acknowledge our own nothingness before God... You, human being, no matter who you are, you are God's child, you are included in God's love, out of the pure, incomprehensible grace of God." He then adds, "accept this word, believe in it, trust in his rule rather than in yourself ... rather than your own work or your own religion. "He concludes the entire message with a final statement, "In your struggles with fate, keep your eyes on the cross, the most wonderful emblem of your God, and be assured that only in this sign will you be victorious."[22]

On the other hand, in his last lecture in Barcelona, while he incorporated thoughts on ethics that would emerge in what is typically regarded as his magnum opus, the unfinished *Ethics*, Bonhoeffer also clung to a nationalistic ethic that rejected the Christian pacifism suggested in the Sermon on the Mount, defending a traditional German view of war. Bethge states that only two years later, Bonhoeffer had come to regret this message.[23]

Return to Berlin and First Journey to the U. S.

After his sojourn in Spain, Bonhoeffer returned to Berlin. While he expected that he might likely serve as a parish pastor, his theological restlessness continued to grow, and he wanted to keep the option of a university position open. He was not yet twenty-five, and could not be ordained as a pastor, so he chose to pursue the second dissertation required in Germany for a university professorship. He recognized that his theology had moved beyond the provincial and liberal position of his first dissertation director who had just retired, and the faculty placed him under the supervision of Wilhelm Lutgert. Lutgert had little influence upon Bonhoeffer's second dissertation, *Act and Being*. Eberhard Bethge summarizes it by connecting it with *Sanctorum Communio*. Bethge writes, "*Act and Being* gave the social and ethical transcendence of one's neighbor, which had already been maintained in *Sanctorum Communio* as against philosophical-metaphysical transcendence, the magnificent formulation 'Jesus, the man for others.'" At the time he completed *Act and Being*, Bonhoeffer had *Sanctorum Communio* with a publisher and soon found a publisher for his second work. Unfortunately, while well-received by friends and approved by the faculty at the university, neither work made much of a theological splash at the time. However, it is important to note as Marsh does that while some of Bonhoeffer's ideas disappeared during the subsequent years, some of the better concepts resurfaced in his prison letters. As Green and DeJonge summarize, he dealt with the backdrop of the philosophy of Immanuel Kant and Martin Heidegger, interacted with Karl Barth's theology, rejected the liberal theology of Karl Holl, and discussed critical theological issues like original sin, sin, and the person. The latter provided themes he returned to when faced with the crisis of the 1940s. Subsequently, he completed his final examinations, trial sermon, trial lecture, and inaugural lecture to finalize this phase of his education. Suffice it to note, however, that probably of greater lasting importance to Bonhoeffer was the resumption of a lasting friendship with a brilliant young student, Franz Hildebrandt, the son of a prominent history professor and a baptized Christian but Jewish mother, and the continued growth of the Bonhoeffer family when his brother Karl Friedrich married Greta von Dohnanyi, the sister of Hans von Dohnanyi, who later connected Dietrich to the conspiracy against Hitler. Additionally, his sister Susanne married his good friend Walter Dress and Klaus married Emmi Delbruck, also the sister of a friend. Each of these individuals would continue to play an important role in Bonhoeffer's life as did his converted Jewish brother-in-law, Gerhard Leibholz, married to his twin sister Sabine.[24]

Even with these accomplishments and family developments, Bonhoeffer remained restless. While working on his second dissertation, he had served as a voluntary assistant lecturer and dealt with the drudgery of grading seminar papers. He remained uncertain as to a career pathway. A delay for this decision came when Union Theological Seminary in New York City admitted him for a year of study. The opportunity to travel and study in America intrigued him in part because of continued wanderlust and the reported experiences of study in America of his brother. The move proved to be providential, not so much for his study at Union which in typical Germanic confidence he believed poorer than his education in Germany, or even for his exposure to broader American culture, but because of his experiences among students less concerned with theology (much to his chagrin) and more concerned with social action and piety. During his year at Union, He did encounter the leading neo-orthodox American theologian of that time, H. Reinhold Niebuhr, but as Marsh writes, he "never acknowledge[d] a theological debt to Niebuhr" and the two disagreed on theological methodology. However, the two continued to correspond for most of the remainder of Bonhoeffer's life. When Bonhoeffer considered leaving Germany at the beginning of the war, Niebuhr provided the possible haven that the German scholar ultimately rejected.[25] Instead, his exposure to Christianity in the African American church and to pacifism through his French friend and companion European Sloan Fellow, Jean Lasserre, a Reformed French pastor, proved to be the redeeming features of this sojourn more than any classroom activity. These two ongoing encounters shaped Bonhoeffer in ways that would constantly re-emerge through his years of struggle.

In the case of Lasserre, the French pastor exposed Bonhoeffer to a Christian pacifism that contrasted distinctly with the Christian nationalism that the young German had imbibed so deeply in the German church and university education. Lasserre later wrote "both of us discovered that the communion, the community of the Church is much more important than the national community."[26] The two initiated an ongoing discussion on the Sermon on the Mount as they continued their studies and as they vacationed on a long car trip with two other colleagues across the heartland of the United States to Mexico. Bonhoeffer returned to the themes of the Sermon on the Mount, but particularly the passage on loving enemies, frequently throughout the remainder of his ministry, especially in his writing and most importantly in the *Cost of Discipleship*. Bonhoeffer spoke vigorously at ecumenical meetings in the 1930s in favor of peace, undoubtedly drawing upon these discussions and his continued study of the Sermon on the Mount. The entreaty to "love your enemies" proved to be an ongoing challenge for Bonhoeffer once he became convinced that he must become involved in the plot to overthrow and, if necessary, assassinate Adolph Hitler. He must have reflected often not only on the words of Jesus in Matthew but also upon his own words in *Cost of Discipleship* when he wrote, "Loving one's enemies leads disciples to the way of the cross and into communion with the crucified one."[27]

Bonhoeffer's introduction to the African American Church came through Frank Fisher, an African American seminary student at Union. Bonhoeffer went with Fisher to Abyssinian Baptist Church in Harlem while Fisher did his field work in the largest and probably most influential black church in the country. Bonhoeffer experienced something unique there. Not only did he see a congregation enmeshed in the struggle for social justice, but he also heard Jesus Christ preached in ways he had never heard before. Pastor Adam Clayton Powell, perhaps the most important African American pastor in the United States at that time and outstanding social justice advocate, proved to be most instrumental in this exposure. He experienced a vibrancy of worship that transcended his previous worship experiences and a Christological centrality existed in every aspect of his experience. Bonhoeffer adopted Powell's ideas regarding the necessity of Christians serving as advocates for suffering humanity and, like Powell, came to believe that by encountering suffering among the needy and the oppressed, the Christian encountered Christ at the same time, much in the vein of Matthew 25:31-46. While this interpretation might seem to be commonsensical, it increasingly became a reality for Bonhoeffer. So closely did he identify with this African American community, for a time, he taught Bible study classes there and he began to identify with the oppressed in a way he had never experienced. Without question, this identification with the oppressed would resonate once he began to witness the intense persecution suffered especially first by German Jews in the 1930s and then as the Holocaust unfolded in Europe after 1939. Its influence on his theology may be certainly felt in both the *Cost of Discipleship* and his final work, the incomplete *Ethics*. Likewise, this identification with the oppressed comes through clearly in his essay, "The Church and the Jewish Question," written in 1933, as German Christians first began to experience pressure from the new Nazi regime in the so-called "church struggle."[28]

The Rise of the Nazis and the Beginning of the "Church Struggle"

Upon his return to Germany in 1931, Bonhoeffer busied himself preaching, teaching, and studying, including visits with Karl Barth in Switzerland for the next two years. He became increasingly involved in ecumenism as well. The Great Depression had begun in the United States with the collapse of the stock market in 1929 had spread to Germany, however, and democracy in that beleaguered nation suffered dramatically. The despair of a defeated Germany from World War I, the instability of the economy and the government under the Weimar Republic, the cultural decadence that existed in those years, the coming of the Great Depression, and a long-standing German desire for greatness and strong leadership, among other things, all conspired to bring Adolph Hitler to power.

A complete discussion of how the rise of National Socialism affected Christians in Germany falls outside the scope of this chapter. Suffice to say that, like all aspects of German life, Adolph Hitler and the Nazis sought to bring both Protestants and Catholics under the control of the German state. Finding Roman Catholics resistant due to their ties with the papacy, the Nazi party sought to bring all Protestant churches under the authority of the German Christian Church, seeking to include all German Protestants into a unified church that embraced ethnic purity and uniformity under Ludwig Muller as Reich bishop. This meant converts like Bonhoeffer's friend Franz Hildebrandt and his brother-in-law Gerhard Leibholz would be forced to worship separately in a Jewish Christian congregation. It also brought Bonhoeffer into open conflict with Hitler and his cronies only a few weeks into Hitler's rule as German chancellor. As Marsh writes, the young theologian was "on his way to becoming the nation's most notorious theological dissident."[29]

Over the next few months, Bonhoeffer wrote and presented a series of essays attacking the German Christian Church's positions on race and Christianity. Specifically, his three publications, "The Church and the Jewish Question," "The Jewish-Christian; Question as *Status Confessionis*," and "The Aryan Paragraph in the Church," laid out his primary assertion that "The church cannot allow the state to prescribe for it the way that it treats its members. A baptized Jew is a member of our church." He added, "being a Jewish Christian is a religious and not a racial concept." Towards the close of the essay he concluded, "In reality it is the duty of Christian proclamation to say: here, where Jew and German together stand under God's Word is church; here it will be proven whether or not the church is still church."[30] Although some of Bonhoeffer's arguments in these essays would later be superseded by more progressive statements than those published in these, he had thrown down the gauntlet. After a radio broadcast attacking Hitler only a short time after his rise to power, Marsh records that Bonhoeffer began referring to Hitler "as the Antichrist."[31]

As pressure grew on both Jews and Christian pastors who opposed the German Christian Church, some Protestant pastors, led by World War I veteran U-Boat captain and Protestant pastor, Martin Niemoller, organized the Pastors' Emergency League. Ultimately, the supporters of the League adopted the name of the Confessing Church in opposition to the German Evangelical Church led by Ludwig Muller. The Confessing Church held its first national meeting in May 1934 and issued what came to be known as the Barmen Declaration. The Barmen Declaration, primarily authored by Karl Barth, rejected the Führer Principle advocated by the German

Christians and Muller and declared allegiance to the rule of Christ over the church while denouncing the sin of idolatry. The signatories of the declaration did not include Bonhoeffer because the previous summer, Theodore Heckel, director of the Lutheran Church's Foreign Office, had offered Bonhoeffer the pastorate of a German-speaking congregation in London, accepting the pastorates of two small congregations in London.[32]

Bonhoeffer in London and the Underground Church in Germany

Undoubtedly, Heckel and Muller believed that removing Bonhoeffer from Germany with an appointment would marginalize Bonhoeffer in the church struggle. In reality, it empowered him. While Niemoller and others organized the Pastors' League, they also experienced intense scrutiny from the German Church hierarchy and increasing pressure from the Gestapo. Bonhoeffer held the luxury of being hundreds of miles away in a safe haven in London. While it removed him physically from the struggle and prompted his absence from Barmen, it failed to distance him from the opposition. It allowed him to work in freedom and to develop ecumenical relationships like the one that he established with Bishop George Bell of Chichester, whom Metaxas regards along with Barth, as the closest person to a mentor that Bonhoeffer ever found. In serving the two small congregations, Bonhoeffer prepared and preached, as if he preached to multitudes, advanced the cause of German ecclesiastical opposition to Hitler, and improved ecumenical friendships that ultimately proved to be a channel, not just for spiritual refreshment, but important political connections once opposition to Hitler solidified. He corresponded at length with Barth and flew to meet with Niemoller and other leaders of the Pastors' League. In these actions, he helped plant the seeds of the Confessing Church in Germany. When the Confessing Church issued the Barmen Declaration, Bonhoeffer and Bell saw that it was widely distributed in Britain and other locations in the West. He then traveled to a conference in Fano, off the coast of Denmark. Metaxas accurately appraises that this trip finalized Bonhoeffer's break with the German Church, prompted him to greater activism, sealed his decision to embrace ecumenism at the cost of his German nationalism, and led directly to what transpired at Flossenbürg. Metaxas writes, "There was no question that his brothers and sisters in Christ around the world were closer to him than the pseudo-Christian Nazis in the Reichskirche

(German Church)... The radical nature of what Bonhoeffer said and did at Fano is difficult to overstate. One may draw a direct line from Fano to Flossenbürg eleven years later."[33]

As pressure increased on the Confessing Church, so did Nazi control over Protestant churches in Germany. After the "Night of the Long Knives," in which Hitler squelched remaining opposition to his rule, the state-run seminaries began to require all seminarians to prove their Aryan lineage and open hostility towards Jews began to increase dramatically. At this point, Bonhoeffer, torn between the struggle in Germany, his academic background, and multiple offers for his talents or opportunities for study, such as one offered by Mohandas Gandhi to study non-violent resistance in India, faced a decision. What next for him? Finally, he decided to accept a new position that might well have been created especially for him, the director's position for a new Confessing Church seminary beginning in the Spring of 1935, to open at Zingsthof on the Baltic Sea.[34]

In many ways, Bonhoeffer's time as director of the underground seminary at Zingsthof, which soon moved to Finkenwalde, fulfilled an unmet longing for community in his life. Even though initially the regional church officially supported the seminary, Bonhoeffer felt free to experiment on an almost blank slate with his ideas regarding the Christian community outside the rigidity of both official Lutheran tradition and the oppressive Nazi regime. An attempt to form a type of Protestant monasticism, the seminary allowed Bonhoeffer to integrate his theology and his philosophy of life while he sought to nurture and educate the young seminarians. While the foundations of his theology remained intact, Bonhoeffer attempted to create a seminary community based upon the Sermon on the Mount. He would later discuss many of these ideas in his section on Matthew 5-7 in *The Cost of Discipleship* that he published in 1937. He developed many of the concepts that he advocated in his 1938 publication, *Life Together,* in this quasi-monastic atmosphere. Unaware of his pacifist orientation, the seminarians found themselves stretched outside the boundaries of their typical German patriotism and almost blind obedience to the state. He forged a vital friendship with a local German aristocrat, Ruth von Kleist-Retzow, who later became a critical supporter of the German resistance to Hitler. He also found an irreplaceable friendship with Eberhard Bethge, who became one of his best-known biographers and, beginning at the end of April 1944, the recipient of his invaluable and soul-searing *Letters and Papers From Prison.*[35]

Some scholars have speculated about the nature of the relationship between Bonhoeffer and Bethge.[36] Such speculation falls outside the scope of this essay. However, it should be noted that an intimacy existed between the two that eclipsed any relationship that had existed for Bonhoeffer once he and his twin Sabine reached adulthood and she married Gerhard Leibholz. Bethge quickly became not only Bonhoeffer's student, but also his closest friend, mentee, confidante, confessor, and traveling companion. He provided the kind of emotional intimacy that Bonhoeffer had always craved and a void that neither family, other friends, and students, nor fellow scholars and colleagues had ever filled. Likewise, for over two years as leader of the underground seminary before the Gestapo closed the seminary, Bonhoeffer found his work the most fulfilling he had experienced to that point. During this same period, he helped his twin sister and her husband escape Germany and persecution because of his Jewish identification, despite his baptism as a Christian. At the same time, he continued his ecumenical contacts and continued to travel, speak, and write against the Nazi regime that ultimately resulted in his being declared an enemy of the state, the loss of his teaching privileges at the Berlin University, being forbidden to live in Berlin, and eventually in 1941, losing his publishing privileges. For a time, he sought to replace his teaching at the seminary with the leadership of "collective pastorates," but the Gestapo ultimately closed even that avenue of ministry for him in 1940, after the war had begun. As Europe moved rapidly from one crisis to the next, Bonhoeffer went briefly to the United States for a speaking tour in 1939. Tempted by an offer to remain in the U. S. and teach in safety, Bonhoeffer opted to return to Germany as a spiritual shepherd to suffer with his sheep if necessary. He recognized that if he hoped to have a role in serving the German people when Nazism finally died, he had to serve his homeland and risk persecution and possible death. As he wrote Reinhold Niebuhr, "I must live through this difficult period of our national history with the Christian people of Germany. I will have no right to participate in the reconstruction of Christian life in Germany after the war if I do not share in the trials of this time with my people." He added, "Christians in Germany will face the terrible alternative of either willing the defeat of their nation in order that Christian civilization may survive or willing the victory of their nation and thereby destroying our civilization." He determined then, "I know which of these alternatives I must choose; but I cannot make that choice in security."[37]

From Crisis to Conspiracy

Before World War II even began in Europe, Bonhoeffer decided upon his return to make connections with the conspiracy to remove Hitler from power. Largely led by Hans Oster and Wilhelm Canaris, the conservative leaders of the *Abwehr*, the German military intelligence agency existed outside the control of the Nazi party. The scope of support for the conspiracy among German leaders outside of Nazism depended on the level of criminality that they discovered in Hitler's regime and the string of successes achieved by German armies in the Fall of 1939, throughout 1940, and most of 1941. His brother-in-law, Hans von Dohnanyi, served as his key connection with the conspiracy, both in the sense of providing him and others with information about the gross atrocities committed by the Gestapo, and the S.S. and in helping him avoid participation in violence on behalf of the Third Reich through direct service in the military. Ultimately, not only did the conspiracy involve von Dohnanyi and Bonhoeffer, but also his brother-in-law Rudiger Schleicher and his brother Klaus. Immediately before the invasion of Poland in September of 1939, Canaris and Oster managed to appoint Bonhoeffer as civilian agent for the *Abwehr*, utilizing the excuse of Bonhoeffer's ecumenical contacts as the rationale for his assignment and draft deferment, while also providing him an excuse to travel on behalf of the conspiracy. As the conspiracy evolved, a key function Bonhoeffer performed was to make people like Bishop Bell aware that opposition to the Nazis existed, though largely powerless and completely underground. Throughout much of 1942, he traveled on behalf of the resistance, including one trip to Sweden where he met with Bishop Bell to relay messages from the conspiracy that might be carried on to British intelligence. Primarily, the shadowy and nascent conspiracy hoped to persuade the Allies that, in the event of a coup successfully directed against the Nazis, that there were Germans who were not Nazis with whom the Allies could peacefully negotiate and end the catastrophic war. As Bosanquet notes, it was during the early part of this period that Bonhoeffer resolved that to participate in a violent overthrow of a ruthless dictator and his henchmen should be preferred to continuing support for a criminal regime and allowing even the perpetuation of even greater violence. By this time, he and others like Canaris had become increasingly aware of some of the worst of atrocities being carried out on the eastern front, especially against the Jews of Eastern Europe. Also, during this same time, he began writing his landmark but ultimately uncompleted *Ethics*, even though in 1941 the regime forbade his publishing because of the nature of his previous publications and his earlier public speaking that the Reich Writers' Guild ruled subversive.[38]

During this same period as he took every opportunity to work on *Ethics* and traveled on behalf of the conspiracy, Bonhoeffer fell in love with the granddaughter of his old friend and supporter Ruth von Kleist-Retzow, the attractive and far younger Maria von Wedemeyer. In part mystified by this experience, since he had never even had a girlfriend, his attachment to her may have been hastened by the traumatic times in which they lived as well as the engagement of his close friend Eberhard Bethge to Bonhoeffer's equally young niece, Renate Schleicher. Likewise, von Wedemeyer's attraction to Bonhoeffer may have come from the long family connection, her sense of personal loss of loved ones in the war, and the attractiveness of the Bonhoeffer family as well as the favorable attentions of a man much older and with a well-regarded reputation. Regardless of the reasons, Bonhoeffer and von Wedemeyer surprisingly became engaged in mid-January 1943.[39]

Arrest and Imprisonment

Only about two weeks prior to his engagement to von Wedemeyer, Bonhoeffer had written a reflection on the previous ten years to Bethge, Oster, and Dohnanyi. In it, he summarized a call for what Marsh describes as "a return to aristocrats of conscience" and a "bygone code of chivalry" as well as "a renewal of quality" that "demanded a return from the newspaper and radio to the book" and a move "from feverishly acquisitive activity to contemplative leisure and stillness, from frenzy to composure, from the sensational to the reflective." Two weeks later, he was engaged and exactly two months from the date of his engagement a plot to destroy Hitler on board his airplane failed, and the S. S. discovered the failed bomb. Within three weeks, the Gestapo arrested Dietrich and Klaus Bonhoeffer, Hans von Dohnanyi, and Bonhoeffer's sister Christine von Dohnanyi, followed by their brother-in-law Rudiger Schleicher and Eberhard Bethge in the following months.[40]

The months that followed cemented Bonhoeffer's legacy in many regards. His imprisonment for many months came in the Tegel Prison in

Berlin. While there, Bonhoeffer managed to receive some of the advantages of being a privileged inmate despite the charges brought against him and intense interrogation by Nazi authorities. He received some visitors through bribes provided to the guards, occasionally received food, flowers, books, and letters, and sent letters to Maria von Wedemeyer and Eberhard Bethge. In isolation, he read as he had been unable to read for years. For months, the family hoped that evidence or lack of evidence against him and the continued delays surrounding Hans von Dohnanyi's trial might allow his release. Unfortunately, his imprisonment forced him to suffer through Allied bombing raids of Berlin while trapped in his prison cell. While frightening, the attacks demonstrated the continued decline of the Reich. Over the months that followed, Bonhoeffer read, wrote, reflected, and waited. He wrote a series of letters to Bethge that have been labeled his "prison theology." In these letters, he called for a more authentic Christianity, asking questions like, "what is Christianity, or who is Christ actually for us today?" or reminding his friend that "God is the beyond in the midst of our lives. The church stands not at the point where human powers fail, at the boundaries, but in the center of the village."[41]

About three weeks later, he sent Eberhard and his niece Renate a meditation he had written for their son, his great-nephew, and namesake, in honor of young Dietrich's baptism, hoping that the boy might someday read it. Identifying his godson as "the first of a new generation in our family," Bonhoeffer wrote that he currently shared "the fate of many other good Germans and Protestant Christians" and he also "tried to keep up the spirit" that the family represented. He also reminded Dietrich that he had been born into a "cosmopolitan culture of the old middle-class tradition represented by [his and Renate's family]" that had "created, in those who inherit it, a proud awareness of being called to high responsibility in public service, intellectual achievement and leadership" as well as "a deep-rooted obligation to be guardians of a great historical and intellectual tradition." Furthermore, he added, "This will endow you, even before you are aware of it, with a way of thinking and acting that you can never lose without being untrue to yourself."[42]

In this simple but deep statement written to his godson, Bonhoeffer essentially defined much about himself and how he had reached this point in his life. His family, the tradition in which they had reared him and his siblings, and the calling that was placed upon his life had laid the foundation upon which he had built his life. But he explained further the Christian component of this "great historical and intellectual tradition" of which he wrote. He admitted that "for the greater part of our lives, pain was a stranger to us. Avoiding pain, as far as possible, was one of our subconscious guiding principles." Bonhoeffer further confessed that he, like others of his generation, sought to guide their lives also "with reason and justice, and when they both failed us, we no longer saw any way forward" and that they had repeatedly "overestimated" their importance. But the pastor-theologian then called his godson back to what it meant to be baptized as a Christian, stating clearly that he and other Christians like Eberhard and Renate were "being thrown back all the way to the beginnings of their own understanding." He dreamed that "the day will come—when people will once more be called to speak the word of God in such a way that the world is changed and renewed." He concluded his meditation with a quotation from Proverbs 4:18 and the words, "Until then the Christian cause will be a quiet and hidden one, but there will be people who pray and do justice and wait for God's own time."[43] This message of hope and light in the midst of darkness and despair typifies who Bonhoeffer had become.

After more than a year's imprisonment in which he experienced his thirty-eighth birthday, he and his loved ones still hoped for his release. Unfortunately, on July 20, 1944, the most nearly successful coup and assassination attempt led by Count Claus von Stauffenberg failed, and the Gestapo began mass arrests and executions. During the course of their thousands of arrests, Nazi investigators uncovered the connection between the Canaris, Oster, and von Dohnanyi conspiracy and that of the von Stauffenberg assassination attempt, including uncovering Abwehr files that implicated Bonhoeffer. More arrests followed including those of Renate's father, Rudiger, and Bonhoeffer's brother, Klaus, and his relocation to a more restricted and harsher Gestapo prison in Berlin. A few months later, a series of moves took place that carried Bonhoeffer and other members of resistance like Canaris and Oster to concentration camps at Buchenwald, Regensburg, and eventually to Schonberg and Flossenbürg and the final trial and execution. Though the traditional eye-witness account is given above, research by Charles Marsh suggests that the actual hangings may have been far more barbaric and painful. A few days later the SS executed Klaus Bonhoeffer and Rudiger Schleicher by firing squad.[44]

Conclusion

Just as people sometimes seek to re-make God in their own image, so do we also want to re-make our heroes in our own images. Bonhoeffer is one such hero. As we look at his life, writings, theology, and leadership, we must be careful not to re-make him in our own image. At certain difficult times in the course of humanity, key individuals have stepped on the stage of human history to shape the direction of the future in one manner or another. Some examples might be Augustine and the collapse of the Roman Empire, Catherine of Siena and the terror of the Black Death, Martin Luther and the upheaval of the Protestant Reformation, Abraham Lincoln and the great trial of democracy and freedom, Clara Barton and the crisis of modern warfare, Mohandas Gandhi and the death of colonialism, William Wilberforce, Martin Luther King, Jr., and Nelson Mandela and the course of human dignity, Mother Teresa and the perpetual profanity of poverty, Winston Churchill and Franklin Roosevelt and the challenges of modern tyranny and global war, and of course, Dietrich Bonhoeffer and those two challenges as well as the horror of genocide. As we admire him (or them), to understand either Bonhoeffer or these others or those like them, we must continue to seek to understand those elements which made them who they are and try to both emulate them and to encourage others to do so as well. We cannot be them, but they can encourage us to be better at who we are and who God calls us to be.

Was Bonhoeffer liberal, conservative, moderate, centrist, modernist, or was he something else? Was he most influenced by classical liberalism, or by the neo-orthodoxy of Barth and Brunner, or by Tillich and Bultmann? Or was he something entirely unique? At the end of the day, this writer concludes that Dietrich Bonhoeffer cannot be neatly categorized, in part because of his distinctive experience within the context of World War II, response to Nazism, and ultimate imprisonment and death. At thirty-nine, he died all too early much the way that Martin Luther King, Jr. or even Abraham Lincoln died much too early, before the full development of his thought could play out and be recorded. Bonhoeffer was Bonhoeffer in a way that only the greatest of men and women can only be unique beyond other great men and women. Like these heroes and heroines, we must be careful not to lapse into hagiography. He, like they, was human with human weaknesses and foibles as well as many admirable traits. Acknowl-

edging this should encourage us with our weaknesses and foibles to persevere in seeking to fulfill our callings.

At the close of his brief "Memoir" of Bonhoeffer at the beginning of
the 1949 edition of *The Cost of Discipleship*, his brother-in-law Gerhard
Leibholz wrote, "Thus Bonhoeffer's life and death have given us great
hope for the future. He has set a model for a new type of true leadership
inspired by the gospel, daily ready for martyrdom and death… The victory
which he has won was a victory for us all, a conquest never to be undone,
of love, light, and liberty."[45]

Endnotes

[1] Eric Metaxas, *Bonhoeffer: Pastor, Martyr, Prophet, Spy* (Nashville, TN: Thomas Nelson, 2010), 532; Eberhard Bethge, trans., Rosaleen Ockenden, *Costly Grace: An Illustrated Biography of Dietrich Bonhoeffer* (New York, NY: Harper & Row Publisher, 1979), 92-107, 132; and Mary Bosanquet, *The Life and Death of Dietrich Bonhoeffer* (New York, NY: Harper & Row Publisher, 1968), 277-78.

[2] Geffrey B. Kelly and F. Burton Nelson, *The Cost of Moral Leadership: The Spirituality of Dietrich Bonhoeffer* (Grand Rapids, MI; Cambridge, MA: William B. Eerdmans Publishing Company, 2003), xi.

[3] See Metaxas, *Bonhoeffer: Pastor, Martyr, Prophet, Spy.*

[4] Eberhard Bethge, *Costly Grace*, 18.

[5] Dallas M. Roark, *Dietrich Bonhoeffer* (Waco, TX: Word Books, Publisher, 1972), 13; Gerhard Leibholz, "Memoir" in Dietrich Bonhoeffer, *Cost of Discipleship* (New York, NY: The MacMillan Company, 1949 edition), 9; Renate Bethge, "Foreword," in *Cost of Moral Leadership*, viii; and Kelly and Nelson, xii.)

[6] Charles Marsh, *Strange Glory: A Life of Dietrich Bonhoeffer* (New York, NY: Alfred A. Knopf, 2014), 9; Roark, 13-14; Dietrich Bonhoeffer, "Eulogy for Adolf von Harnack ," in Clifford J. Green and Michael P. DeJonge, eds., *The Bonhoeffer Reader* (Minneapolis, MN: Fortress Press, 2013), 16-17; Dietrich Bonhoeffer, "The History of Twentieth Century Systematic Theology," in Green and DeJonge, 160ff; Dietrich Bonhoeffer, "The Nature of the Church," in Green and DeJonge, 183; Dietrich Bonhoeffer, "History and Good," in Green and DeJonge, 659; and Dietrich Bonhoeffer, "Letters from Prison," April 30, 1944 and June 8, 1944, in Green and DeJonge, 777, 794, 797.

[7] Marsh, 14,15, 16-17 and Eberhard Bethge, *Dietrich Bonhoeffer: Man of Vision, Man of Courage,* translated by Eric Mosbacher, *et al* (New York, NY: Harper & Row, 1970), 9-10. Bonhoeffer quotation as cited in Bethge.

[8] Bethge, 27-28 and Marsh, 11, 12, 39-40.

[9] Bethge, *Costly Grace*, 29-33; Marsh, 22-23; and Kelly and Nelson, 7.

[10] Ibid., 31-33.

[11] Eberhard Bethge, *Bonhoeffer*, 37-42 and Marsh, 34-38.

[12] Bethge, *Bonhoeffer*, 44; Marsh, 43-46; and James Woelfel, *Bonhoeffer's Theology: Classical and Revolutionary* (Nashville, TN Abingdon Press, 1970), 19.

[13] Marsh, 32, 44; Bethge, *Bonhoeffer*, 46-47; and Dietrich Bonhoeffer, *Act and Being* in Green and DeJonge, 93-109.

[14] Bethge, *Bonhoeffer*, 47-49 and Marsh, 50-60.

[15] Bethge, *Bonhoeffer*, 45-46; Marsh, 43, 44, 45; Woelfel, 17; and Bonhoeffer, "Eulogy for Adolf von Harnack," in Green and DeJonge, 16, 17.

[16] Roark, 14-15; Bethge, *Bonhoeffer*, 50-55; Marsh 51-57 and Woelfel, 89.

[17] Woelfel, 72-74, 83-88.

[18] Marsh, 48.

[19] Bethge, 23.

[20] Bethge, *Bonhoeffer*, 57-59; Marsh, 57, 59; and Bonhoeffer, *Sanctorum Communio,* in Green and DeJonge, 20ff.

[21] Bethge, *Bonhoeffer*, 70-89 and Marsh, 62-87.

[22] Dietrich Bonhoeffer, "Jesus Christ and the Essence of Christianity," in Dejonge and Green, 73.

[23] Marsh 84-86.

[24] Bethge, *Dietrich Bonhoeffer*, 94-102; Metaxas, 89-91, 94; Dietrich Bonhoeffer, *Act and Being*, 93-104 in Dejonge and Green; see also Dejonge and Green's editorial comments, 93; and Marsh, 93-101.

[25] Marsh, 108.

[26] Jean Lassere as quoted in Marsh, 110.

[27] Dietrich Bonhoeffer, *The Cost of Discipleship*, in Green and Dejonge, 498. See the entire section on the Sermon on the Mount in *Cost of Discipleship*, in Green and Dejonge, 490-510. See also Marsh, 109-10, Kelly and Nelson, 101-02; Michael Pasquarello, III, *Dietrich Bonhoeffer and the Theology of a Preaching Life* (Waco, TX: Baylor University Press, 2017), 68; and Geffrey Kelly, "The Life and Death of a Modern Martyr," and F. Burton Nelson, "Friends He Met in America," in *Christian History*, X:32:10, 37.

[28] Reggie L. Williams, *Bonhoeffer's Black Jesus: Harlem Renaissance Theology and the Ethic of Resistance* (Waco, TX: Baylor University Press, 2014), 19, 39, 101-02, 123; Metaxas, 108-10; Pasquarello, 72-79; Bonhoeffer, *The Cost of Discipleship*, in Green and Dejonge, 461, 477; and Dietrich Bonhoeffer, "The Church and the Jewish Question," in Green and Dejonge, 371-78.

[29] Marsh, 157-73. See also Michael Burleigh, *The Third Reich: A New History* (New York, NY: Hill and Wang, 2000), 719-20.

[30] Dietrich Bonhoeffer, "The Church and the Jewish Question," in Green and Dejonge, 376. See also Dietrich Bonhoeffer, "The Jewish-Christian Question as *Status Confessionis*" in Green and Dejonge, 379-81 and Dietrich Bonhoeffer, "The Aryan Paragraph in the Church," in Green and Dejonge, 382-88.

[31] Marsh, 160.

[32] Burleigh, 720-21; and "The Barmen Theological Declaration," at http://www.sacred-texts.com/chr/barmen.htm, accessed March 9, 2019

[33] Metaxas, 195-204, 236, 237.

[34] Richard Evans, *The Third Reich in Power* (New York, NY: The Penguin Press, 2005), 31-41 and Metaxas, 246, 247.

[35] Marsh, 227-35, 237-47 and Bonhoeffer, *The Cost of Discipleship*, in Green and Dejonge, 490-510. See also Bonhoeffer, *Life Together*, in Green and Dejonge, 514-61; Kelly and Nelson, 145-72; and Bonhoeffer, *Letters and Papers From Prison*, in Green and Dejonge, 775-817.

[36] Marsh, 305-318. Chapter 12 of Marsh's biography on Bonhoeffer discusses in detail the relationship with Bethge, and Marsh has had conflict on this matter with the other prominent Bonhoeffer biographer, Eric Metaxas. An excellent overview of the matter

is the blog post by Trevin Wax from 2014 entitled *"Was Bonhoeffer Gay?" and Other Adventures in Missing the Point* found at thegospelcoalition.org.

[37] Marsh, 231-62; Bethge, *Bonhoeffer*, 558-59; and Dietrich Bonhoeffer letter to Reinhold Niebuhr as cited in Bethge, 559.

[38] Marsh, 288-91, 345-47; Metaxas, 369-78; and Bosanquet, 220-38. One of the most fascinating individuals in the entire conspiracy against Adolph Hitler was Admiral Wilhelm Canaris, director of the *Abwehr*. For more see, Richard Bassett, *Hitler's Spy Chief: The Wilhelm Canaris Mystery* (London, England: Weidenfeld & Nicolson, 2005).

[39] Marsh, 332-38 and Metaxas, 405-21.

[40] Ibid., 340-44.

[41] Ibid., 348-66 and Dietrich Bonhoeffer to Eberhard Bethge, April 30, 1944, in Dejonge and Green, 777, 779.

[42] Dietrich Bonhoeffer, "Thoughts on the Day of Baptism of Dietrich Wilhelm Rudiger Bethge," ca. May 16-18, 1944, in Dejonge and Green, 783.

[43] Ibid., 787-788.

[44] Marsh, 382-92.

[45] Gerhard Leibholz, "Memoir," in Dietrich Bonhoeffer, *The Cost of Discipleship*, 27.

Chapter 4

THE PHENOMENOLOGY OF A LEADER

Dr. Jordan Davis

The question considering if a leader is born or made persists even in modern leadership discussions and is certainly applicable to Dietrich Bonhoeffer. The broader discussion on leadership takes different approaches and for example, Angela Duckworth writes in her widely popular book entitled *Grit,* that talent (natural-born ability) does matter and also the willingness of an individual to persevere also matters and according to Duckworth, may matter more than natural talent and ability.[1] Then, for Dietrich Bonhoeffer, was he born exceptionally gifted, or did he develop leadership abilities and skills along the way? Throughout this chapter, it will become clear that Dietrich Bonhoeffer was born with exceptional academic abilities and also having experiences and opportunities which supported his development as a scholar and a courageous leader.

Early Life and Development

Dietrich Bonhoeffer was raised in an affluent, upper-middle-class family. His father, Karl, was a well-educated man who expected much from his children. The elder Bonhoeffer was a psychiatrist and, perhaps above all else, an intellectual. As a medical doctor, Karl placed his faith in science and empirical study. His focus on the world he could *see* most certainly influenced the eventual formulation of Dietrich's humanistic theology.[2]

Additionally, Karl created an atmosphere of open discussion with his children, allowing for disagreement if a clear and concise argument could be made to support one's opinion. He often entertained other academic minds from Berlin, including theologians, who would teach Dietrich later in life in rousing intellectual discussions around the dinner table. Marsh identified Dietrich as outstanding in his academic pursuits as a child and teenager and graduated high school two years before his classmates. The family focus on academic achievement helped him excel across different disciplines, and this environment of academic discourse may very well have set the stage for Dietrich's journey into theology and philosophy.[3]

Dietrich's mother, Paula, came from a family of theologians, and she was the primary source of religious and spiritual influence in his early life.[4] However, Dietrich's father did not share his wife's interest in religion. A dutiful Lutheran, Paula Bonhoeffer was the nurturer of Dietrich's early spiritual development. She educated all her children at home until the family moved to Berlin, offering special consideration to Dietrich's religious studies, and Dietrich announced he would become a theologian at the age of thirteen. At fifteen years old, he began signing his name including the self-given title of theologian.

The interest in matters of God came directly from his mother's influence as others in his family were not fond of spiritual matters. Mrs. Bonhoeffer's faith was, however, more of an exercise in tradition than a relationship with an Almighty God. She shared her husband's interest in science, especially when providing care for her children. She was well-versed in developmental psychology, and this influenced how she disciplined her children. While Paula was strict in her own way, she encouraged her children to explore and grow as individuals. Charles Marsh stated that, to Paula, "the point of discipline and order was to inspire free exploration and invention."[5] His parents' authoritative parenting style provided Dietrich with an ideal environment for healthy psychological development. He was provided with clear, consistently reinforced boundaries, and was given freedom within those boundaries to develop an independent sense of self.[6] Dietrich's mother's presence and care also created a secure attachment, which set the stage for Dietrich's independence and desire to explore later in life.[7]

Dietrich also found interest in theological matters from thoughts and experiences outside the direct influence of his parents. As young children, he and his twin sister shared a room, and they would thoughtfully ponder death and eternity as they watched funeral processions march toward the nearby cemetery. At such a young age, Dietrich routinely rehearsed his last words, imagining what it would be like to confront death and stand at the gates of Heaven.[8]

There is no way to know exactly why Dietrich was fascinated with spirituality as a child. His father categorically rejected spiritual matters. Marsh's comments on this provide insight to Karl's view of the spiritual: "Karl subscribed to an enlightened skepticism toward the miraculous and the supernatural, toward any belief that contradicted the laws of reason."[9] Amid this type of home, Dietrich Bonhoeffer seemed to have this innate interest in spiritual matters especially life after death. Perhaps, this mortality salience was further deepened when Dietrich's brother, Walter, died after only a month of service in World War I. This privileged family, which had never really experienced suffering up to this point, was unexpectedly thrust into a period of disequilibrium as the tranquil homeostasis that was so carefully crafted by Karl and Paula Bonhoeffer suddenly disappeared with news of the death of a son.[10] Karl reacted by repressing his grief but expressing emotion in ways the children had never seen, and Paula became so depressed that she moved out of the house so that her children would not be subjected to her suffering. As Murray Bowen postulated, a new balance must be found within a family unit when homeostasis is lost.[11] As a result, new roles were inevitably established among the members of the family. This may be why, not long after Walter's death, Dietrich chose to reveal his intentions to become a theologian to his family.

Dietrich sought to stand out in everything he did. He excelled academically, but still competed for recognition with a young female classmate, Maria Wiegert, who was the top student in the class and beloved by all her teachers. Dietrich resented the fact that his academic success was qualified as being "top among boys."[12] Dietrich also struggled to stand out in his family. All his older siblings were high-achieving and successful, and they followed their father's humanistic example. Church and religion were frivolous pursuits to the elder Bonhoeffer men, but Dietrich found them fascinating. While many in his family expected Dietrich to pursue a career in music, Dietrich surprised everyone (except, perhaps, his mother) when he declared his intention to study theology. When his brothers protested by pointing out the flaws of the church as an institution, Dietrich stated that he "shall reform it."[13] There was no shortage of pride or ego with the drive to succeed in young Dietrich. The successful family life certainly helped to cultivate these desires in this young man.

Dietrich did have a yearning to not just succeed but to have success in a particular fashion. It was not just simply to excel, but to excel in something that truly stood out from the rest of his siblings. His drive and desires aligned with other research on this area of the family dynamic. The youngest children, especially in large families, commonly have several parental figures, primarily in the form of older siblings. Along with being among the youngest of the Bonhoeffer children, Dietrich was also a twin which may have intensified his pursuit of distinction among his siblings. Twins often struggle with differentiation of self and identity formation that is separate and unique from the other sibling.[14] Dietrich was not immune from this common family dynamic. His drive toward theology seemed to be a reaction to, or perhaps in some ways a rejection of, the expectations placed on him as a Bonhoeffer child. His declaration as a young adolescent male that he would be a theologian who would reform the institution of the church was an assertion of self and individual identity. Ironically, this drive toward individuation was most likely a culmination of the installation of independence, exploration, and free thought that was so greatly emphasized by his parents. In an unexpected way, Karl and Paula Bonhoeffer helped lead Dietrich to the doorstep of theology and church ministry simply by allowing him to arrive there on his own accord.

Dietrich also seemed to possess a strong sense of social responsibility and a desire for justice. This was primarily influenced by his father, who expected his children to "stand by the weak."[15] The younger Bonhoeffer described himself as being "like a fierce lion" when standing up for a cause that he considered being just. Marsh stated that Dietrich was "aware of his privilege and its obligations."[16] However, according to his reflections later in life, at a young age, Dietrich's desire for justice was born more out of ego than a love for his fellow man. At this point in young Dietrich's development, he demonstrated a desire for social justice in a way that was mature beyond his years. However, his motivations revealed a somewhat stunted development of moral reasoning. He admitted that his desire at the time was to gain recognition for being morally superior rather than to promote a just cause or protect his fellow man.

This type of motivation aligns with Kohlberg's conventional stage of moral development, wherein the person conforms to socially acceptable norms and rules to win the approval of others.[17] This may reflect the life of privilege that Bonhoeffer experienced up to this point. Karl and Paula instilled in Dietrich a strong moral compass, but his experience did not allow for a true empathetic understanding of the people around him. The Bonhoeffers hardly noticed the Turnip Winter of 1917, when many in the country were starving and food was being rationed, and while Dietrich was in seminary, he paid little attention to the economic crisis occurring in Germany, focusing instead on a trip to Italy.[18] It would not be until later in life that his desire for justice and sense of social responsibility would be sharpened into love for his fellow man and a true understanding of suffering.

Despite his self-proclaimed shortcomings in terms of pride, ego, and privilege, young Dietrich was described by his twin sister Sabine as a sensitive and caring boy. Sabine shared a story of Dietrich carrying her knapsack through deep snow and walking before her to create a path so she could walk uninhibited.[19] Sabine also noted that Dietrich was more affable toward family than classmates, with his twin sister being his primary playmate, affirming the developmental assumption that the family is the most important source of socialization for most children until they reach adolescence.[20] In addition, Sabine stated that "Dietrich was warmly attached to every member of his family."[21] Yet Sabine seemed to recognize a greater calling on Dietrich's life, concluding that "he must have felt that the atmosphere was too narrow for his spirit."[22]

Bonhoeffer was truly exceptional in his desire to grasp the meaning of the ultimate existential questions of life. He sought to fully understand eternity, life after death, and God Himself. These were not ordinary musings for a young, affluent, upper-middle-class boy. While his family created an environment for healthy cognitive development, and his mother, Paula, fanned the flames of Dietrich's spiritual inquisitions, it seemed that his desire to understand God was more intrinsically motivated. In a memoir for the revised edition of *The Cost of Discipleship*, Leibholz asserted that the call to theology was in Dietrich's blood, citing the number of prominent theologians on his mother's side.[23] It may be more accurate to say that this call to study theology, the Church, and Christ was in Dietrich's soul.

Encountering the Gospel

Bonhoeffer began his theological studies in Tübingen at the age of 18. He would spend a year there, joining a fraternity deemed *Der Igel* (The Hedgehog) mostly out of a sense of obligation. His father and uncle were both former members of this fraternity, and, consequently, Dietrich was doing what was expected of him. Dietrich's older brothers, Klaus and Karl-Friedrich had both rejected *Der Igel* on moral grounds. Klaus found the fraternity life to be "undemocratic and woefully nationalistic."[24] Karl-Friedrich, who spent his time in Tübingen after returning from The Great War, disagreed with his fellow pledges on political views, especially the benefits of communism. One of Dietrich's fellow pledges resigned because he could not reconcile the requirements of the fraternity to his Christian faith. Dietrich, however, showed no real interest in or awareness of "politics and human rights."[25]

At the age of eighteen, Dietrich continued to demonstrate a very underdeveloped sense of moral reasoning, remaining primarily fixed in Kohlberg's conventional stage.[26] Never mind that the fraternity was denounced by both of his older brothers, or that another pledge pointed out the problematic relationship between fraternity life and the practical expression of his faith. Dietrich was expected to join, and so he did. For Bonhoeffer, responsibility was born out of a desire to please or to be excellent in the eyes of others, and justice remained more of an intellectual concept than a practical reality for young Dietrich. Interestingly, he had disappointed his family (especially his father) by choosing to study theology but chose to please his family by joining the fraternity despite the advice of others and potential conflicts with burgeoning religious faith.

During his time in Tübingen, Bonhoeffer also spent a transformative semester abroad in Italy. He traveled to Rome and studied the wonders of the Catholic Church. His visit to Rome produced quite different results than the visit to Rome of another well-known German minister, Martin Luther. While Rome created a sense of awe and wonder of the grandeur and global nature of the church, Luther "did not leave Rome with a sense of spiritual renewal; instead, he departed disappointed and doubtful."[27] Bonhoeffer's privilege and worldliness were never more evident as, while his country was steeped in a terrible economic depression, he planned his itinerary for a holiday in a foreign country. Little thought was given to the suffering of his fellow countrymen, which is a stark contrast to the Bonhoeffer of later years. This may be in part a result of the egocentrism that is characteristic of late adolescence,[28] as well as a product of the privilege to which Bonhoeffer was accustomed.

From Tübingen, Dietrich moved to Berlin. While in Berlin, he studied theology under some of the most prominent names in Germany, and, again, stood out among his peers and classmates. Bonhoeffer was known as "an exceptional thinker, applying himself to both theology and philosophy."[29] He was deeply influenced by Luther and Barth, as reflected in his theology throughout the course of his life. During this time, Bonhoeffer's focus on humanism, which was so intentionally instilled in him by his father's teachings, was also apparent in his theology. Bonhoeffer wrote his doctoral dissertation on the communal nature of the church. He also authored a book, *Act and Being*, a work that is both theological and philosophical, in which he discussed "the church as the community in which the act of God's revelation and ontology find their unity."[30] The person of Christ, however, was not yet the central figure of this community.

Although the central theme of the communal aspect of the church remained a primary aspect of Bonhoeffer's theology in his early works, his evolving view of Christ served to provide a more sharply focused theological understanding. It appeared that Bonhoeffer's theology regarding community did not fulfill his desire to *experience* community. He struggled with the nationalistic culture in which he was raised in Germany, and this culture would insidiously matriculate into his theology and teaching.[31] However, a turning point in Bonhoeffer's life came when he left his comfortable existence in Germany to study for a year in America. Outwardly, Bonhoeffer reacted to the opportunity to travel to Union Seminary in New York as simply another chance to see the world. Inwardly, however, there seemed to be something more for which Bonhoeffer searched. As he would write to a friend, he went to America looking for the cloud of witnesses that he had studied about in Hebrews 12.[32]

Unfortunately, his expectations were not met, and the negative attributes of his ego were on display. His initial reaction to the students he encountered at Union Seminary was one of disdain and frustration. His excellent German theological education left him underwhelmed at the weak, liberal ideology that seemed to pervade the campus. "There is no theology here" he would eventually conclude."[33] Ultimately, Bonhoeffer found the community he was searching for outside of the academic circles to which he was so accustomed. Two different friendships in particular fashioned

Bonhoeffer's worldview into something he had not before seen. The first was with a French pastor, Jean Lasserre. The relationship between Bonhoeffer and Lasserre was forged through the overcoming of grievances between their national identities. As the two fought over the implications of the Treaty of Versailles and wrestled with their innate identities as German and French, they learned to see that "the communion, the community of the church is much more important than the national community."[34]

In Lasserre, Bonhoeffer encountered "an obedience to Jesus' demand for peace such as he had never experienced before."[35] While Bonhoeffer never identified himself as a pacifist, Lasserre's influence on Bonhoeffer's view of the German war effort and his view of nationalism, which had before weaved its way into Bonhoeffer's preaching, is undeniable. Bonhoeffer became an advocate for peace. Eberhard Bethge wrote that even though Bonhoeffer had been aware of pacifist movements in Germany, it was not until he met with Lasserre that he became a vocal supporter of peaceful dissidence in his native country.[36] Through Lasserre's influence, Bonhoeffer developed a significant departure from the nationalist culture in which he had been raised. Lasserre's impact on Bonhoeffer's phenomenology cannot be understated. This relationship between a German and Frenchman laid the foundation for the ideas of Bonhoeffer's future peaceful rebellion.

While at Union Seminary, Dietrich experienced another aspect of American life that he was not expecting. He developed a close friendship with African American seminarian Franklin Fisher. This relationship was monumental in Dietrich building the psychological and emotional schemas on which Bonhoeffer's theological, ethical, and spiritual views were based for the rest of his life.[37]

Before Fisher befriended Dietrich at Union Seminary, Bonhoeffer had no real contact or experience in dealing with other races or cultures apart from his own. When Bonhoeffer attended Abyssinian Baptist Church with Fisher, he discovered a profound new teaching of the Gospel that moved him deeply. Bonhoeffer was transfixed by the music, the presentation of the Gospel, the emotional aspect of the faith, and the tradition of the African American church.[38] The Negro spirituals became his anthems, and he would later lead his congregation in his underground church in Germany in singing these songs.[39] Music may have been Bonhoeffer's strongest connection to the African American church experience initially, as he was so musically inclined himself. It deeply connected with a part of him that academic theology never did.

Over the course of the next six months, Bonhoeffer immersed himself in the culture of Harlem. He engaged with the culture, and, perhaps for the first time in his life, grew to understand oppression and suffering as real, practical matters as opposed to academic concepts. He engaged with the youth of Harlem and identified so deeply with the African American community that he was accepted as though "he had never been an outsider at all."[40]

During his time in Harlem, Bonhoeffer also met with various ministries to marginalized people groups, including the American Civil Liberties Union, the Women's Trade Union League, and the Worker's Education Bureau of America. Bonhoeffer seemed to not only be immersing himself in marginalized culture but also identifying with it as well. It is an interesting juxtaposition to observe this privileged German boy, who grew up safely sheltered from the suffering of his fellow countrymen, now discovering a newfound sense of purpose in identifying with the suffering of a foreign people group.

Fisher positively recounted a story of an evening dinner with Bonhoeffer where Bonhoeffer was disgusted at how Fisher was treated due to the color of his skin. When Bonhoeffer discovered that Fisher would not be served in the same manner as everyone else in the restaurant, Bonhoeffer "ostentatiously left the place."[41] Bonhoeffer's moral development had grown beyond the conventional stage and into Kohlberg's postconventional stage of moral reasoning. Bonhoeffer identified universal ethical ideals that directly rejected the law of the land, and he chose to no longer conform to principles he now considered unethical.[42] He condemned injustice and stood up for others, not out of a sense of pride, but out of a genuine desire to see that which was wrong made right. This growth was born out of a friendship. A simple friendship had a profound impact.

Bonhoeffer also traveled into the southern United States with his friend Jean Lasserre. Together, they encountered racism on a level neither had experienced before. Bonhoeffer was disillusioned by the white pastors he heard speaking so hatefully regarding African Americans in southern states. He wrote of the "terrible miscarriage of justice" and stated that "the way that the southerners talk about Negroes is simply repugnant…and the pastors are no better."[43]

Bonhoeffer experienced a respite from the oppressive hatred while worshipping with the black congregations in the South. He found their joy to be both refreshing and convicting. The freedom with which these oppressed people worshipped had a profound impact on Bonhoeffer's theology.[44] He saw the person of Jesus as the galvanizing figure within this community of believers, and this observation led Bonhoeffer to elevate Christ to the central figure in his theology. The lessons he internalized from Harlem and the southern United States significantly influenced his opposition of Hitler in Germany.

As a young adult, Bonhoeffer was moving out of the stage of finding his identity, and into the stage of searching for intimacy with others.[45] Marsh wrote that Bonhoeffer returned to Germany "ready at last to put away childish things…and begin to search the Christian and Jewish traditions for inspiration to peace-making, dissent, and civil courage."[46]

Choosing to Lead

Erik Erikson, a student of Sigmund Freud, delineated a theory of psychological development that encompasses the entire lifespan. Erikson's developmental theory is comprised of eight unique stages. In each stage, the person is confronted with a task, or psychosocial crisis, that he or she must face. Bonhoeffer left America at age twenty-five, during the young adult stage of life in which, according to Erikson, a person is faced with the task of finding intimacy.[47] When he left for America, Bonhoeffer was enraptured by the idea of community that he read about in Hebrews 12. He found his cloud of witnesses in Harlem, the African American churches in the southern states, and a French pacifist. Bonhoeffer found intimacy with those who suffered, and he carried that connection and concern with him back to Germany.

A change in Bonhoeffer's worldview upon his return to Germany is evident in his teaching. During his brief time lecturing in Berlin, Bonhoeffer began to share his view of Christ as the center of the community of the church. His writings revealed a deeper reflection on and interaction with Scripture. What was once an intellectual exercise for Bonhoeffer had become a relationship with a living God. The centrality of Christ in the community of the church also guided Bonhoeffer's resistance to the Nazi regime.

Bonhoeffer observed the church in Germany become a tool for the government. His newfound conviction regarding *costly grace* would not allow him to follow the example displayed by church leaders in his homeland.[48] He watched with disgust as the university and the church turned their loyalty to Hitler and his vision of a pure race. Bonhoeffer looked for support from his theological comrades, but found, to his surprise and disappointment, that issues such as the ethnic cleansing of the German race were a little more than problematic and not worthy of dissent or rebellion.[49]

Bonhoeffer's experiences in the United States directly impacted his response to Hitler's nationalistic proclamations. When other theologians and seminary students wondered aloud that the suffering being wrought on the Jews by the Reich was part of "the curse that had haunted the Jews since Jesus's death on the cross," Bonhoeffer's rebuke was sharp, and he declared the persecution of the Jews in Germany to be an act of unadulterated violence brought on by an evil regime.[50]

Bonhoeffer now viewed Christ as the center of reality and the unifying force through which everything in existence found its meaning, both the sacred and the secular. To Bonhoeffer, the supernatural and the natural could not be separated.[51] Intrinsic in this view of Christ is that the recognition of evil is met with the responsibility to act against it. Bonhoeffer began to look forward to what the Church would become after Hitler's regime was gone, and he desired to ensure a future in which the Church could thrive within the community. Bonhoeffer wrote in his work on ethics that "when Christianity is employed as a polemical weapon against the secular, this must be done in the name of a better secularity and, above all, it must not lead back to a static predominance of the spiritual sphere as an end in itself."[52]

Before his first venture into America, Bonhoeffer's sense of justice and morality was primarily conventional in nature as he sought to please others, perhaps just to show them that he was morally superior. He was not callous or unsympathetic, but his worldview was limited by his experiences. As previously mentioned, his privileged upbringing may have played a significant role in these feelings. As paradigms shifted and Christ's centrality became paramount in Bonhoeffer's theology, he progressed into what Kohlberg would describe as the postconventional stage of moral reasoning. Bonhoeffer's sense of morality was now motivated by universal standards that superseded any nationalism and moral superiority he may have once felt.[53] It may be more accurate to say that he was motivated by the universal standard, which he came to understand was Christ.

This change in thinking and belief led Bonhoeffer to involve himself in many different resistance movements against the Reich. He was the main teacher and leader of illegal seminaries first in Zingst, then in Finkenwalde until it was shut down in 1937 by the Gestapo, and he was among the pastors of the Confessing Church who opposed the state-sponsored Protestant Church who were commonly referred to as the German Christians. He traveled to London to preach and teach, but also to help Germans who were fleeing the oppression of the Nazi regime.[54] His rebellious acts were not part of an organized conspiracy but were his own actions of faith and conscience. The well-known German theologian Karl Barth wrote that Bonhoeffer did not see himself as some great heroic leader of a German rebellion, but as "an accomplice conscious of his guilt," and that he determined to "establish a space within the chaos of the conspiracy for Christian reflection."[55]

Bonhoeffer's faith and conscience about the situation in his home country were exhibited again as he traveled to America a second time in 1939. During this trip, he made what proved to be his most important life decision. America offered Bonhoeffer an opportunity for safety. If he stayed in America, he would be protected and would not be conscripted into the German military nor would he be arrested and imprisoned for his opposing beliefs. Marsh provided background to the reality faced even by pastors, "One factor in his abortive decision to go to American had not changed: he still lived under imminent threat of call-up to active combat duty. Protestant clergymen were receiving their orders every day in large numbers; nearly all theology students and seminarians would be sent to the front within the year."[56] He could stay far from the war while continuing to provide support to German resistance efforts from a distance. He could speak freely against the Nazis and the state of the German Christian church. The officials of the Third Reich would not be able to reach Bonhoeffer in America, but Bonhoeffer would not be able to reach the suffering German community with whom he now felt such a strong kinship. However, while traveling to American, he realized that he must return to German and be part of the resistance and, in his mind, part of the rebuilding of Germany after the demise of the Nazi regime.

In his classic work, *The Cost of Discipleship*, Bonhoeffer outlined a phenomenology that directly supported his ultimate choice to return to

Germany. To truly be Christ's disciple, Bonhoeffer believed he had to follow Christ even unto death.[57] He felt strongly that he could have no part in the post-war community in Germany if he did not also partake in its suffering. Bonhoeffer did not know that the choice to leave America and return to Germany would lead to his death. He was not actively seeking martyrdom but believed that his presence back in Germany could be a part of the solution. He acted out of obedience to Christ and service to Christ's community, the Church.

The Development of a Leader

How did Dietrich Bonhoeffer become such an influential leader? Was he more talented than others? Was his family upbringing the catalyst that propelled him to greatness? Did he make decisions amid situations that positioned him for a meaningful legacy? The answer to this exploration of his development as a leader is that all these factors played significant roles in his leadership development. The culmination of Bonhoeffer's life and work can be understood clearly by his fateful decision to return to Germany, as well as by his actions upon his arrival back in his homeland. His desire at a young age to understand the ultimate questions regarding eternity, his grounding in humanistic ideals by his parents, his tireless academic work ethic, and, finally, his exposure to and desire for communion with Christ and other believers, directed him to the one choice that sealed his legacy. With an opportunity for comfort and safety, Dietrich Bonhoeffer returned to the dangers of Nazi Germany. He chose to lead, not out of a sense of duty or obligation, but out of what he believed was obedience to Christ who was at the central focus of the cloud of witnesses for which he longed to partake and commune.

Endnotes

[1] Angela Duckworth. *Grit: The Power of Passion and Perseverance,* (New York, NY: Scribner, 2016).

[2] Charles Marsh. *Strange Glory: A Life of Dietrich Bonhoeffer.* (New York, NY: Alfred A. Knopf, 2014), 10.

[3] Marsh, 20.

[4] Ibid., 9.

[5] Ibid., 9.

[6] A. Bernier, S. M. Carlson, and N. Whipple. From External Regulation to Self-Regulation. Early Parenting Precursors of Young Children's Executive Functioning. *Child Development*, 81:326-339, (2010).

[7] Marsh, 11.

[8] Marsh, 4 and G. Posada and G. Kaloustian, *Attachment in Infancy* (Malden, MA: Wiley-Blackwell, 2010).

[9] Marsh, 8.

[10] Murray Bowen. *Family Therapy in Clinical Practice* (New York, NY: Jason Aronson, 1978).

[11] Murray Bowen. *Family Therapy in Clinical Practice* (New York, NY: Jason Aronson, Inc., 1993).

[12] Marsh, 11.

[13] Ibid., 17.

[14] Henry Stein. *Classical Adlerian Depth Psychotherapy, Volume 1: Theory and Practice: A Socratic Approach to Democratic Living* (Bellingham, WA: The Alfred Adler Institute of Northwestern Washington, 2013).

[15] Eric Metaxas, *Bonhoeffer: Pastor, Martyr, Prophet, Spy* (Nashville, TN: Thomas Nelson, 2010), 12.

[16] Marsh, 11.

[17] Lawrence Kohlberg, *The Philosophy of Moral Development* (New York, NY: Harper Collins, 1981).

[18] Marsh, 23.

[19] Wolf-Dieter Zimmerman and Ronald Gregor Smith, *I Knew Dietrich Bonhoeffer*, trans. Käthe Gregor Smith (New York, NY: Harper & Row, Publishers, Incorporated, 1966).

[20] S. J. Racz and R. McMahon, The Relationship Between Parental Knowledge and Monitoring and Child and Adolescent Conduct Problems: A 10-Year Update. *Clinical Child and Family Psychology Review.* 14, 377-398 (2011).

[21] Zimmerman & Smith, 33.

[22] Ibid., 33.

[23] Dietrich Bonhoeffer, *The Cost of Discipleship* (New York, NY: The Macmillan Company, 1949).

[24] Marsh, 24.

[25] Ibid., 24.

[26] Kohlberg.

[27] Jay Harley, *Luther as a Transformational Leader* in Luther on Leadership: Leadership Insights from the Great Reformer, ed, David Cook (Eugene, OR: Wipf and Stock, 2017), 119.

[28] P. Schwartz, A. Maynard, and S. Uzelac. (2008). *Adolescent Egocentrism: A Contemporary View.* Adolescence. 43:441-448.

[29] Joel Lawrence, *Bonhoeffer: A Guide for the Perplexed* (New York, NY: T&T Clark International, 2010), 3.

[30] Ibid., 4.

[31] Marsh, 68.

[32] Metaxas, 104-106.

[33] Marsh, 104.

[34] Ibid., 110.

[35] Zimmerman & Smith, 47.

[36] Ibid.

[37] Marsh, 115.

[38] Ibid., 119.

[39] Zimmerman & Smith, 49.

[40] Ibid., 49.

[41] Ibid., 49.

[42] Kohlberg.

[43] Marsh, 133.

[44] Ibid., 119.

[45] Kohlberg.

[46] Marsh, 134.

[47] E. Erikson, *Elements of a Psychoanalytic Theory of Psychosocial Development* (Madison, CT: International Universities Press, Inc., 1989).

[48] Wolf-Dieter Zimmerman and Ronald Gregor Smith, *I Knew Dietrich Bonhoeffer*.

[49] Marsh, 189.

[50] Zimmerman & Smith, 150.

[51] Dietrich Bonhoeffer, *Ethics*, ed. Eberhard Bethge, trans. Neville Horton Smith (New York, NY: The Macmillan Company, 1955).

[52] Ibid., 199.

[53] Kohlberg.

[54] Lawrence, *Bonhoeffer*.

[55] Marsh, 326.

[56] Ibid., 286.

[57] Dietrich Bonhoeffer, *The Cost of Discipleship*.

Chapter 5

BONHOEFFER AND THE FÜHRER PRINCIPLE

Dr. Jack Goodyear

In "Selling Hitler: Propaganda and the Nazi Brand," Nicholas O'Shaughnessy describes the setting and desired effect of the Nazi brand which culminated in the adulation for Adolf Hitler through his use of imagery and political spectacle:

> A Hitler speech has been described as one of the best possible evening's entertainment in the Germany of the early 1930s. It was a process of seduction, and as with seduction the performance would rise slowly to a crescendo, the role of mystical visionary blending with heavy sarcasm and brutal denunciation...accompanied by a symphony of gestures, now fey, now harsh, and that famous relentless stare...All of this was designed to trigger the adulatory excess of the masses...Hitler was a professional image maker...a professional actor with a vast range of gestures and an uninterrupted flow of tumbling ideas and words.[1]

How was Hitler able to captivate the German society so successfully? During the rise of the Third Reich, the mood of the German people bent toward a desire for a strong central authority, national allegiance to Germany, a rejection of communism, and a commitment to traditional Germanic values. Pluralism was deemed a threat to the preservation of German society and culture. As a result, the German populace yearned for a strong leader to provide the answers for the upheavals felt within the country. Hitler filled the void, as he was proclaimed as the lone authority that could reclaim German significance and purpose. With Hitler coming to power, nationalism increased and impacted all segments of society, including the Christian church. Authorities in Germany began to declare that only those who fully trusted and supported Hitler could be true leaders in society, including in the church. The Christian church set aside its ethical questions concerning the practices of the Third Reich in exchange for stability and a promised future for German society, valuing temporal security and political efficiency over theological faithfulness.[2] Noted American theologian, Reinhold Niebuhr, criticized the church in Germany for developing a theology sympathetic to governmental power:

> It gave government and principle of order an absolute preference over rebellion and political chaos. This one exception had morally catastrophic consequences. It tended to ally the Christian church too uncritically with the centers of power in political life and tempted to forget that government is frequently the primary source of injustice and oppression.[3]

However, not all Christians followed this practice. Dietrich Bonhoeffer, a colleague of Niebuhr, resisted the temptation to ignore the atrocities of the Nazi party in exchange for personal stability. Instead, through his speeches and writings, Bonhoeffer specifically called upon the church in Germany to question the injustices and oppression that the Nazi Party was inflicting upon groups in Germany, including the Jewish people. As Germany enjoyed a resurgence of national pride and status, Bonhoeffer warned of the unintended and devastating consequences of the rise of the Third Reich:

> The cult of reason, the deification of nature, faith in progress and a critical approach to civilization, the revolt of the bourgeoisie and the revolt of the masses, nationalism and anti-clericalism, the rights of man and dictatorial terror – all this together erupted chaotically as something new in the history of the western world.[4]

His call for the church to resist the state ultimately cost him his life, but the leadership Bonhoeffer displayed continues to inspire people today. This chapter will examine Bonhoeffer's reaction and rejection of the Führer Principle to the point that he declared, "I pray for the defeat of my country, for I think that is the only possibility of paying for all the suffering that my country has caused the world," and for which he ultimately died.[5]

Following WWI and the perceived humiliation of Germany, Adolf Hitler set out to instill a new sense of nationalism among the German people. The emerging sentiment of the importance of the German race, focusing on "blood and soil," found favor among the people.[6] The Führer became the supreme law of the land, whose will was to be followed independent of state law.[7] As Rudolf Hess declared, "Hitler is Germany and Germany is Hitler. Whatever he does is necessary. Whatever he does is successful. Clearly the Führer has divine blessing." The Party was protected by the judicial branch, appointed by Hitler, and unable to declare any ruling as final without Hitler's approval.[8] To oppose Hitler risked one's safety and position within society. As Nazism grew in public acceptance, the totalitarian tendency of the movement became increasingly influential over all aspects of society, including not just politics, but social and religious activities as well.[9] The Führer Principle, then, meant that no one could question Hitler's authority or judgment. Anything he chose to do was deemed correct, and any dissenting voices were met with social rejection or physical violence. This supreme authority extended beyond the political realm into all German society, including the church.

As Hitler's power increased, the Führer, not the church, captured the spiritual and religious mantle, claiming that any enemies of Hitler are godless. Hitler manipulated the public through a propaganda campaign, effectively persuading the church to submit to his authority. During the reign of Hitler, Nazism was not just a political movement, but a life philosophy, overtaking all aspects of a German citizen's being. Tolerating no dissent, the Nazi party pushed nationalism to secure "honor, purity, and internal strength" in both the party as a whole and the individual party member.[10] The inclusion of spiritual language into his rhetoric worked to blend the two spheres, rendering church authority impotent against the superior position of the Führer. As Bonhoeffer described, "Hitler's rhetoric was religious…He dissolved politics in a religious aura, and all the theological terms which had been previously secularized [became] the great standards of his appeal…He did all that in the name of Providence, for he believed that Providence had chosen him to deliver the German people."[11] One of the dangers of a society determining that a leader is divinely chosen whether they are viewed as King David or King Cyrus, is that the ability of spiritual authority to hold that power accountable is diminished, because the standard of righteousness or justness morphs to become whatever that "chosen" leader determines it to be.

Although Bonhoeffer urged the church to reject Hitler's philosophy and influence by rejecting Nazism, Hitler's sway overtook the German church as a whole, leading to Hitler's call for national church elections, flooding those elections with pro-Hitler candidates, and resulting in the newly elected church leaders fully supporting the Nazi regime.[12] Instead of pursuing the unity of the universal Church, the Christian church in Germany placed nationalism as the paramount aim, concluding that German culture should supersede a global calling of the church: "No action may be approved by a German national Church which does not first of all serve the security of the German people."[13] The Führer, capitalizing on the Führer principle, controlled church polity. To be a good Christian meant to support Hitler, the Nazi policy, and the nationalism and populism that Nazism promoted.

One of the ways the church succumbed to acquiesce governmental authority and Nazism was through an interpretation of Romans 13:1-7: "Let every person be subject to the governing authorities, for there is no authority except that which God has established. The authorities that exist have been established by God."[14] Throughout history, a misapplication of this passage has led to deleterious effects and "have constantly been misapplied by oppressive rightwing regimes, as if Scripture gave rules carte blanche to develop a tyranny and to demand unconditional obedience."[15] Partly, this capitulation by the church to Nazism was influenced by Lutheran thought. Martin Luther, who strongly advocated for *cuius region, eius religio (whose realm, their religion* in Latin), once said, "It is better for the tyrant to wrong them a hundred times than for the mob to treat the tyrant unjustly but once."[16] This sentiment gripped the church during the rise of Hitler, which in turn mounted pressure on church leaders to secure church authority by voicing full support of Hitler and Nazism.[17] Those who did not were labeled as "enemies of the state."[18] As a result, Protestant churches in Germany sought ethnic uniformity and "common blood" as part of the theological unity.[19] With the church subjugated to the power of Hitler, to be a Christian in Germany took on a racial identity rather than a spiritual one. This, of course, helped secure the nationalism Hitler sought for the nation.

With the acquiescence of the church, Hitler was able to incorporate religious imagery and sacred symbols into support for his control.[20] Manipulating religious language to support a nationalistic cause provides justification and cover for actions that, in normal times, moral authority may otherwise question or reject. Upheld as a symbol of absolute authority, Hitler, viewed as a cultural hero and political savior, utilized the Führer principle to rally the people to support Nazism through the utilization of religious emotions and by making sacred national symbols, namely the Nazi flag: "Let us therefore take care that in the honoring of the flag, youth is overcome by reverential thrill, through which the ultimate and deepest meaning of the flag is revealed…which inspire the inner and outer behavior which corresponds to the Being of the Eternal Germany, which we all serve as followers of the Führer."[21] With the flag sacred, not saluting the flag meant not supporting Nazism or Hitler, and ultimately meant that one was not a good German or a good Christian. Hitler spread nationalism through military parades, honoring the Nazi flag, and the elevation of German culture as preeminent.[22] Additionally, Hitler conducted a "process of seduction" through his speech, gestures, and mannerisms, all designed to entertain and "trigger the adulatory excess of the masses."[23]

The German people were not forced to follow Hitler; they chose to, and as a tragic result, the church was not immune to his seduction. Hitler practiced successfully a certain type of charisma, or charismatic leadership, which is defined as possessing "exceptional powers [that are] of divine origin…the personality characteristics of a charismatic leader include being dominant, having a strong desire to influence others, being self-confident, and having a strong sense of one's own moral values."[24] However, he did not practice charismatic leadership to inspire all people, but rather, "he played to people's basest needs and fears. If he inspired people toward the common good of Germany, it was the good of a truncated and exclusive society feeding off others."[25] Bonhoeffer's resistance to the Führer principle aimed at bringing the church to an awareness of this reality; however, the seduction of Hitler met too many Germans where they wanted to be.

The German people began to view themselves, through Hitler, as God's chosen people, possessing "a strong church of muscular virtues—a manly church," convincing themselves that Jesus was not Jewish, and that Jews must be rejected as a part of the German culture.[26] Even Jews that had converted to Christianity could no longer hold leadership positions in the church. In essence, the Protestant church in Germany was rooted in ethnic and racial identity rather than through faith in Christ.[27] Through all this, the German church at large bowed subserviently to Hitler's coopting of faith and symbols.[28] Dietrich Bonhoeffer viewed this tragically: "We are about to witness a great reorganization of the churches…the most intelligent people have totally lost both their heads and their Bible."[29] The tragedy that Bonhoeffer was witnessing tested his teachings in *The Cost of Discipleship,* which called for patient endurance in the face of evil.

Bonhoeffer warned his fellow Christians against falling for the seduction of the Führer, chastising the acceptance of state idolatry and deification of rulers.[30] In a radio address in 1933, Bonhoeffer criticized the notion of the Führer principle and the idea that political authority should only flow, unquestioned, from the top down.[31] In a sermon Bonhoeffer delivered shortly after Hitler's rise to power, Bonhoeffer declared, "In the church we only have one altar—the altar of the Most High, the One and Only, the Almighty, the Lord, to whom alone be honor and praise, the Creator before whom all creation bows down, before whom even the most powerful are but dust. We don't have any side altars at which to worship human beings."[32] Bonhoeffer witnessed firsthand the capitulation by church leaders of the faithful witness in return for temporary security and perceived influence in Hitler's Germany.

However, Bonhoeffer did not contain his criticism of Nazism to general complaints; he also forcefully spoke out against the conduct of the Nazi regime towards the Jews. Increasingly becoming a lone voice, Bonhoeffer lamented the fact that no official word of protest concerning this violence came from any of the Protestant churches in Germany. Bonhoeffer desired for the church to probe constantly the role the Christian church should play in opposing tyranny.[33] While some church leaders fell in line behind Hitler, others felt the church should remain silent and simply endure, suggesting that perhaps protest was not the avenue to pursue either. In a sermon, Bonhoeffer preached the following:

"I feel that Christianity is doing too little in making these points than doing too much. Christianity has adjusted itself much too easily to the worship of power. It should give much more offence, more shock to the world, than it is doing.

> Christianity should take a much more definite stand for the
> weak than for the potential moral right of the strong."[34]

Bonhoeffer's enduring legacy of resistance, his "being on the right side of history," in looking back today, was not just formed by his theological education, but by his life experiences and encounters as well. For instance, during one of his times in the United States, Bonhoeffer studied at Union Theological Seminary in New York. During his studies, he spent time in Harlem, where he "witnessed the historic black church's passionate commitment to social justice, racial equality and human rights."[35] This experience undoubtedly influenced his views on Nazi Germany's treatment of the Jewish people, driving Bonhoeffer to embrace a commitment to social justice as part of his Christianity, which includes a commitment to public resistance when needed.[36]

In 1939, Bonhoeffer, fearing for his life, fled from Germany back to Union Theological Seminary; however, the guilt he felt from being away from his people was too great. He confided in Reinhold Niebuhr: "I have made a mistake in coming to America… I will have no right to participate in the reconstruction of Christian life in Germany after the war if I do not share the trials of this time with my people."[37] In facing the seductive power of the Führer in Germany, Bonhoeffer concluded that the only way to save Germany and its values was to defeat Germany and its values:

> Christians in Germany will face the terrible alternative of either willing the defeat of their nation in order that Christian civilization may survive, or willing the victory of their nation and thereby destroying our civilization. I know which of these alternatives I must choose; but I cannot make that choice in security.[38]

He trusted in the spiritual power to overcome the evils of Nazism; however, prayer was not enough—Bonhoeffer advocated that the church must act and surrender its privilege, security, and safety. The church must do more than "simply minister" to those affected by evil but must openly oppose and work for the removal of Hitler from power. As Bonhoeffer said, "If a drunken driver drives into a crowd, what is the task of the Christian and the Church? To run along behind to bury the dead and bind up the wounded? Or isn't it, if possible, to get the driver out of the driver's seat?"[39]

Bonhoeffer allowed his theology to drive his political convictions, refusing to allow politics to drive his theology. Through multiple sermons, Bonhoeffer promoted weakness, reminding his listeners that according to Scripture, God works powerfully through weaknesses. Political strength is no match for spiritual dependence on Christ, therefore, for Bonhoeffer, the church should detach itself from power and advocate for the oppressed and against the oppressor.[40] Attraction to a leader other than Jesus is devastating for the Christian faith, as Bonhoeffer preached during his final sermon in Berlin, "No human being builds the church, but Christ alone. Anyone who proposes to build the church is certainly already on the way to destroying it, because it will turn out to be a temple of idolatry."[41]

Specifically, Bonhoeffer called on the church to question the legitimacy of the state's actions, to assist victims regardless of their faith, and to take direct political action to break the political power of Hitler.[42] To be a good German and Christian, Bonhoeffer refused to be a nationalist. That was not the way to ultimate obedience to the call of God on his life. Bonhoeffer viewed the practice of nationalism as the opposite of how Christians should respond. He lamented that the German church recast the Christian narrative of death and resurrection as a German narrative of defeat during WWI and rebirth under Hitler and Nazism. Bonhoeffer questioned the state of the nation's soul.[43] The wrapping of Christianity in Germany with the Nazi flag, which led many German Christians to abide by the Führer principle against Christian teachings, ran counter to Bonhoeffer's views: "The church is not to be a national community like the old Israel, but a community of believers without political or national ties."[44] As previously mentioned, Bonhoeffer not only rejected the populism and nationalism of Hitler's reign but prayed for the defeat of Germany so that the church and Germany might survive.[45] Whereas the Führer principle promoted nationalism among the German people and its churches, Bonhoeffer refused the seduction of the temporal political power that pressured all Germans to acquiesce to the political power. Bonhoeffer attempted to persuade German Christians to resist the seduction of Nazi Germany. In a discussion of the Beatitudes from the Book of Matthew, Bonhoeffer, in reference to "Blessed are the poor in spirit, for theirs is the kingdom of heaven," wrote the following:

This beatitude is poles removed from the caricatures of it, which appear in political and social manifestos. The Antichrist also calls the poor blessed, but not for the sake of the cross, which embraces all poverty and transforms it into a source of blessing. He fights the cross with political and sociological ideology. He may call it Christian, but that only makes him a still more dangerous enemy.[46]

He refused to concede that God had placed Hitler in power for a reason or that the church should support the ruler and abide by the Führer's authority. He rejected the faulty interpretation of Romans 13 and continued to call out the cowardice and prejudice in the German church, along with its overly rigid theological interpretations of secular authority:

The essence of the church is not to practice theology but to believe and obey the word of God…the community needs clarity about what constitutes true and false preaching—it needs theology not as an end in itself but as a means to help keep its proclamation authentic and combat false preaching.[47]

Bonhoeffer remained steadfast in his faith, committed to boldly speaking and living, even when it placed him at odds with authority and ultimately led him to his death.

Today's society and leadership would do well to learn from and model the example of Bonhoeffer. Martin Luther King, Jr. said the following about Bonhoeffer: "If your opponent has a conscience, then follow Gandhi and non-violence. But if your enemy has no conscience like Hitler, then follow Bonhoeffer."[48] As the world today wrestles with values, truthfulness, and character, and as events unravel throughout the world that cry out for leaders to strive for justice, one Bonhoeffer scholar says the following:

As long as we face intolerable situations—that is, as long as human history exists—we have to find the courage to say no, for radical opposition. To prepare such an eventual resistance, an example like Bonhoeffer's is of great value, particularly at a time when we notice a certain emptiness, a vacuum of deeply rooted convictions in our Western society.[49]

One of the values Bonhoeffer sought, and a value modern society could continue to embrace that can protect a community from falling prey to something similar to the Führer principle is the continued support and practice of separation of church and state. Maintaining distinct spheres, keeping the church from embracing one political group or party, can help protect the society as a whole from devolving into fanaticism or political holy wars that justify mistreatment of people through the name of religion.[50] While society and the church must embrace the separation of church and state, the church must continue to embrace the Christian discipleship of its members, filling congregants with love, justice, patience, faith, and hope. While in this world Christians will experience suffering, even perhaps resulting in death, the church must resist the seductive pull of political power, remembering that her calling is obedience to Christ. As Bonhoeffer wrote:

> If our Christianity has ceased to be serious about discipleship, if we have watered down the gospel into emotional uplift which makes no costly demands and which fails to distinguish between natural and Christian existence, then we cannot help regarding the cross as an ordinary everyday calamity, as one of the trials and tribulations of life. We have then forgotten that the cross means rejection and shame as well as suffering...When Christ calls a man, he bids him come and die.[51]

Endnotes

1 Nicholas O'Shaughnessy, "Selling Hitler: Propaganda and the Nazi Brand," *Journal of Public Affairs 9* (2009), 58.

2 Raymond Mengus, "Dietrich Bonhoeffer and the Decision to Resist," *The Journal of Modern History 64* (1992), S136.

3 Reinhold Niebuhr, *The Nature and Destiny of Man: A Christian Interpretation,* Vol. 1: Human Nature, (Louisville, KY: Westminster John Knox Press, 1996), 221.

4 Jean Bethke Elshtain, "Bonhoeffer on Modernity: 'Sic et Non,' *The Journal of Religious Ethics 29* (2001), 348.

5 Alex Rankin, "Dietrich Bonhoeffer, A Modern Martyr: Taking a Stand Against the State Gone Mad," *The History Teacher 40* (2006), 115.

6 Charles Marsh, "The Overabundant Self and the Transcendental Tradition: Dietrich Bonhoeffer on the Self-Reflective Subject," *Journal of the American Academy of Religion 60* (1992), 665.

7 John Brown Mason, "The Judicial System of the Nazi Party," *The American Political Science Review 38* (1944), 99. Brown describes, "The Fuhrer has the supreme power in all party matters."

8 Ibid., 102.

9 John Brown Mason, "Christianity Faces Caesarism," *The Sewanee Review 47* (1939), 469.

10 Mason, "The Judicial System of the Nazi Party," 97.

11 Bonhoeffer, quoted in Charles Marsh, *A Strange Glory,* (New York, NY: Alfred A. Knopf, 2014), 160.

12 Dietrich Bonhoeffer, *The Collected Sermons of Dietrich Bonhoeffer*, ed. Isabel Best, (Minneapolis, MN: Fortress Press, 2012), 81. See also, George J. Walmer, "Hitler and the German Church," *The North American Review 237* (1934), 138.

13 Mason, "Christianity Faces Caesarism," *The Sewanee Review* 47 (1939), 467-8.

14 Romans 13:1 (NIV). See also Romans 13:2: "Consequently, whoever rebels against the authority is rebelling against what God has instituted, and those who do so will bring judgment on themselves."

15 John Stott, *The Message of Romans,* (Downers Grove, IL: InterVarsity Press, 1994), 341.

16 Sockness, "Luther's Two Kingdoms," 106.

17 John Stroup, "Political Theology and Secularization Theology in Germany, 1918-1939: Emanuel Hirsch as a Phenomenon of His Time," *The Harvard Theological Review* 80 (1987). 350-1.

18 Brown, "Christianity Faces Caesarism," 464.

19 Marsh, 158-9.

20 Simon Taylor, "Symbol and Ritual under National Socialism," *The British Journal of Sociology* 32 (December 1981), 514-5.

21 Taylor, 518-9.

22 Taylor, 506.

23 O'Shaughnessy, 58.

24 Peter G. Northouse, *Leadership,* 188.

25 Ronald Heifetz, *Leadership Without Easy Answers,* 24.

26 Marsh, 158.

27 Marsh, 162.

28 Stroup, 351.

[29] Bonhoeffer, quoted in Marsh, 165.

[30] Elshtain, 348.

[31] Marsh, 159.

[32] Bonhoeffer, *Collected Sermons*, 68-9.

[33] Rankin, 113.

[34] Bonhoeffer, *Collected Sermons*, 169.

[35] Rankin, 112.

[36] Mengus, S141.

[37] Bonhoeffer quoted in Rankin, 113.

[38] Bonhoeffer quoted in Mengus, S142.

[39] Bonhoeffer quoted in Rankin, 115.

[40] Bonhoeffer, *Collected Sermons*, 170.

[41] Ibid., 85.

[42] Marsh, 165.

[43] Marsh, *A Strange Glory*, 159.

[44] Bonhoeffer, *The Cost of Discipleship*, 141.

[45] Bonhoeffer quoted in Ranking, 115.

[46] Bonhoeffer, *The Cost of Discipleship*, 108.

[47] Bonhoeffer quoted in Weber, Manfred, ed., *Dietrich Bonhoeffer Reflections on the Bible*, Hendrickson Publishers, 2004.

[48] Martin Luther King, Jr. quoted in Rankin, 116.

[49] Mengus, S135.

[50] Stroup, 353.

[51] Bonhoeffer, *The Cost of Discipleship*, 88-9.

Chapter 6

BONHOEFFER AS A PROPHETIC LEADER

Dr. David Cook

"Dare to quit anxious faltering and enter the storm of events, carried alone by your faith and by God's good commandments..."[1]

Written from the confines of Tegel Prison in 1944, months before his death, these words of Dietrich Bonhoeffer serve as a deeply convicting reminder of the cost of discipleship. Penned amidst the "storm" of World War II and Hitler's despotic reign of terror, they show the heart of a man who had courageously entered a raging tempest, just as the prophets of the Bible had done millennia before him. Few of his early contemporaries would have guessed that this mild-mannered theologian from Berlin would have become one of the most courageous leaders of his day. Yet as the storm clouds drew nearer in his homeland, he felt a deep conviction to stand for truth and prophetically lead others to do the same. "Carried alone by [his] faith and by God's good commandments,"[2] he shared a message of justice, love, mercy, and righteousness that was desperately needed both in his day and our own.

The example of his life provides a strong illustration of the type of prophetic leadership that Jesus calls His disciples to project into the world around them. This concept of prophetic leadership is not discussed extensively in the leadership literature of today. While countless texts have been written about transformational leadership, authentic leadership, power, and even servant leadership in the last fifty years, few authors have discussed the harsh necessity for prophetic leadership in times of strife. In many ways, this may be because this prophetic function of leadership is not as necessary in times of bounty and success; it has the peculiar function of being most vital in times of strife, discord, and hopelessness. In those times of turmoil and distress, there exists a great need for leaders who will call their people back to justice, mercy, peace, and righteousness—back to God himself. It is not an enviable job, for many prophetic leaders' careers end prematurely with their own demise. Nonetheless, it is a type of leadership that is intensely needed at certain key junctures in history.

Just such a pivotal moment in history occurred in Germany in the 1930s and 1940s. At a time when the country was adrift in a sea of economic misery, national pain, violent upheavals, and racial tensions, the German people needed a great prophet to speak truth amid the storm. Amidst the rise of Adolf Hitler and the tyrannical reign of terror he unleashed, there was an urgent need for someone to courageously proclaim the truth. While God raised up several Christian leaders during this time, perhaps none was more compelling than Dietrich Bonhoeffer, who left a legacy of prophetic leadership that has had reverberations that stretch even to the present day.[3]

This chapter will explore the role of prophetic leaders from the lens of the life and ministry of Dietrich Bonhoeffer. In arguing for the need for prophetic leadership, this chapter will first focus on how the role of a leader as a prophet is outlined in Scripture. What will follow is a discussion of five Scriptural themes for prophetic leadership that emerge from the Biblical narrative. Next, the chapter will take the step of applying these themes to the life and leadership of Dietrich Bonhoeffer. Finally, the end of the chapter will analyze how modern-day Christian leaders can serve a prophetic function by speaking truth into the present-day culture of modern America.

Prophetic Leadership in Scripture

Throughout the Bible, God consistently calls his people back to a right relationship with Himself.[4] Amidst the Israelites' grumbling, disobedience, wandering, and exile, God sent dozens of prophets in Old Testament times to share His message of repentance, judgment, and hope. What we see is that God used a variety of people, from shepherds (Amos)[5] to priests

(Ezekiel)[6] to royal officials (Daniel)[7] to share his message. While the Bible recounts the lives and leadership of a broad cross-section of prophetic leaders, none more fully exhibited the prophetic nature of leadership than Jesus Christ Himself. Throughout His ministry, Jesus shared a message of hope, redemption, and mercy alongside a clear call to repentance, holiness, and righteous living. Perhaps no section of Scripture is more emblematic of the Lord's call to prophetic leadership than Jesus' very own Sermon on the Mount.[8] Spoken as a call to radical discipleship, this decisive address is thus highly profitable as a starting point for any discussion of the true nature of prophetic leadership. Bonhoeffer himself wrote extensively about this passage in his book *The Cost of Discipleship*.[9]

While the primary passage in the Sermon on the Mount relating to prophetic leadership can be found in his metaphorical discussion of salt and light in Matthew 5:13-16, it is instructive to note that the overarching theme of the Sermon on the Mount was a radical realignment of the disciples' hearts towards a true right relationship with God. Within the sermon, found in chapters 5–7 of the Gospel of Matthew, Jesus discusses topics ranging from divorce to murder, prayer, fasting, and more. But all the admonitions He gives to His disciples revolve around a singular desire to see them in a right relationship with God and right relationships with others.[10] Out of this righteousness, Jesus called His disciples to bring His peace, justice, mercy, and love into the world around them in a way that was both prophetic and winsome. His discourse reveals five key lessons for prophetic leaders which will serve as the foundation for this chapter's discussion of the role of prophetic leaders in society.

Lesson #1: The heart condition of a leader precedes his/her effectiveness as salt and light in the world.

While it may seem counterintuitive to our modern, action-oriented American mindset, Jesus began His sermon not with a call to righteous living, but to a heart condition that was wholly trained on God.[11] Just as the Ten Commandments in the Old Testament had begun first with ordering a right relationship with God that would lead to right relationships with other humans, so, too, did Jesus focus His listeners on having a heart ready to commune with God first and foremost. He knew that only out of the overflowing of the love they had for God would they be able to enact the type of deep righteousness that He was espousing in His sermon.

Thus, He began His discourse on the heart condition of a leader by centering on the blessings that flow from an understanding of one's fallen condition: "Blessed are the poor in spirit…" (v. 3) and "Blessed are those who mourn…" (v. 4). From a leadership perspective, these first two beatitudes should serve as a reminder that, as a disciple of Christ, prophetic leaders are called first to recognize that they are sin-stained individuals, spiritually bankrupt before a just and mighty God and that those around them are likewise spiritually bankrupt without the cleansing power of Jesus' sacrifice on the cross.[12] Such a stark reality—a separation from our loving father because of sin—is a sobering and gut-wrenching fact that must cause the prophetic leader to mourn his fallen condition and the condition of the sinners right around him.[13]

Yet at the same time, the prophetic Christian leader has the hope that, even in the realization of that condition, he is "blessed" because of Christ's substitutionary atonement on the cross. In acknowledging his brokenness and turning to Jesus, the prophetic leader receives the blessing of being clothed in Jesus' righteousness. Yet the knowledge of his spiritual bankruptcy without Christ should make the prophetic leader humble both in his relationship with God and his dealings with others. Thus, Jesus continues His beatitudes by noting: "Blessed are the meek…" (v. 5) and "Blessed are those who hunger and thirst for righteousness…" (v. 6). Any true disciple of his, after mourning his own spiritual bankruptcy, stands in a posture of meekness and humility before a sovereign God, realizing that without Christ's beautiful sacrifice, he would stand utterly condemned.[14] The meekness and humility evident in such a heart can be seen in the prophet Isaiah's exclamation in Isaiah 6:5 (NIV): "'Woe to me!' I cried. 'I am ruined! For I am a man of unclean lips, and I live among a people of unclean lips, and my eyes have seen the King, the Lord Almighty.'" Such a meek attitude before our almighty Heavenly Father should not only make the prophetic leader humble before God, but it should compel him to "hunger and thirst" for a right relationship with Him. In humbly realizing that he needs the living water that only Jesus provides, the prophetic leader should thus have an overwhelming desire to stay close to Christ and drink of His goodness and mercy each day.[15]

Through these first four beatitudes, Jesus showed His disciples the type of heart condition they should have before God, and this can be instructive in our understanding of prophetic leadership. The pivotal lesson we learn is that any disciple of Christ, much less one who is called to serve as a prophetic leader for him, must first have a heart condition that is right before the Lord. This heart condition and the blessings it produces precede one's ability to effectively function as a prophetic voice of salt and light to a fallen world.

Lesson #2: The prophetic leader feels a deep conviction to take Jesus' message to those around him.

The second element of prophetic leadership that we see from Jesus' Sermon on the Mount is that, out of a right relationship with God, the true prophetic leader feels a deep sense of mourning over the decaying condition of the world around him.[16] As he looks at the sin-soaked people around him, he grieves for their spiritual poverty and brokenness. This leads the prophetic leader to a deep conviction to take action to do his part to prevent that decay and draw others to a right relationship with God.[17] But to be effective, this conviction must be manifested in a call from God to lead prophetically in a particular time, place, and culture.

Here, Jesus' call to be "salt" and "light," found in verses 13-16 of Matthew 5, serve to illustrate the type of conviction that prophetic leaders should have. The two images of salt and light provide a clear picture of both the state of the world and of the Christian's duty to live prophetically in the world. First, these images speak to the condition of the world as dark and rotten.[18] Being mired in sin, the people of this world are in darkness—shrouded from God by the screen of their shame. Jesus told His disciples in the Beatitudes that they would be "blessed" when they realized their spiritual bankruptcy, mourned over it, and turned to him, but they are also to realize that there are many others who have not accepted Christ and therefore are mired in darkness. Jesus tells His disciples in John 8:12 (ESV): "I am the light of the world. Whoever follows me will not walk in darkness but will have the light of life." It is the job of the disciples, therefore, to take this light to the darkest regions of the world in Jesus' name. In the same way, Jesus uses the image of salt to highlight the condition of the world. Salt is used to prevent decay, and Jesus is here telling His disciples that the world is in a state of decay—literally rotting in its sin. As salt, is disciples are there to prevent this decay by turning people to Jesus.[19]

A second important element of these metaphors is that they call the disciples to engage the world but be distinct from its sin.[20] These two images provide a vivid portrayal of this concept. Salt is not effective unless it engages with the meat it is meant to preserve, and in the same manner, light is only effective when it is brought near to the darkness. In the same way, Jesus was calling His disciples not to sequester themselves away from the sin of the world, but to actively live among the sinful people who needed God's love the most.[21] Only by living in and among lost people could His disciples ever truly share His love with them. But through these images, He also gives them a warning: to be effective, both salt and light must be distinct from the medium they are trying to change. Salt can only preserve meat if it is in its pure form, untainted by impurities that reduce its chemically distinct properties.[22] Likewise, light is meant to provide a contrast to the dark, not merely a reflection of the darkness that already exists. Here, Jesus is showing His disciples that they must interact with lost people daily while also retaining their distinctness as Christians.

A third important element of these metaphors is that they have the paradoxical effect of bringing both comfort and conviction to the world. While salt is important in preserving meat, it is also used to heal wounds. Inevitably, though, the salt that is used to heal a person's wound will also sting as it purifies the open lesion. While the result of the healing properties of salt may be the ultimate comfort of the individual, Jesus was counseling that His message of hope would naturally sting those whose gaping wounds of sin were touched by the salt.[23] In the same way, those whose eyes are accustomed to the darkness will be initially blinded by any strong light that enters the room. Ultimately, that light will be a comfort to them, dispelling the enveloping darkness. But at the outset, it stings the eyes of the one who is trapped in a dark place. Thus, Jesus was telling His disciples that, even amid bringing His message into the world, they would be persecuted and reviled by those who could not stand the sting of their salt and light.[24]

Finally, Jesus used these images as a way to draw His disciples' attention to the beautiful joy that His message could bring to the world. The disciples would have understood that salt inherently brings out a rich flavor in the meat it touches, providing a savory sensation to all who enjoy the meat thereafter. Likewise, light brings joy, peace, and comfort to those in a room. It is a sign of merriment, happiness, and cheer. In the same way, Jesus had told His disciples to "rejoice" because of His Good News, even if it meant that they would be persecuted in the end. For He knew that His message of restoration and hope would be a sweet aroma to those who truly understood their filthy condition. Thus, the disciples were meant not just to bring peace, but a fullness of life—a joyful message—to the world around them.[25]

In the same way Jesus calls His disciples to exhibit the qualities of salt and light in the world, the prophetic leader must have a conviction to bring God's righteousness to the world around him. This leads to a deep sense of mission to live incarnationally among the hurting world around the prophetic leader and to speak truth into that culture.[26] While a heart for God precedes the prophetic leaders' actions, the actions must follow if the prophetic leader is to try to preserve and heal the world around him in Jesus' name.

Lesson #3: The prophetic leader brings a message of shalom.

The third lesson for prophetic leaders that can be drawn from the Sermon on the Mount is that they must bring a message of peace to the decaying world around them. This message of peace is best understood as bringing the *shalom* of Christ into the world.[27] Therefore, Jesus tells His disciples in verse 9 of Matthew 5 that "blessed are the peacemakers..." This verse echoes Micah 5:5, which foretold the coming of Christ, who would be the peace that the world so desperately needed. His peace was all-encompassing, not merely denoting the absence of strife, but true *shalom*. This Jewish concept of *shalom* encompassed a much broader concept of wholeness—of having a singular focus on God that caused one to emanate God's justice, integrity, holiness, peace, and righteousness to the world around them.[28]

Throughout the Sermon on the Mount, one of Jesus' key themes was the coming of the Kingdom of God on earth, and thus His admonition to be peacemakers had a much deeper meaning. Not only were the disciples to work to end strife in the world around them, but they were also to speak out against injustice, division, hypocrisy, and immoral living.[29] From a leadership perspective, this means that the prophetic leader is called to bring the message that unites people together in their pursuit of righteousness. He is thus to call out sin in all its forms but does so as an act of love and mercy for those around him. Out of the mourning that Jesus admonished His disciples to have in the second beatitude, then, He reminded them in the fifth and sixth beatitudes that they would be "blessed" if they brought His message in a spirit of mercy and purity of heart that made the message winsome and inviting. Only by engaging the world around them in this type of merciful, pure way could the disciples truly bring Christ's peace as outlined in the seventh beatitude. Thus, the prophetic leader must likewise not only share a message of Christ's *shalom* but must also do so in a way that is pure and merciful.[30]

Lesson #4: The prophetic leader's message must be shared through both words and actions.

A fourth lesson on prophetic leadership from the Sermon on the Mount is that the message of *shalom* must be communicated through both words and actions. In many respects, the living example of the prophetic leader is just as important as his vocal message. He must show people what it means to live virtuously in Christ and to share in His sufferings. In essence, because the *shalom* of which He speaks is so anathema to the sinful condition of the world, the prophetic leader must live his life as an example of what that *shalom* truly means.[31] To show them what this *shalom* looks like, the prophetic leader must live on the "edge of the inside"[32]— being close enough to the people that they can see him, but not so close that he actively engages in the debased actions they take. He must be distinct, just as salt is distinct from the meat it cures. His message cannot be one example only: he must boldly proclaim through his words the Gospel message of sin, redemption, and justification in Christ. Yet this message must be shared in love. The prophetic leader's words and actions must be so winsome that they draw others to listen more deeply and hear the Holy Spirit's promptings. Thus, the prophetic leader's words and actions must be filled to the brim with a mixture of meekness, mercy, purity of heart, and bold conviction.[33]

This lesson of prophetic leadership can be seen in much of the remainder of Matthew 5, which describes the type of deeper righteousness Jesus calls His disciples toward. Thus, Jesus tells His disciples it is not enough not to murder; one must also not bear deep-seated anger in his heart (v. 21-22). Likewise, He exhorts them that it is not enough to refrain from adultery if one is inwardly lusting in his heart (v. 27-28). Similarly, Jesus implores His disciples that they are not to take an "eye for an eye," but instead to "turn the other cheek" (v. 39-40) and to even go so far as to "love your enemies and pray for those who persecute you" (v. 44). In all, He calls them to bring His message of *shalom* by being "perfect…as your heavenly Father is perfect" (v. 48).

Thus, the prophetic leader must realize that his actions many times speak as loudly as his words. His singular focus on God, found in the very first lesson discussed above, must cause an overflow of love and righteousness into every facet of the prophetic leader's life. Out of this wellspring, the prophetic leader should live a life that displays Christ's message of *shalom* to the world around him.

Lesson #5: The prophetic leader must be ready for persecution.

Finally, the prophetic leader must be ready for persecution, not shying away from being a co-heir with Christ in His sufferings.[34] Just as Jesus' message was welcomed by some and reviled by others, so, too, must the prophetic leader be ready to be opposed by those who cling to their evil ways. Just as salt stings in the wound it tries to heal, the message of the prophetic leader will cause pain in the hearts of those that hear it—a pain that is rooted in understanding their guilt and shame. Some will respond righteously to this realization, clinging to God and accepting His gift of salvation. But many will not. Thus, the prophetic leader must be prepared to face the ire of those who not only reject the Lord but those who proclaim the Lord's message.[35]

Jesus made it clear to His disciples in His beatitudes that "Blessed are those who are persecuted because of righteousness" (v. 10) and "Blessed are you when people insult you, persecute you and falsely say all kinds of evil against you because of me" (v. 11). This reminder was important, for Jesus knew that, in a paradoxical twist, the very people who were shown mercy, love, and *shalom* would be the ones to persecute His disciples the most. He reminded His disciples of this fact in John 16:33 when He told them: "In this world you will have trouble. But take heart! I have overcome the world."

Similarly, the prophetic leader must walk in the realization that his message of peace will naturally sting the hearts of the sinful people around him. While some will turn to Christ, others will recoil from his call to righteousness. The prophetic leader must be prepared to suffer at the hands of evil people whose sin causes them to lash out at the very peacemakers that are trying to help them. While this fact is quite sobering for the prophetic leader, he can and should take heart that Jesus has not only "overcome the world,"[36] but will come again one day in power to deal with the righteous and the unrighteous alike.[37] Thus, it is not for the prophetic leader to strike back against those who persecute him; instead, he is to leave justice in the hands of God[38] and press forward to the end just as Jesus did: in meekness and truth.

Applying the Elements of Prophetic Leadership to the Life of Dietrich Bonhoeffer

While a variety of German Christian leaders spoke out against the tyrannical reign of Adolf Hitler during the 1930s and 1940s, one of the best examples of prophetic leadership during this time was Dietrich Bonhoeffer. Likewise, the books, sermons, poems, and letters that he wrote have continued to have a broad-ranging prophetic impact in our culture even today. The section that follows will thus utilize his life and ministry as an example of the elements of prophetic leadership found in the biblical narrative described above.

Element #1: The heart condition of a leader precedes his/her effectiveness as salt and light in the world.

One of the qualities that made Bonhoeffer unique amongst his peers in the Lutheran church of the day was his devotion to a personal relationship with God that formed the basis for his relationships with others in the community.[39] While the family that Bonhoeffer grew up in was not overtly religious and did not advocate for a personal relationship with God, Bonhoeffer was drawn to a deep personal walk with the Lord through his experiences during and after his college years. Beginning with his dissertation, *Sanctorum Communio*, Bonhoeffer began to see the deep importance of Christian community and personal devotion in the life of a Christian.[40] This interest in growing both deeper in his faith and in learning how to live faithfully in community with others led him on a circuitous journey of discovery that started during his time as an associate pastor in Spain, to his time as a student in the United States (specifically in his involvement in Abyssinian Baptist Church), and to his days leading youth movements in Germany before the rise of Adolf Hitler.[41]

Through all of these experiences, Bonhoeffer began to develop a Christo-centric theology of the cross and a theology of community that far transcended those of many of his contemporaries. He became convinced that "the call to discipleship is a commitment solely to the person of Jesus Christ,"[42] and that this commitment was at the core of the Christian experience. Throughout his book *The Cost of Discipleship*, we can see that Bonhoeffer had developed a personal conviction to follow Christ with all his heart and this devotion led him to see his walk with the Lord at the root of his very existence. As he noted, "Only when we have really forgotten ourselves completely, when we really no longer know ourselves, only then are we ready to take up the cross for his sake."[43] Throughout his later years, one can see that he continued to engage in spiritual disciplines such as prayer, Bible reading, and meditation, which kept God at the center of his daily life.[44] It is clear from his writings that he saw a genuine relationship with God at the core of his call in the world.[45]

Likewise, from his work, *Life Together*, written while he was leading an underground seminary before World War II, we can see that he had developed a strong sense of the importance of living out one's Christian faith with Christ at the center of the church:

> Christian community is not an ideal we have to realize, but rather a reality created by God in Christ in which we may participate. The more clearly we learn to recognize that the ground and strength and promise of all our community is in Jesus Christ alone, the more calmly we will learn to think about our community and pray and hope for it.[46]

As a part of the training program for pastors, Bonhoeffer led his pupils in daily spiritual rituals designed to elicit the type of personal devotion to God that they would need to effectively lead their congregations during times of strife. This included the disciplines of silent meditation, prayer, corporate singing, meals together, and a variety of other spiritual disciplines that were intended to focus their individual and corporate hearts towards God.[47] His goal was not merely to show them how to live lives of outward obedience to Christ, but to place him at the center of their lives and community. As he noted:

> The more genuine and the deeper our community becomes, the more everything else between us will recede, and the more clearly and purely will Jesus Christ and his work become the one and only thing that is alive between us.[48]

Finally, we can see from some of his later writings that he had become convinced that his heart for the Lord required such a devotion to God's will that all else—even normal ways of thinking about ethical theories—was subsumed under one's relationship to God.[49] In all, his heart for the Lord preceded his actions and allowed him to be one of the most effective prophetic leaders of his day. While his words and actions were certainly powerful, they were preceded by his daily walk with God and a heart that was ready to put God's agenda at the top of his list of priorities.

Element #2: The prophetic leader feels a deep conviction to take Jesus' message to those around him.

From the beginning of Hitler's despotic reign, it is clear that Bonhoeffer had a deep conviction to call his people back to holiness that was centered on God, not the Führer. While many other German Christians at that time took a wait-and-see approach to Hitler, Bonhoeffer felt an immediate conviction to call the German people back to a proper view of government under God. In a radio address delivered mere days into Hitler's rule, Bonhoeffer prophetically noted:

> ...if the leader tries to become the idol the led are looking for—something the led always hope from their leader—then the image of the leader shifts to one of a misleader, then the leader is acting improperly both toward the led as well as toward himself...There is currently a terrible danger that, in the crying out for authority, for a leader or office, we forget that the human being is an individual before the ultimate authority, and that everyone who misappropriates this breaks an eternal law and takes on superhuman responsibility, which in the end will crush him...Leader and office that turn themselves into gods mock God and the solitary individual before him who is becoming the individual, and must collapse. Only the leader who is in the service of the penultimate and ultimate authority merits loyalty.[50]

While even Bonhoeffer could not have foreseen the totality of the evil that Hitler would unleash on the world, even in 1933, Bonhoeffer saw the "terrible barbarization of our culture" that had begun.[51] Thus, he took the courageous stand to make his radio address as a reminder to his people that they were under God's rule, not the Führer's. Ultimately, his address was cut off by the radio station as Bonhoeffer went deeper and deeper into his discourse about the dangers that the "Führer Principle" posed.[52] But his early inclination to do something was merited, for as he wrote towards the end of his life about how Hitler had manipulated the German people:

The weaknesses of human nature appear more clearly in a storm than in the quiet flow of calmer times. Among the overwhelming majority of people, anxiety, greed, lack of independence, and brutality show themselves to be the mainspring of behavior in the face of unsuspected chance and threats. At such a time the tyrannical despiser of humanity easily makes use of the meanness of the human heart by nourishing it and giving it other names. [53]

Thus, from the very beginning, Bonhoeffer had a deep conviction to enter the "storm of events" and speak Jesus' truth. As he wrote in his book *The Call of Discipleship*, "To flee into invisibility is to deny the call. Any community of Jesus which wants to be invisible is no longer a community that follows him."[54] He saw his role and the role of the church as taking a stand to bring Christ's love into the forefront of public discourse:

Jesus' community ought to examine whether it has given a sign of Jesus' love, which preserves, supports, and protects lives, to those whom the world has despised and dishonored. Otherwise the most correct form of worship, the most pious prayer, and the bravest confession will not help, but will give witness against it, because it has ceased following Jesus. We are not allowed to separate God from our sister or brother. God does not want to be honored if a sister or brother is dishonored. [55]

As he noted, fleeing from the troubles of the world was "unnaturalness, irrationality, triumphalism, and arbitrariness" for the true Christian.[56] Instead, in taking a step of prophetic leadership, he acted upon the conviction that he must bring Christ's message of truth, love, justice, and mercy, to the decaying world around him. As he wrote in his *Cost of Discipleship*:

The world will be overcome not by destruction but by reconciliation. Not ideals or programs, not conscience, duty, responsibility, or virtue, but only the consummate love of God can meet and overcome reality. Again, this is accomplished not by a general idea of love, but by the love of God really lived in Jesus Christ. This love of God for the world does not withdraw from reality into noble souls detached from the world, but experiences and suffers the reality of the world at its worst...the abyss of the love of God embraces even the most abysmal godlessness of the world.[57]

Element #3: The prophetic leader brings a message of shalom.

Throughout his prophetic ministry, Bonhoeffer sought to call his people back to righteousness that was rooted in God alone. As he noted in *Ethics,* "To participate in the indivisible whole of God's reality is the meaning of the Christian question about the good."[58] For him, the goodness of God was the answer for the dying world around him, and it was the calling of each Christian to bring that goodness to bear in their community. At the center of that call to righteousness was a relationship with God himself, for "everything we may with some good reason expect or beg of God is to be found in Jesus Christ."[59] While speaking about social issues was important, the core of Bonhoeffer's prophetic message was a call to know God on a deeper level. In living out this call to righteousness, Bonhoeffer attempted to create a community at Finkenwalde that would draw his seminarians into a deep relationship with God that would then pervade all their actions towards others around them. Only out of this deep love for God would they be able to endure the evil around them and speak the truth in love into their culture. As he noted in one of his letters from prison near the end of his life, his clarion call had always been: "May God lead us kindly through these times, but above all, may God lead us to himself."[60]

Out of this call to love God, Bonhoeffer also felt a deep conviction to bring the *shalom* of God to bear in the world around him. As he noted, "The abyss of the love of God embraces even the most abysmal godlessness of the world."[61] Thus, the Christians could not stand idly by while oppression and evil pervaded their very own public square. Bonhoeffer stated that "the church stands not at the point where human powers fail, at the boundaries, but in the center of the village."[62] Thus, throughout his ministry, Bonhoeffer preached and wrote against the evils of the Nazi regime. Perhaps his most overt attempt to do this was in his courageous work in helping to draft the Bethel Confession, which was an early, but ultimately unsuccessful attempt to draft a strong statement by the Confessing Church against the outlandish and malevolent ideology of the Nazi regime. Time and again in the first drafts of the document, Bonhoeffer and his co-authors wrote the statement "we reject the false doctrine that..." in denouncing a variety of false teachings that made up the core of Nazi ideology. While his attempt to denounce the poison of Nazi ideology was ultimately too strong for many of his counterparts in the Confessing Church, they show the heart of a man who was crying out for justice, love, and mercy in the face of an evil ideology.

Element #4: The prophetic leader's message must be shared through both words and actions.

While Bonhoeffer's words were not always heeded, his actions spoke volumes to the people of his day and to those who have studied his life since. One of the foremost ways that he exhibited this resolve was in his ministry of presence. Many of his colleagues strongly urged him to escape from Germany, especially as the war drew nearer and Hitler's tactics became more evident. Twice, it appeared that Bonhoeffer would flee to a refuge of safety. The first happened in 1933 when he left Germany a dejected man after his Bethel Confession was rejected by the Confessing Church. While he was able to do much good in London during his almost two years of service as a pastor of a German congregation, one wonders if his first inclination in taking this post was out of frustration at what was happening in Germany rather than the promise of leading the congregation in London. Nonetheless, by 1935, Bonhoeffer was again heeding the call back to the storm of events in Germany by founding an underground seminary at Finkenwalde. If his early retreat was out of frustration, this bold move back to Germany was certainly a courageous act that put him right back into the fray of German society.

During his time at Finkenwalde, Bonhoeffer worked earnestly to show his seminarians how to live a life that exhibited true Christian community amid a dying world. His words from *Life Together* serve as a reminder of exactly what he was trying to show them through his lessons at Finkenwalde:

> Jesus Christ lived in the midst of his enemies. In the end all his disciples abandoned him. On the cross he was all alone, surrounded by criminals and the jeering crowds. He had come for the express purpose of bringing peace to the enemies of God. So Christians, too, belong not in the seclusion

of a cloistered life but in the midst of enemies. There they find their mission, their work.[63]

Eventually, even his work at the seminary was shut down by the Gestapo and he lived much of the rest of his life moving from place to place, ministering to others while he stayed one step ahead of the Gestapo. At one point, after fervent entreaties from his friends abroad to leave Germany and take a teaching post in America, he went so far as to get on a ship bound for the U.S. Yet his resolve to remain in the storm of events in Germany was too strong, and his conviction too great to allow him to truly make that move. Shortly after arriving, he quickly boarded the last ship back to Germany, where he would re-enter the chaotic caldron of German society and eventually be imprisoned.

Through it all, Bonhoeffer showed the world the courage of a Christian who, while frustrated and despondent over the state of his nation, could not leave his people very long as they wrestled with the enormous issues that Nazism brought. His courage to return to Germany more than once, to lead an underground seminary, and to continue to write compelling books, spoke volumes not only to the people of his day but to those who have studied his life in the years since. Even today, they remind us that the true prophetic leader must not only speak words of *shalom* but live in such a way that he shows his people what God's *shalom* truly means.

Element #5: The prophetic leader must be ready for persecution.

Courageous in both words and actions, Bonhoeffer was aware of the persecution he would likely face because of his bold stands. Instead of shying away from what was going on in Germany, he made the conscious choice twice to return to Germany and stand amidst the furor of what was going on around him. Even amid the great terror that Hitler unleashed during this time, Bonhoeffer remained firmly committed to speaking the truth and facing the wrath of those who did not agree. As he noted in *The Cost of Discipleship*:

> There is no thinkable deed in which evil is so large and strong that it would require a different response from a Christian. The more terrible the evil, the more willing the disciple should be to suffer. Evil persons must be delivered to the hands of Jesus. Not I but Jesus must deal with them.[64]

He understood his clarion call back to Jesus would be unpopular in a nation that was turning away from Christian piety and towards the perceived strength of the Führer principle. Nonetheless, he believed it was the Christian's duty to continue to share God's truth amidst the lies and be ready to face the opposition of sinners who did not wish to hear that truth. In fact, he even went so far as to note in *The Cost of Discipleship* that:

> ...suffering becomes the identifying mark of a follower of Christ. Those who do not want to take up their cross, who do not want to give their lives in suffering and being rejected by people, lose their community with Christ. They are not disciples.[65]

Hounded by the Gestapo for much of the 1930s and the early 1940s, Bonhoeffer was finally arrested and imprisoned for the final two years of his life. Yet even in the dark circumstances, he faced during this time, he continued to seek God and write extensively to his friends and colleagues. One of his most enduring works is the compilation *Letters and Papers From Prison* that his friend, Eberhardt Bethge, assembled after his death. In these letters, poems, and other writings, readers gain a glimpse of what it truly meant for Bonhoeffer to suffer for Christ, all the while knowing that, as he had preached in one of his earlier sermons, "death [would be] swallowed up in victory." To the end of his life, he continued to serve God and others, leaving a lasting legacy of prophetic leadership amidst great persecution.

Bonhoeffer's Life as a Model for Modern-Day Prophetic Leadership

While many Christians in the West today may not face the horrors that Bonhoeffer and other Christians faced in Nazi Germany, there is still a great deal that we can learn from the prophetic leadership of this courageous man. First, as a Christian community, we must learn from the lessons of Bonhoeffer's *Sanctorum Communio* and *Life Together* as we seek to develop individual and corporate disciplines that will allow us to mirror the love of Christ in our lives.

Reading these works from an American individualistic mindset, one is immediately struck by Bonhoeffer's insistence that the Christian life is best lived not individually, but in community with other Christ-followers. As Bonhoeffer noted, the essence of Christian fellowship is "Christ existing as the church community."[66] It is convicting to notice how individualistic and materialistic we have allowed our 21st-century churches to become, and yet the words of Bonhoeffer give us hope that there is so much more to the Christian life—a life lived humbling walking together with other Christians as we seek each day to become more like Jesus.

Second, we need a revival of conviction to engage a dying world for Christ. Too often our churches have become merely isolationist, watching on as the embers of sin smolder in their community. Bonhoeffer's words and actions remind us that the call of Christ is to feel a firm conviction to be salt and light in the decaying world around us. As we seek to be a body that mirrors Christ, we must focus not just on our inward growth, but also on bringing the Good News of Jesus into the dying world around us.

Third, we must be ready to bring a message not just of peace and prosperity, but of true, holistic justice, mercy, and love in the name of Christ. All too often our churches speak out about certain sins but fail to also speak out about injustices that run rampant in their communities. If we are to follow Jesus, we must always mesh the ministry of healing with our teaching and preaching, just as Jesus did throughout His ministry. The message of God's *shalom* must be at the forefront of our message as we call people back to a holistic life centered on the goodness, integrity, justice, love, mercy, and grace of our Heavenly Father.

While we must bring God's message with our words, we must also be ready to do so through our actions. Before we can feed the spiritual souls of our neighbors, we must first show that we care about them by healing their physical and emotional wounds. We must be actively working to do good in society not merely for the sake of doing good, but to bring God's *shalom* to bear through our actions. We should be inspired by the life of Bonhoeffer, who did not merely preach sermons and write books but tried to live intentionally for Christ within the German community.

Finally, Bonhoeffer's example should serve as a reminder that even as we serve and love the world around us, there will be those who recoil at our saltiness. Though we may not face imprisonment and death like Bonhoeffer, we will nonetheless be subjected to opposition as we seek to bring God's message into the decaying world around us. We must remember that, as Paul tells us, we are co-heirs with Christ in His suffering,[67] and that thus "…suffering becomes the identifying mark of a follower of Christ."[68] Yet even in this, as Bonhoeffer so prophetically preached, our own "death[s] [are] swallowed up in victory"—the victory of Christ.[69]

Endnotes

[1] Dietrich Bonhoeffer, *Letters and Papers From Prison*, ed. Victoria J. Barnett, trans. Isabel Best et al., Reader's ed. vol. 8, *Dietrich Bonhoeffer Works* (Minneapolis, MN: Fortress Press, 2015), 513.

[2] Ibid., 495.

[3] Charles Marsh, *Strange Glory: A Life of Dietrich Bonhoeffer* (New York, NY: Vintage Press, 2014).

[4] Deuteronomy 4:29-31; 1 Samuel 7:3-4; 2 Chronicles 15:4, 30:9; Nehemiah 1:9; Isaiah 31:6; Jeremiah 3:12; Ezekiel 18:30-32; Hosea 14:1; Joel 2:13; Zechariah 1:3; Malachi 3:7; Matthew 3:1-2; James 4:8; 1 Peter 2:25

[5] Amos 1:1.

[6] Ezekiel 1:1.

[7] Daniel 1:3-7.

[8] John R. W. Stott, *The Message of the Sermon on the Mount (Matthew 5–7): Christian Counter-Culture*, (Leicester; Downers Grove, IL: InterVarsity Press, 1985), 14-15. While two Gospels recount the Sermon on the Mount, in Matthew 5–7 and Luke 6:17-49, this chapter will primarily focus on the account of this sermon found in the Gospel of Matthew.

[9] Dietrich Bonhoeffer, *Discipleship*, ed. Victoria J. Barnett, trans. Barbara Green and Reinhard Krauss, Reader's ed. vol. 4, *Dietrich Bonhoeffer Works* (Minneapolis, MN: Fortress Press, 2015).

[10] Stott, *The Message of the Sermon on the Mount*, 18.

[11] Ibid., 45.

[12] Ibid., 39.

[13] Ibid., 41.

[14] Jonathan T. Pennington, *The Sermon on the Mount and Human Flourishing: A Theological Commentary* (Grand Rapids, MI: Baker Academic: a division of Baker Publishing Group, 2017), 197.

[15] Ibid., 91.

[16] Stott, *The Message of the Sermon on the Mount*, 41.

[17] Ibid., 42.

[18] Ibid., 57.

[19] Ibid., 60.

[20] Ibid.

[21] Dietrich Bonhoeffer, *Ethics*, ed. Victoria J. Barnett, trans. Reinhard Krauss and Charles C. West, Reader's ed. vol. 6, *Dietrich Bonhoeffer Works* (Minneapolis, MN: Fortress Press, 2015), 12.

[22] Stott, *The Message of the Sermon on the Mount,* 210.

[23] Pennington, *The Sermon on the Mount and Human Flourishing*, 157.

[24] Bonhoeffer, *Discipleship*, 54.

[25] Stott, *The Message of the Sermon on the Mount,* 64.

[26] Bonhoeffer, *Ethics,* 18.

[27] Pennington, *The Sermon on the Mount and Human Flourishing,* 72.

[28] Ibid.

[29] Stott, *The Message of the Sermon on the Mount,* 66.

[30] Bonhoeffer, *Ethics,* 31.

[31] Bonhoeffer, *Discipleship,* 91-92.

[32] David Brooks, "At the Edge of the Inside." *New York Times,* June 24, 2016.

[33] Bonhoeffer, *Ethics,* 31-33.

[34] Pennington, *The Sermon on the Mount and Human Flourishing,* 97.

[35] Stott, *The Message of the Sermon on the Mount,* 66.

[36] John 16:33.

[37] Revelation 19:1-12.

[38] Romans 12:19.

[39] Dietrich Bonhoeffer, *Life Together*, ed. Victoria J. Barnett, trans. Daniel W. Bloesch, Reader's ed. vol. 5, *Dietrich Bonhoeffer Works (*Minneapolis, MN: Fortress Press, 2015), 9.

[40] Eberhard Bethge, *Dietrich Bonhoeffer: A Biography*, ed. Victoria J. Barnett, trans. Betty and Peter Ross, Frank Clarke, and William Glen-Doepel, and Eric Mosbacher, Rev. ed. (Minneapolis, MN: Fortress Press, 2000), 81.

[41] Marsh, *A Strange Glory*, 66-193.

[42] Bonhoeffer, *Discipleship*, 19.

[43] Ibid., 51.

[44] Bonhoeffer, *Letters and Papers From Prison*, 279.

[45] "Genuine prayer is not a deed, an exercise, a pious attitude. Rather it is the request of the child to the heart of the Father." Dietrich Bonhoeffer, "On the Hidden Nature of the Christian Life," in *Discipleship*, ed. Victoria J. Barnett, trans. Barbara Green and Reinhard Krauss, Reader's ed. vol. 4, *Dietrich Bonhoeffer Works* (Minneapolis, MN: Fortress Press, 2015), 123.

[46] Bonhoeffer, *Life Together*, 13.

[47] Ibid., 13-50.

[48] Ibid., 9.

[49] "Those who wish even to focus on the problem of a Christian ethic are faced with an outrageous demand—from the outset they must give up, as inappropriate to this topic, the very two questions that led them to deal with the ethical problem: 'How can I be good?' and 'How can I do something good?' Instead, they must ask the wholly other, completely different question: what is the will of God? This demand is radical precisely because it presupposes a decision about ultimate reality, that is, a decision of faith." Bonhoeffer, *Ethics*, 1-2.

[50] Dietrich Bonhoeffer, *Berlin: 1932–1933*, ed. Carsten Nicolaisen, Ernst-Albert Scharffenorth, and Larry L. Rasmussen, trans. Isabel Best, David Higgins, and Douglas W. Stott, vol. 12, *Dietrich Bonhoeffer Works* (Minneapolis, MN: Fortress Press, 2009), 280-282.

[51] Ibid., 94. [Letter to Reinhold Niebuhr – Feb 6, 1933]

[52] Marsh, *Strange Glory*, 160.

[53] Bonhoeffer, *Ethics*, 33.

[54] Dietrich Bonhoeffer, "On the 'Extraordinary' of Christian Life," in *Discipleship*, ed. Victoria J. Barnett, trans. Barbara Green and Reinhard Krauss, Reader's ed. vol. 4, *Dietrich Bonhoeffer Works* (Minneapolis, MN: Fortress Press, 2015), 81.

[55] Bonhoeffer, "On the 'Extraordinary' of Christian Life," 92–93.

[56] Bonhoeffer, *Ethics*, 12.

[57] Ibid., 31.

[58] Ibid., 6.

[59] Bonhoeffer, *Letters and Papers From Prison*, 497.

[60] Ibid., 473.

[61] Bonhoeffer, *Ethics*, 31.

[62] Bonhoeffer, *Letters and Papers From Prison*, 356.

[63] Bonhoeffer, *Life Together*, 1.

[64] Bonhoeffer, "On the 'Extraordinary' of Christian Life," 104.

[65] Bonhoeffer, *Discipleship*, 54.

[66] Geffrey B. Kelly, "Editor's Introduction to the Reader's Edition of Life Together," in *Life Together*, ed. Victoria J. Barnett, trans. Daniel W. Bloesch, Reader's ed. vol. 5, *Dietrich Bonhoeffer Works* (Minneapolis, MN: Fortress Press, 2015), viii.

[67] Romans 8:17.

[68] Bonhoeffer, *Discipleship*, 54.

[69] 1 Corinthians 15:54.

Chapter 7

THE LEADER'S RESPONSIBILITY TO ACT

Dr. Mark Bloom

> ...under the pressure of anti-Christian forces there came together groups of men who confessed the faith unequivocally and who were impelled to seek a clear decision for or against Christ in strict discipline of doctrine and of life. In their struggle these confessing congregations could not but perceive that the greatest of all the dangers which threatened the Church with inner disintegration and disruption lay in the neutrality of large numbers of Christians; they saw in this the true hostility to Christ.[1]

Dietrich Bonhoeffer (1906-1945) was born in Breslau, Germany, and came of age during the rise of the Third Reich. His upbringing and family heritage specially prepared him for the authentic and inspiring leadership that he demonstrated in reaction to the rise of Adolf Hitler and Hitler's commandeering of the German church. His parents, Karl and Paula, raised their children to maintain control of their emotions, speak only when they had something valuable to offer, and speak out against injustice.[2] Further, many members of his father's family tree were theologians, and some from both his mother's and father's side had suffered for speaking out about religious issues. His maternal grandfather, Chaplain for Kaiser Wilhelm, was fired for disagreeing with the Kaiser's political opinions, and his maternal great grandfather and paternal grandfather were imprisoned for their liberal and subversive ideologies.[3] Speaking out against what one perceives as wrong was in Bonhoeffer's blood. Bonhoeffer's heritage and upbringing laid the foundation for the development of his "Christian, humanitarian, and liberal" ideology that would guide his actions throughout his short life.[4] Bonhoeffer became an ordained minister in 1931, at the age of 25. Only two years later, in 1933, Adolf Hitler was appointed Chancellor of Germany and the course of Bonhoeffer's life changed dramatically. Bonhoeffer staunchly opposed Hitler's racism and the principles of National Socialism and openly spoke out against them. However, Hitler quickly sought to gain control of the German church by appointing sympathetic leaders into positions of power within the church, and, as such, the church began to accept the direction in which Hitler was leading the country. In response, Bonhoeffer and several other theologians who opposed the Third Reich drafted the *Barmen Declaration*, in which, the newly founded Confessing Church, "…trumpeted its rejection of the Nazi's attempts to bring their philosophy into the German church."[5] It only took a few years before the Nazis increased pressure against Bonhoeffer and the Confessing Church. In 1940 the Gestapo closed the Finkenwalde seminary in which Bonhoeffer taught the Confessing Church theology and just three years later, after a short stint outside of Germany, Bonhoeffer was arrested by the Gestapo and sent to Tegel military prison. Bonhoeffer spent the rest of his life in one concentration camp or prison after another. It was during this time that he wrote *The Cost of Discipleship*. In 1945, he was transferred to the Buchenwald death camp and months later to Flossenbürg concentration camp. In April of 1945, just two weeks before the arrival of the American forces that would eventually contribute to the end of the war, Bonhoeffer was tried for treason and hanged. *The Cost of Discipleship* provides some valuable insights into Bonhoeffer's leadership within the church during a time when, as he put it, Christians were settling for "cheap grace" rather than suffering the cost of following the example of Jesus Christ.[6] In the words of G. Leibholz, the example Bonhoeffer gave of how to live *costly grace* provides:

> …a model for a new type of true leadership inspired by the gospel, daily ready for martyrdom and death and imbued by a new spirit of Christian humanism and a creative sense of civic duty. The victory which he has won was a victory for us all, a conquest never to be undone, of love, light and liberty.[7]

Indeed, Bonhoeffer's inspiration for speaking up and acting out against the Third Reich came from his devotion to the Gospel. Bonhoeffer recognized how far the church had strayed from its core precepts. In *Ethics*, Bonhoeffer addresses the culpability of the church in the inhuman acts of the Nazis:

> The Church confesses that she has witnessed the lawless application of brutal force, the physical and spiritual suffering of countless innocent people, oppression, hatred and murder, and that she has not raised her voice on behalf of the victims and has not found ways to hasten to their aid. She is guilty of the deaths of the weakest and most defenseless brothers of Jesus Christ.[8]

Bonhoeffer's words indicate that it was his commitment as a follower of Christ, partnered with witnessing the Church abandoning its core values, that inspired him to step forward and act. In other words, it was his exemplary followership of Christ that compelled him to exercise his courageous conscience despite the imminent risk it entailed.[9] As such, a closer look at Bonhoeffer's theology, and how it influenced his leadership, is warranted.

The Theology and Leadership of Dietrich Bonhoeffer

Prior to the reformation, Christians bought their way to absolution of sins through the purchasing of indulgences; such indulgences, provided by priests, would assure the pious believer of a shorter stay in purgatory upon their death. Such indulgences could also be purchased in the name of lost loved ones to hasten their release to Heaven.[10] With the Reformation, however, faithful believers recognized the sacrifice of Jesus offers mankind salvation from sins solely by His grace, regardless of works. While the Protestant Reformation was the most influential and positive event in Christian history since the birth, death, and resurrection of Jesus, it brought with it at least one noteworthy negative outcome: *cheap grace*. *Cheap grace* is the acceptance, by Christians, that Jesus' sacrifice was sufficient to provide salvation from sin and death, which is true, but to then let that fact allow them to continue through life unrepentant and unchanged.

It is, according to Bonhoeffer, "...the justification of the sin without the justification of the sinner" and is, therefore, "...the deadly enemy of our Church."[11] Once a person embraces the idea of 'cheap grace' as justification for their sins, the sense of responsibility to model the actions and behaviors of Christ in face of modern-day problems diminishes; instead, when following Christ's example becomes too painful or difficult, one can simply rely on God's grace. Bonhoeffer warns, however;

> The only man who has the right to say that he is justified by grace alone is the man who has left all to follow Christ. Such a man knows that the call to discipleship is a gift of grace, and that the call is inseparable from the grace. But those who try to use this grace as a dispensation from following Christ are simply deceiving themselves.[12]

Bonhoeffer viewed cheap grace as the poison that killed true discipleship. Christians had taken Luther's recommendation to "sin boldly[13]" too literally and were embracing their cheap grace by becoming hardened in their sin natures and abandoning their followership of Christ.

Bonhoeffer witnessed widespread evidence of German Christians, deceiving themselves and clinging to cheap grace during the 1930s and 1940s across Germany as they faced the rise of the Third Reich. Leading theologians spoke out against the Nazi movement; Karl Barth described Christianity as separated "...by an abyss from the inherent godlessness of National Socialism."[14] Despite such public proclamation of the anti-Christian nature of the new regime, rather than stand up to the Nazis, many within the church, out of a sense of self-preservation at best or their inherent racism at worst, became tolerant, or even supportive, of the movement. Combatting the negative portrayal of the Nazi regime put forth by Barth, Bonhoeffer, Niemöller, and others, the supporters of the Führer sought to align Nazi ideology and growing anti-Semitism with a "religious fervor for 'purity' in the churches," and even called Hitler a "new spiritual leader who would restore Germany's cultural greatness and initiate a new thousand-year reign of Aryan Christianity throughout Europe."[15] These self-named German Christians portrayed Jesus as an anti-Semite and preached a Christianity that was antithetical to the Scripture and identified the Jewish people as the enemy of the Christian Germans. They also called the Old Testament a "saga of racial defilement."[16] Solberg explains, "Pastors, theologians, and ordinary churchgoers alike appear to have understood their faith in terms that permitted or even encouraged attitudes and practices that now seem utterly to contradict the most basic ethical precepts of Christianity."[17]

Despite the clear misrepresentation of the Scriptures, the German Christians met little opposition. The church had "grown comfortable with its position in the world" and was "either unwilling or unable to speak out against Hitler and the German Christians."[18] For Bonhoeffer, however, witnessing his church twist the Scriptures this way was more than he would bear. Bonhoeffer felt the need to stand up against the new regime and he, along with other prominent theologians who were willing to fight for the church, drafted the Barmen Declaration in 1934. This declaration contained the articles of faith held by all evangelical churches in Germany and warned them

> ...that what they hold in common in this Confession is grievously imperiled, and with it the unity of the German Evangelical Church. It is threatened by the teaching methods and actions of the ruling Church party of the 'German Christians' and of the Church administration carried on by them.[19]

This declaration, in stark opposition to the Nazi party and the German Christians, drew a line in the sand, in which Bonhoeffer would begin to experience the cost of discipleship as he embraced the "costly grace" by which he claimed his salvation.

The Cost of Discipleship

Practicing discipleship means accepting the Word of God and following in the footsteps of Jesus Christ as one develops his faith. To do so authentically, one cannot embrace cheap grace. Rather, *costly grace* requires sacrifices. Bonhoeffer describes *costly grace* this way:

> ...it is costly because it calls us to follow, and it is grace because it calls us to follow Jesus Christ. It is costly because it costs a man his life, and it is grace because it gives a man the only true life. It is costly because it condemns sin, and grace because it justifies the sinner.[20]

Denying oneself. Bonhoeffer identifies the first cost of discipleship as one mandated by Jesus Christ Himself: "If any man will come after me, let him deny himself" (Matthew 16:24, KJV). When one accepts the grace of forgiveness, with it comes the responsibility of following God's calling for one's life. After drafting the *Barmen Declaration*, Bonhoeffer left Germany for America, largely to avoid being drafted into the military. Safely outside the grasp of the Gestapo, Bonhoeffer could have lived out his days without risking his life. However, he felt called to return to Germany, despite the pleas of those who loved him. Denying his own safety, he was intent on returning to his home to help fight for the restoration of the church. In his words:

> I will have no right to participate in the reconstruction of Christian life in Germany after the war if I do not share the trials of this time with my people. ...Christians in Germany will face the terrible alternative of either willing the defeat of their nation in order that Christian civilization may survive, or willing the victory of their nation and thereby destroying our civilization. I know which of these alternatives I must choose; but I cannot make the choice in security![21]

Suffering. Just as Jesus suffered, so must the follower of Christ when he embraces the *costly grace* of forgiveness. In Bonhoeffer's opinion, suffering was a critical aspect of Christ-followership. In fact, without suffering, one's relationship with Christ is lost; "If we refuse to take up our cross and submit to suffering and rejection at the hands of men, we forfeit our fellowship with Christ and have ceased to follow him."[22] As difficult as it might seem to accept the necessity of suffering in one's discipleship, Bonhoeffer truly practiced what he preached. Instead of viewing his suffering negatively, he openly rejoiced in his suffering as evidence of his continued faithfulness to his walk with God. Bonhoeffer describes the paradoxical nature of suffering: "Suffering means being cut off from God. Therefore, those who live in communion with him cannot really suffer."[23] Bonhoeffer certainly experienced more than the average amount of suffering in his short life. His school was closed due to his teachings. Later, he was prohibited from teaching anywhere. He lost family members at the hands of the Nazis and was separated from his fiancé.[24]

Forgiving. In forgiving mankind's sins, Jesus took upon Himself the burden of others' sins. Likewise, followers of Christ are similarly commanded to "Bear ye one another's burdens, and so fulfill the law of Christ" (Galatians 6:2, KVJ). Bonhoeffer was especially moved by the Sermon on the Mount and particularly took to heart the admonition by Jesus to "Love your enemies, bless them that curse you, do good to them that hate you, and pray for them which despitefully use you, and persecute you" (Matthew 5:44, KJV). With regards to the insults and curses, Bonhoeffer made clear that they would, "…do us no harm"[25]; rather than resist or fight back, Bonhoeffer advised blessing the persecutors, stating, "We are ready to endure their curses so long as they redound to their blessing."[26]

Leadership of Bonhoeffer

Servant leadership. In *Servant Leadership: A Journey into the Nature of Legitimate Power & Greatness*, Greenleaf describes two noteworthy qualities that are characteristic of servant leaders, "…great integrity and a profound sense of the mystical." Servant leaders, he says, are "guided by the heart."[27] Northouse further explains that servant leaders "demonstrate strong moral behaviors toward followers, the organization, and other stakeholders."[28] At the age of 14, Dietrich Bonhoeffer already felt called to ministry.[29] Through continual communication with God through prayer, accompanied by his intensive study of Scripture, Bonhoeffer found clarity in his call to serve God. As a disciple of Christ, Bonhoeffer realized the implications such a role would have on his life:

> The disciple is dragged out of relative security into a life of absolute insecurity (that is, in truth, into the absolute security and safety of the fellowship of Jesus), from a life which is observable and calculable (it is, in fact, quite incalculable) into a life where everything is unobservable and fortuitous (that is, into one which is necessary and calculable), out of the realm of finite (which is, in truth, infinite) into the realm of infinite possibilities (which is the one liberating reality).[30]

And yet, Bonhoeffer embraced this new role, giving up his desires and freedoms to become a slave to God's will for his life. In *Life Together*, Bonhoeffer emphasizes the authority of Scripture when determining the course of one's discipleship; "It is not our heart that determines our course, but God's Word."[31] He goes on to explain how deep understanding is critical as the Word often points in the opposite direction of what one might arrive at when using life experiences or intuition to make decisions. Throughout Bonhoeffer's short life, he consistently adopted the role of servant to others (both individuals and the church itself), putting their needs before his own, following God's direction communicated to him through prayer.

Northouse[32] outlines several characteristics that are central to servant leadership; some of these are particularly identified in Bonhoeffer's life. Bonhoeffer first and foremost *listened* to God's direction for his life. Bonhoeffer also spent time *healing* or making whole, his followers. Even in the darkest times of his imprisonment, Bonhoeffer sought opportunities to minister to others to help restore their spirits as well as physical health. Bonhoeffer demonstrated an acute *awareness* of the social and political climate as well as the impact that his actions could have to inspire up-and-coming theologians who could join his efforts to restore the church. Arguably, Bonhoeffer also demonstrated *foresight* in his premonitions of what likely outcome he would face if he returned to Berlin. His willingness to knowingly walk into the dangerous situation in Germany, while predicting it might cost him his life, is a testimony to his foresight and commitment to his servant role. Bonhoeffer also quite clearly demonstrated his *commitment to the growth of people* and the importance of *building community*. His efforts to teach young seminarians at the seminary of the Confessing Church, despite the laws prohibiting such teaching, communicates how important he knew this job was. Without a community of individuals working together to accomplish change, Bonhoeffer knew the church would be lost.

Transformational leadership. While Bonhoeffer never lived to see the outcome of the war between the Confessing Church and the German Christians, or the long-lasting impact that his life still has today on the people who learn his story, his leadership can also be considered transformational. Bonhoeffer has been called a modern-day prophet. Some may take the characterization a bit too far and portray him in an almost messianic sense[33], and his popularity among both Christians and non-Christians, and with both liberals and conservatives, demonstrates the inspirational nature of his life and testimony. Northouse describes transformational leadership as, "…a process that changes and transforms people" and concerns itself with, "emotions, values, ethics, standards, and long-term goals."[34] The testimony of Dietrich Bonhoeffer fits these criteria quite nicely; in fact, those who explore the life of Bonhoeffer will finish with a challenge to live their own lives more authentically and courageously and will be inspired to live more selflessly, practicing *costly grace* in their service to others.

Followership as a Pathway to Leadership

Bonhoeffer's writings clearly describe how his theology formed the foundation of his opposition to the actions of Hitler and the Third Reich and his lasting legacy provides evidence of his transformational servant leadership. The question that remains is what compelled Bonhoeffer to act as he did, in such a dangerous time and in the face of such personal costs. Indeed, fellow Christian leaders turned a blind eye to the atrocities enacted upon the Jews and other marginalized groups. Famously, the German Lutheran pastor, Martin Niemöller, described his own inaction:

First they came for the Socialists, and I did not speak out—
Because I was not a Socialist.
Then they came for the Trade Unionists, and I did not speak out—
Because I was not a Trade Unionist.
Then they came for the Jews, and I did not speak out—
Because I was not a Jew.
Then they came for me—and there was no one left to speak for me.[35]

Niemöller was a contemporary of Bonhoeffer, and although an early supporter of Hitler, later rejected the anti-Semitism of Hitler's regime and was one of the founders of the confessing church. Like Bonhoeffer, Niemöller was also imprisoned for resisting Hitler's forces. Sadly, vast numbers of German Christians never outwardly opposed the Third Reich – either out of fear of retribution or because they inwardly approved of the Nationalistic change within the church.

So, what explains Bonhoeffer's immediate rejection of the changes occurring in the German church? What compelled Bonhoeffer to act in such a way that he became the transformational servant leader who continues to inspire over seventy years after his death? Perhaps a look at other transformational leaders from the past, who also led in difficult circumstances, can shed light on what sets leaders like Bonhoeffer apart from others. History is filled with examples of leaders who risked much to stand up for their values and to defend injustices. Two such examples are the German monk Martin Luther and his modern namesake Reverend Martin Luther King, Jr. Both of these extraordinary men, similar to Bonhoeffer, risked all to stand up against injustice.

It was in 1517, that the insignificant monk, Martin Luther, nailed his 95 Theses to the door of the Palace Church in Wittenberg, Germany in defiance of the Catholic Church. Included in the theses was, among other criticisms, an abject rejection of the practice of the church selling indulgences. Pettegree describes the castle church in which Luther studied as deep in the theology of indulgence, possessing, "…a very rare indulgence that offered general remission from sins for all those who made an act of worship there on All Saints' Day."[36] These indulgences promised forgiveness from sins in the hereafter—sins that might impede one's soul from reaching paradise. Luther eschewed the practice of selling pardons for sins and knew that until people could have direct access to Scripture, they would be constrained to hearing whatever theology church leaders provided. To this end, Luther worked tirelessly to translate the New Testament into German so people could read the Scripture directly.[37] Luther's actions and teachings eroded the authority of the church and empowered believers to have direct access to God.[38] Such radical speaking out was at great risk to Luther, yet despite facing excommunication and even execution, he publicly held firmly to his beliefs and refused to recant his statements.[39] At the Diet of Worms, the trial in which he was to recant his teachings about indulgences, Luther explained why he could not; "…my conscience is captive to the Word of God … I cannot and will not recant, because it is neither safe nor wise to act against conscience."[40] Luther's conscience was guided by his understanding of the Scripture. His commitment to following the guidance of Scripture compelled him to defend his teachings despite the grave risk to his wellbeing.

A little more than 400 years after Luther's courageous leadership, Martin Luther King, Jr. ascended to leadership within the civil rights movement in the American South. Also, like Luther, King Jr. would have to address a misalignment between the church and the message of Scripture in how church leaders turned a blind eye, or even openly supported, injustice towards – not towards Socialists, Trade Unionists, or Jews, but rather towards African Americans. On top of the extreme segregation widespread throughout the South, African Americans also faced extreme abuse from their white counterparts. In time between the end of the Civil War and the Civil Rights movement, close to 5,000 African Americans had been lynched in the American South.[41] Strangely, during this same time, the church largely ignored the injustice. Indeed, Ku Klux Klan members, who were responsible for the murders, justified their actions by asserting that they were doing God's work.[42] Many Southern ministers openly defended segregation from the pulpit, teaching that Negroes were pre-Adamite animals or the descendants of Noah's son Ham from the Genesis Flood. Even the churches that were accepting of black members sought to minimize conflict by avoiding the issue. For instance, when white civil rights activist Reverend Ed King asked permission to bring black college students to worship at First Baptist Church in Tougaloo, Mississippi, his request was met one week later with a resolution from church leaders to limit their worship services to only non-Negroes until "cordial relations could be reestablished."[43] Martin Luther King, Jr. grew up during this segregated period and was raised by a strong-willed and outspoken minister who taught him to never accept racial injustice.[44] In his early 20s, while studying at Crozer Theological Seminary, he was strongly influenced by the writings of Reinhold Niebuhr, which maintained that oppression could only be restrained through coercive means. Niebuhr emphasized that individuals could act morally in the sense that they can consider the needs of others, put aside their self-interests (egoism), and act with goodwill to others despite the cost to themselves.[45] Niebuhr's sentiments were reflected in King's speech before the Montgomery bus boycott:

> If we protest courageously, and yet with dignity and Christian love, when the history books are written in the future, somebody will have to say, 'There lived a race of people... who had the moral courage to stand up for their rights. And thereby they injected a new meaning into the veins of history and civilization.'[46]

In the afterword to *Why We Can't Wait*, Reverend Jesse Jackson, Sr. describes how King's focus was, "...not merely black and white. It was not merely the racial gap. It was the ethical challenge of wrong and right."[47] Like Bonhoeffer and Luther, King's actions were strongly influenced by his ethics – ethics that were intimately connected to their religious faith.

Perhaps Bonhoeffer best explains the motivation behind these three great leaders in how he characterizes the confessing church's opposition to Hitler's regime,

> In their struggle these confessing congregations could not but perceive that the greatest of all dangers which threatened the Church with inner disintegration and disruption lay in the neutrality of large numbers of Christians; they saw in this the true hostility to Christ.[48]

Bonhoeffer, Luther, and King each began their leadership journeys as relatively insignificant individuals with little or no positional power. Yet each went on to accomplish transformational leadership by speaking out when so many other Christians would not. Their leadership actions, which derived from their committed followership (of Christ) continue to impact people today. These three leaders each faced great risks, yet courageously stepped forward and spoke their truth as an obligation to their Christian witness.

Robert Kelly describes how "star followers" think for themselves and give their full support to advance the agenda of their leader.[49] Blackaby and Blackaby assert, "If anything can revolutionize today's Christian leaders, it is when they understand God's design for those he calls to lead."[50] Bonhoeffer, Luther, and King all recognized God's plan for their leadership. Following the example set by Christ, each man risked all, acted upon their "courageous consciences,"[51] and never compromised their values. They each spoke out against the church when religious leaders strayed from core Christian values and allowed and even promoted unethical and unjust practices—"a crucial aspect of followership."[52] Their actions inspired revolutions that continue to resonate today and provide an example for future transformational biblical servant leaders.

Endnotes

[1] Dietrich Bonhoeffer, *Ethics* (New York, NY: Touchstone Books, 2005), 59-60.

[2] Eric Metaxas, *Bonhoeffer: Pastor, Martyr, Prophet, Spy* (Nashville, TN: Thomas Nelson Publishers, 2011).

[3] Dietrich Bonhoeffer. *The Cost of Discipleship* (New York, NY: Touchstone Books, 2005).

[4] Ibid., 13.

[5] Metaxas, 61.

[6] Bonhoeffer, *The Cost of Discipleship*, 43.

[7] Gerhard Leibholz. *"Memoir,"* in *The Cost of Discipleship* (New York, NY: Touchstone, 1995), 33.

[8] Bonhoeffer, *Ethics*, 114.

[9] Robert Kelley, *The Power of Followership* (New York, NY: Doubleday, 1992).

[10] Andrew Pettegree, *Brand Luther: How an Unheralded Monk Turned His Small Town into a Center of Publishing, Made Himself the Most Famous Man in Europe, and Started the Protestant Reformation* (London, England: Penguin Books, 2015).

[11] Bonhoeffer, *Cost of Discipleship*, 43.

[12] Ibid., 51.

[13] Let Your Sins Be Strong: A Letter From Luther to Melanchthon Letter no. 99, 1 August 1521.

[14] Metaxas, 171.

[15] Michael Van Dyke. *Radical Integrity: The Story of Dietrich Bonhoeffer.* (Uhrichsville, OH: Barbour Publishing, Inc, 2001), 76.

[16] Metaxas, 172.

[17] Mary Solberg, *A Church Undone: Documents from the German Christian Faith Movement 1932-1940* (Minneapolis, MN: Augsburg Fortress Publishers, 2015), 11.

[18] H. Barker. *The Cross of Reality; Luther's Theologia Crucis and Bonhoeffer's Christology.* (Minneapolis, MN: Fortress Press, 2015), 421.

[19] Arthur Cochrane. *The Church's Confession under Hitler.* (Philadelphia, PA: Westminster Press, 1962), xx.

[20] Bonhoeffer, *The Cost of Discipleship*, 45.

[21] Van Dyke, 134.

[22] Bonhoeffer, *The Cost of Discipleship*, 91.

[23] Ibid., 92.

[24] Metaxas.

[25] Dietrich Bonhoeffer. *Life together.* (New York, NY: HarperCollins, 1954), 149.

[26] Ibid., 149.

[27] Robert Greenleaf. *Servant Leadership: A Journey into the Nature of Legitimate Power & Greatness* (New York, NY: Paulist Press, 1977), 262.

[28] Peter Northouse. *Leadership: Theory and Practice, 7th Edition.* (Newbury Park, CA: Sage Publications, 2015), 226.

[29] Bonhoeffer, *Life Together*.

[30] Bonhoeffer, *The Cost of Discipleship*, 58.

[31] Ibid., 55.

[32] Northouse.

[33] Metaxas.

[34] Northouse, 161.

[35] Marcuse, "The Origin and Reception of Martin Niemöller's Quotation 'First They Came for the Communists...'," 173.

[36] Pettegree, 16.

[37] David Cook, James Harley, and Brent Thomason. *Luther on Leadership.* (Eugene, OR: Wipf & Stock, 2017), 103.

[38] Cook, 71-86.

[39] Ibid, 10-13.

[40] Robert Kelly, *Luther's Works*, ed. Jaroslav Pelikan and Helmut T. Lehman. (Philadelphia, PA: Fortress, 1955-86), 105-31.

[41] Charles Marsh. *God's Long Summer: Stories of Faith and Civil Rights.* (Princeton, NJ: Princeton University Press, 1997), 82.

[42] Ibid., 3.

[43] Ibid., 101.

[44] Donald T. Phillips. *Martin Luther King, Jr. on Leadership: Inspiration & Wisdom for Challenging Times.* (New York, NY: Grand Central Publishing, 1998), 22.

[45] Reinhold Niebuhr. *Moral Man and Immoral Society: A Study in Ethics and Politics.* (Louisville, MY: Westminster John Knox Press, 1932), xxix.

[46] Phillips, 39.

[47] Jackson, "Afterword," 198.

[48] Bonhoeffer, *Ethics*, 60.

[49] Kelley, *The Power of Followership*, 8.

[50] Henry Blackaby and Richard Blackaby. *Spiritual Leadership: Moving People on to God's Agenda* (Nashville, TN: B&H Publishing Group, 2001), 4.

[51] Kelley, *The Power of Followership*, 14.

[52] Ibid., 15.

Chapter 8

BONHOEFFER AS A LEADER OF STUDENTS: HIS DEVELOPMENT INTO A RELATIONAL LEADER

Dr. Dale Meinecke

One morning when Dietrich Bonhoeffer served as a youth minister in Barcelona, Bonhoeffer heard a knock at the door, and a ten-year-old boy came into his room with something that Bonhoeffer had requested from his parents. The usually cheerful boy was solemn, so Bonhoeffer asked why he was so downcast. The boy broke down in tears and said, "Mr. Wolf is dead," and then continued to cry uncontrollably. Through coaxing and consoling, Bonhoeffer was finally able to learn that Mr. Wolf was the boy's German shepherd dog who had been sick for days and died earlier that morning. The boy sat on Bonhoeffer's knee, and through his tears described the wonderful relationship he had with Mr. Wolf. The two always played together, and the dog awakened the boy every morning. The boy talked with Bonhoeffer about their friendship for some time. The boy lamented, "now that the dog was dead, how was he to go on without him."

Then, suddenly, the boy became very quiet, and he said that he knew Mr. Wolf was not dead and that his spirit was now in Heaven. He then asked Bonhoeffer, "Will I see Mr. Wolf again? He's certainly in heaven." At that moment, Bonhoeffer, as the one who was supposed to know the answer, recalled that he felt quite small next to the boy. He quickly thought through the responses. If Bonhoeffer said, "I don't know," then that would be the same as saying "no." He knew this would crush the boy in his moment of distress. Instead, Bonhoeffer told the boy, "Look, God created human beings and also animals, and I'm sure He also loves animals. And I believe that with God it is such that all who loved each other on earth—genuinely loved each other—will remain together with God, for to love is part of God. Just how that happens, though, we admittingly don't know." After telling the boy this, he stopped crying and said, "So I'll see Mr. Wolf again and we can play together?" Bonhoeffer reminded the boy that he didn't really know how this happened, but the boy was now filled with joy and could only think of being with Mr. Wolf again.

Bonhoeffer told this story through a letter to Walter Dress, his youngest sister's fiancé. This tender and special letter demonstrates how Bonhoeffer "place-shared" with the boy.[1] The story also illustrates relational leadership, which happens as one individual influences another individual through a shared relationship based on compassion for and trust in one another. The term "place-sharing" is Root's translation of Bonhoeffer's *Stellvertretung* from his doctoral dissertation, "The Community of Saints" (*Sanctorum Communio*), describing how people come to experience Christ in community.[2] Biographer Metaxas regards Bonhoeffer's dissertation as a "stunning debut" for a young theologian.[3] The above story, along with Bonhoeffer's "place-sharing" idea from *Sanctorum Communio,* demonstrate Bonhoeffer's belief and practice of *relational leadership*. His experience as a student and as a children's and youth worker offers us a better understanding of relational leadership, as well as how relational leaders develop over time. After this review, a few concluding thoughts on how others can develop into a relational leader will be offered.

What Is Relational Leadership?

To begin, it is necessary to define relational leadership. Two early studies identified *concern for people,* or relationship-oriented behavior, as an effective leadership style for leaders.[4] These studies noted that effective leaders can also be focused on accomplishing tasks and that most leaders tend to function in either a relational or task-oriented way. Blake and Mouton argued that leaders can be most effective by integrating the two behaviors and stressed the importance of both people (relationships) and production (tasks).[5] In other words, leaders should provide support for followers while at the same time noting the importance of tasks and results. Robert Greenleaf focused more on relationships. He suggested a departure from the traditional autocratic, top-down style of leadership in his work, *Servant Leadership*.[6] In this essay, Greenleaf saw the leader as a servant whose followers become wiser, freer, more autonomous, and more likely to lead others through service. This happens when leaders listen and learn about needs, as well as show empathy and share in followers' pain. Through the support of the leader, trust emerges, and followers are empowered to carry out their job tasks.

At about the same time as Greenleaf was writing on servant leadership, Robert Burns, a political leadership theorist, was looking at individual, especially heroic leaders to develop a leadership theory emphasizing the roles and traits of a leader.[7] The result was his seminal work on leadership, in which he developed the concept of the transforming leader. The transforming leader initiates the mobilization of "people for participation in the processes of change, encouraging a sense of collective identity and collective efficacy, which in turn brings stronger feelings of self-worth and self-efficacy."[8] Furthermore, Burns highlighted the role of the leader's personal virtue, the ethical relationship with followers, and a vision that elevates both the leader and the follower's values and hopes.[9] Bass further defined transformational leadership with 4 *I's*: *Idealized Influence, Individualized Consideration, Inspirational Motivation, and Intellectual Stimulation*.[10] Individualized consideration hits the relational aspect the most where leaders provide support, encouragement, and coaching to followers.

Similar to transformational leadership, two other theories examine the influence that occurs between interpersonal interactions, noting how the quality of those interactions can motivate some sort of change in attitude or behavior on the part of the followers. The first is Leader-Member Exchange Theory (LMX). Leader-Member Exchange Theory approaches leadership as a two-way exchange between the leader and follower. The quality of the exchange, which is based on mutual respect and trust, determines the level of influence on followers' actions, decisions, and overall work performance.[11] The research involving LMX reviews how these quality relationships develop, and how out-group members can be drawn into a special relationship with the leader.

Charismatic leadership, on the other hand, emphasizes less the quality of relationship, and more the characteristics of the leader that draw the follower to the leader. Sociologist Max Weber first described the charismatic organization as one led by an individual with personal magnetism.[12] Charisma in leadership is often recognized as leaders who can articulate a compelling vision through engaging storytelling and the use of symbols. But more than this, charismatic leaders bring energy to their work, an undying optimism that promotes the probability of success, and a willingness to take risks and make sacrifices. These characteristics of the leader often draw in followers, motivating them to inspired work performance, and endearing him or her to the leader so much so that they take on characteristics of the leader.[13] Both LMX and charismatic leadership theory stress the interactions between the leader and the follower for influence to occur.

Next, research on the phenomenon of emotional intelligence emerged.[14] Goleman, Boyatzis, and McGee define emotional intelligence as the ability of "leaders to handle themselves and their relationships."[15] This involves the four domains of self-awareness, self-management, social awareness, and relationship management. The goal of emotional intelligence is to manage relationships to create a positive environment for everyone to achieve their best work.[16] This is what Goleman, Boyatzis, and McGee consider *resonate leadership*. Warner and Wilder take it a step further and call it R.A.R.E. leadership.[17] This is leadership that **R**emains relational, **A**cts like one's self, **R**eturns to joy, and **E**ndures hardship. Leadership like this is rare because so few leaders combine all four essential ingredients for effectiveness.

That is a fast trip on the trail to defining relational leadership. What does it mean? In the words of Kouzes and Posner, "leadership is a relationship."[18] Kouzes and Posner's research comes to this—leadership is not relegated to a select few extraordinary leaders, or only the charismatic leaders, or to those naturally gifted at building relationships. Instead, leadership as a relationship means anybody can be an effective leader by learning and practicing relational skills. In his daily relationships and particularly early on, Bonhoeffer could be described as distant, aloof, intense, and measured in dealing with others. The interactions with his family seemed to fill any relational needs, and he did not have close friends until later in life.[19] His professors thought he was distant and even arrogant, although that may have been due to his sharp, fiercely independent mind.[20] Later in life, Bonhoeffer would face pride as a sin and a project for spiritual correction.[21] While studying at Tubingen, he preferred to study in his room because it was quiet, and no one would bother him.[22] Based on this, we might assume that Bonhoeffer was much more of a task-oriented introvert. So, why is he an example of relational leadership?

Bonhoeffer's Leadership Development

In answering this question, it is helpful to consider how leaders develop. Komives and colleagues offer six stages of leadership development as a guide.[23] While the research is mainly geared for college students, these stages apply to various age groups and networks. The first two stages of awareness and exploration/engagement usually occur in an individual's younger years. For Bonhoeffer, there were plenty of opportunities to witness leadership and even try it on. Bonhoeffer's father, Karl Bonhoeffer, held the chair of psychiatry and neurology, first in Breslau and then in Berlin. Karl Bonhoeffer valued and demonstrated adept thinking and expected the same from his children. Bonhoeffer drew from the leadership example of his father's brilliance. He also had numerous opportunities to explore leadership with his seven siblings. Together, they played in the garden, climbed trees, competed in sports, and serenaded one another with music on Saturday nights. Bonhoeffer had a gift for music and even considered becoming a concert pianist. He often led his family in hymns and folk songs.[24] From his early experiences, Bonhoeffer witnessed and explored leadership without necessarily naming it or recognizing it as leadership.

The growth between the third stage (*leader identified*) and the fourth stage (*leadership differentiated*) of leadership development is essential.[25] During the third stage, individuals recognize the positions of leaders and followers and usually attribute leadership to a hierarchical position. Some individuals pursue leadership at this stage to have the position of "leader," or they may avoid this stage because they prefer not to have leadership responsibility. The critical juncture in leadership development happens when a person understands that leadership occurs when anyone from the team contributes to the functioning of the group. Leadership becomes more than a role at this stage; it is recognized beyond titles and positions. In this stage, key leadership elements of trust, teamwork, working in diversity, higher levels of self-awareness, communication, conflict management, collaboration, and networking are learned. This, in turn, results in higher levels of self-efficacy in responsibilities. These two stages seem to dominate Bonhoeffer's early years as a student, children's worker, and minister. A maturity in Bonhoeffer develops as his focus moves away from *self* and onto the role of the church. We see this first on his tour of Rome and the resulting enamor with the Catholic Church. He was only 18 at the time, but his reflections are mature and thoughtful. He was entranced by the beauty, exuberance, and grandeur of Catholicism, so much so that he was tempted to convert.[26] This is what stirred his interest in understanding the community of the church.

In the next section, we will return to stages three and four for a closer look, but we must complete the review of Bonhoeffer's leadership development through the last two stages. Stage five is *generativity*—when leaders are grounded in their understanding of leadership as a process and grasp their role as a leader regardless of position. At this point, leaders know their strengths, their beliefs, and their values that move them to act. These leaders can articulate a sense of purpose and mission in life and feel a sense of responsibility to mentor younger leaders.[27] We see this stage most in Bonhoeffer as director of the Confessing Church seminary at Finkenwalde, and then certainly as he joins as a double agent in the cause to remove Hitler from power.

The final leadership stage is *integration/synthesis*. This stage reflects a person who has a stable identity as a leader and remains focused on leadership as a process. The leader participates in various contexts and can offer value and insight in new settings. Also, this person recognizes the need for learning and welcomes it from others, embracing self-development as a way of life. Relationships and coalitions are an integral part of life. From Tegel prison, Bonhoeffer wrote his enduring friend Eberhard Bethge:

> So it really came off! Only for a moment, but that doesn't matter much...it will be with me for a long time now—the memory of having the four people who are nearest and dearest to me with me for a brief moment. When I got back to my cell afterwards, I paced up and down for a whole hour, while my dinner stood there and got cold...I found myself repeating over and over again, 'That was really great!'...
>
> ...I was taken to the sick-bay for an interview which lasted until noon. The last of the air raid brought some most unpleasant experiences—a land-mine 25 metres away; a sick-bay with no lights or windows, prisoners screaming for help, with no one but ourselves taking any notice of them; but we

too could do very little to help in the darkness, and one has to be cautious about opening the cell doors of those with the heaviest sentences, for you never know whether they will hit you in the head with a chair leg and try to get away. In short, it was not very nice. As a result, I wrote a report of what had taken place, pointing out the need of medical attention during air raids. I hope it will be some use. I'm glad to be able to help in any way with reasonable suggestions.[28]

This excerpt offers us two things. First, the observation of just how important relationships had become to Bonhoeffer. Second, that even in prison, Bonhoeffer took the responsibility and the lead to serve and offer his gifts to the other prisoners. Less than twenty-four hours before he was hanged at Flossenbürg, Bonhoeffer held a church service, preaching and praying for his fellow prisoners.[29] This is the integrated life—Bonhoeffer could not stop being who he was—a relational leader among the community of the saints—even in the direst of conditions.

Bonhoeffer as a Relational Leader

The bulk of Bonhoeffer's development into a relational leader happened as he passed through leader identification (stage three) and leadership differentiation (stage four), which occurred during his time as a student and children/youth worker. Clinton referred to these formative years as sovereign foundations, inner-life growth, and ministry maturing.[30] It is interesting to note how godly influences on Paula Bonhoeffer's (Dietrich's mother's) side of the family may have been what captured Bonhoeffer's attention for theology and ministry. Dietrich's great-grandfather had been a theologian and colleague of Hegel, and his grandfather had been a court chaplain for Wilhelm II at Potsdam.[31] Paula's brother, "Uncle Hans" to Dietrich, was the superintendent of the Liegnitz church in Waldau about forty miles away. Bonhoeffer would visit his cousins and read his uncle's leather-bound theology books.

From an early age, Bonhoeffer was thinking about ultimate questions, of which Paula took note.[32] Bonhoeffer and his twin sister, Sabine, would often lie awake at night and concentrate on the word *eternity*. When he was four, Bonhoeffer asked his mother, "Does the good God love the chimney sweep too?" and "Does God, too, sit down to lunch?"[33] Paula Bonhoeffer led the family in daily Bible readings and songs, and it was Paula who insisted on all her children being confirmed. When Bonhoeffer was twelve, his brother Walter, who had gone to fight in the First World War, was killed. Two years later, Paula gave Dietrich Walter's Bible, which Dietrich would use for his daily devotions for the rest of his life.[34]

At thirteen, Bonhoeffer knew he wanted to study theology, but he did not announce it for another year. Once he did make the declaration, his family pounded him with questions mercilessly. Both his father and older brothers seriously challenged his decision, but Bonhoeffer stood his ground. While there was never a specific mention of "calling," something within Bonhoeffer was certain of his path. In fact, in a perhaps prophetic moment, Bonhoeffer's older brothers Klaus and Karl-Friedrich teased, "Look at the church—a more paltry institution one can hardly imagine!" Bonhoeffer stood his ground and responded, "In that case, I shall reform it!"[35] As Metaxas noted, Bonhoeffer's future work would focus more on the community of the church than any other subject.[36]

At least one other incident certainly made a substantial impact on Bonhoeffer's grasp of leadership. Dietrich attended his first evangelistic meeting at age fifteen. The leader, General Bramwell Booth of the Salvation Army, impressed Dietrich with his joy and ability to bring people to a conversion experience.[37] Booth's ministry involved caring for the needs of the suffering. Bonhoeffer would not see this type of inspiring ministry until ten years later in New York City at Abyssinian Baptist Church. These experiences were foundational to Bonhoeffer's personal growth and understanding of leadership and ministry.

Relational leadership for Bonhoeffer began as he intellectually, spiritually, and practically worked out his understanding of "Christ existing as the church" in his dissertation at Berlin University.[38] For Komives and colleagues, this would still fall under leadership identified,[39] and for Clinton, as inner-life growth.[40] Yet in both systems, we see Bonhoeffer moving toward the end of these stages and into a greater sense of leadership. Kelly noted the groundwork laid in *Sanctorum Communio* would influence his more developed understanding of community in *Life Together* written in 1939.[41] The twelve years between these two great writings is the lifework of an honest individual who, with integrity, attempted to work out what he firmly held to be true about how people came to genuinely experience Christ. In the process, a relational leader emerged.

In *Sanctorum Communio*, Bonhoeffer considered how Christ relates to people both in and through the church. Bonhoeffer suggested personhood as a theological reality. In fact, Bonhoeffer explained that individuals only exist in relationship with other people.[42] Jesus Christ took on the form of personhood, overcoming sin and death so that believers may become children of God. Bonhoeffer explains that people encounter the personhood of Christ through the church—a community of persons in relationships.[43] In the interactions with the church community, individuals come to experience Christ personally.

A good example of how relationships play a key role in people experiencing Christ is Bonhoeffer's understanding of infant baptism. Children are baptized by the will of their parents. The church must then accept the responsibility to "carry" the child through. If not, it is analogous to a mother giving birth and, rather than nourishing the child, deserting him. Root notes, "The kind of 'carrying' that Bonhoeffer calls for can only be done when children are drawn deeply into the life-world of community, when children are known, heard, and prayed for."[44] The story at the beginning of this chapter about the boy and Mr. Wolf perfectly illustrates this point. The boy needed Christ and encountered Him as he was ministered to and served through a relationship with Bonhoeffer. Bonhoeffer entered the boy's suffering and "carried" him. This is relational leadership.

Bonhoeffer's foundational idea of the importance of relationships in the community of the church is further underscored by his idea of *analogia relatonis*. For Bonhoeffer, humanity's likeness to God is reflected in their relationships with one another. The fact that God, a relational being as evidenced in the Trinity, created mankind in His likeness, means that human beings were made for relationship with one another. In human relationships, we mirror the image of God. What's more, Bonhoeffer believed that "only by being in relation with the other am I free," and that freedom means "being-free-for-the-other."[45] While this freedom for the other person bears responsibility, it is nonetheless a free choice to respond to others' needs. Bonhoeffer held convictions from Scripture that informed an understanding of relational leadership.

At nearly the same time as he was intellectually and spiritually developing his understanding of the church community, he was learning practically how community works. He was required as a theological candidate at Berlin University to spend time in local ministry. He chose to lead a Sunday school in Grunewald.[46] This first experience with ministry reflects what would occur in nearly every children/youth ministry role Bonhoeffer would undertake. Bonhoeffer spent a tremendous amount of time preparing for each class and then spent time outside of class with his students. His class at Grunewald became so popular that children started leaving other classes to join Bonhoeffer's. The Thursday Circle grew out of this Sunday school class. Bonhoeffer believed deeply in the need to train the next generation of young men, so he started a class on his own initiative to this end. The group met at his home for about an hour and a half each week and discussed a reading on topics of religion, ethics, politics, and culture. Together, the young men explored topics such as, "What is the purpose of prayer?" "the gods of the Negro tribes," and "famous poets and their God." This was the start of a highly relational ministry.

From Grunewald, Bonhoeffer went to Barcelona in 1928 as assistant vicar of the German congregation. The children's ministry started with just one student. Bonhoeffer resolved to change that by visiting children personally at their homes and inviting them to Sunday school.[47] They did come, and within weeks the Sunday school became large. He spent most of his time with the older boys. He had them to his house, much like he did with the boys and the Thursday Circle, where they listened to music and talked about how he could help them solve problems at school with homework or with issues with teachers. He even bought Christmas gifts, including a bicycle for one of the students.[48] It was during this ministry when Bonhoeffer ministered to the boy who had lost his dog in the opening story.

Bonhoeffer further developed in ministry and as a relational leader on his year-long study visit to New York as a Sloan Fellow at Union Theological Seminary in 1930. New York would radically transform Bonhoeffer's life, not because of the intellectual stimulation he received there, but because of the significant friendships formed.[49] One of those friendships was with Frank Fisher, an African American who introduced Bonhoeffer to Harlem's Abyssinian Baptist Church, resulting in a six-month immersion into American black Christianity and culture.[50] Bonhoeffer believed that both the preaching and the community of Abyssinian deeply reflected the gospel. Dietrich believed that it was only through the relationships and conversations with Frank Fischer and others at Abyssinian Baptist Church that he felt he truly experienced religion. He was moved by the "skill in preaching and the passion of life together."[51] Bonhoeffer searched record shops and purchased the "negro spirituals" that had such a transformative effect on him.[52] Later, he would play these songs for students in Berlin and then at Finkenwalde.

Armed with a new picture of a community of saints who passionately lived life together, Bonhoeffer returned to Germany and took a position as a lecturer at Berlin University. By this time, Bonhoeffer had developed relational giftedness. When he started lecturing, only a few students would show up. Since the classes were small, Bonhoeffer decided to meet in the attic of a nearby church. The meetings that took place in the attic included prayer and song—either Bach, romantic lieder, or Negro spirituals.[53] The class grew over time so that it no longer fit in the attic, and once they returned to campus, his lectures were regularly attended by two hundred students. One student commented, "Sometimes, when we laid our pens down after a lecture, we were literally perspiring."[54]

Bonhoeffer showed love to every student because of his desire to care for the whole person, an uncommon phenomenon by a professor at the time. Bonhoeffer took attention to care for the souls of his students.[55] Marsh offers a photograph of Bonhoeffer with his student from Berlin. In the picture, Bonhoeffer is in the middle, dressed in a sweater and tie. Around him, the students are relaxed and joyful. One student playfully bites a stick and bares his teeth directly behind Bonhoeffer. Two females lean on each other while another plays an imaginary flute with another student looking on and laughing.[56] The scene perfectly reflects Dietrich as a relational leader.

It was also during this time that Bonhoeffer displayed an incredible ability to connect in a difficult situation. He was appointed to a confirmation class in the city of Wedding. Bethge described the class as "out-of-control."[57] Upon his first meeting with them, the boys stomped their feet, threw confetti at him, and chanted "Bon, Bon, Bon" for several minutes. Bonhoeffer let the boys chant and then softly began to tell them a story about Harlem. Slowly, a hush moved through the room. Bonhoeffer continued to tell them stories about New York until it was time to go. The boys wanted to hear more and asked him to share again at their next meeting. Richard Rother, one of the boys in the class, said of Bonhoeffer later, "[Pastor Bonhoeffer] was so composed that it was easy for him to guide us; he made us familiar with the catechism in quite a new way, making it alive for us by telling us of many personal experiences."[58]

Bonhoeffer eventually rented a flat in Wedding and invited the boys over for meals, games, and music. A few of the boys became enthusiastic chess players. Root noted, "Bonhoeffer then was not only relationally connecting these boys to himself, but through his relationship with them, to others. Place-sharing was leading to communion."[59] Bonhoeffer's ministry at Wedding was a clear picture of what he believed to be true—that Christ is experienced in community with one another. Bonhoeffer did not just believe it—he lived it. He practiced *Stellvertretung* and witnessed its power. Root explained, "Bonhoeffer saw his boys confirm their faith, transformed from delinquents to disciples by the act of Jesus Christ in and through their life together; through chess, dinner, walks in the forest, and stories about New York and the New Testament they had encountered the living Christ."[60]

Bonhoeffer would carry this same approach to ministry to Finkenwalde in 1935 when he established the Confessing Church seminary. Here, Bonhoeffer infused the community with a true brotherhood through times of chess, music, and deep conversation, along with a monastic rule of life. This monastic rule of life included calling each other "brother," meditating on Scripture, spending time in quiet reflection, and confessing sin to one another. Another practice was to never speak about a brother in his absence. In this way, the brotherhood shared life and experienced Christ in community with one another. It was at Finkenwalde where Eberhard Bethge and Bonhoeffer first met and developed a deep friendship. This friendship supported Bonhoeffer as he wrote his classics, *Discipleship* and *Life Together*. It was his relationship with Bethge that would also be an encouragement to him through the dangerous years of Bonhoeffer's participation in a conspiracy against Hitler, and later during the dark times of imprisonment that eventually led to his death.

Perhaps one other account should be noted as evidence toward Bonhoeffer as a relational leader. This would be Bonhoeffer's incredible self-denial and consequential decision to return from the safe haven of America to suffer alongside the German Christians. When Bonhoeffer received notice that he must register with the military, he consulted mentors to help him decide what to do. If he took a stand, he would jeopardize the entire Confessing Church, but he could not, in good conscience, fight in the war. So, an alternative option came about through Bonhoeffer's now large and influential network of mentors and friends, including Reinhold Niebuhr, a former professor at Union. Niebuhr was able to secure him a position as pastor and lecturer in New York. With this invitation to serve in America, Bonhoeffer was able to avoid his notice to report for military duty. However, Bonhoeffer was not in America twenty-four hours before he knew he had made a mistake. Not long after, he wrote to Niebuhr,

> I have had the time to think and to pray about my situation and that of my nation and to have God's will for me clarified. I have come to the conclusion that I have made a mistake in coming to America. I must live through this difficult period of our national history with the Christian people of Germany. I shall have no right to participate in the reconstruction of Christian life in Germany after the war if I do not share the trials of this time with my people [61]

Bonhoeffer's convictions of living life together with the people he felt called to minister did not allow him to rest in security while they suffered. This is a true mark of someone who valued people and relationships over self.

Each of the accounts offered above describes an individual deeply committed to people and relationships. Bonhoeffer's obedience to what he believed was God's call to live relationally among others motivated him to sacrifice his well-being. Leadership happens in relationship, and Bonhoeffer tapped into this principle and lived it as an example for all leaders.

Concluding Thoughts on Bonhoeffer's Leadership Development

Bonhoeffer's example of relational leadership inspires us to live relationally in our leadership. However, there is more to learn from Bonhoeffer's leadership development. We have considered the stages of leadership development already, but there were critical factors involved at each stage that provided the necessary encouragement for developing further as a leader. There were at least five of these critical factors that can be easily remembered through the acronym, S.M.A.R.T. Bonhoeffer's development as a relational leader happened as he *Studied* and sharpened his mind, as he met with *Mentors*, took *Action* as a leader, *Reflected* on these experiences through extensive letter writing, and as he allowed *Time* to congeal his beliefs and his behaviors into an integrated whole.

These five critical factors—Study, Mentoring, Action, Reflection, and Time—are key components in the development of relational leaders. Bonhoeffer devoted his mind to serious inquiry, continually seeking to learn more about the Church and how to live out the Christian faith. He surrounded himself with respected men such as Max Diestel, Karl Barth, and George Bell. Each of these men provided key direction and insight for Bonhoeffer while on his leadership journey. Yet, perhaps demonstrated most through this article, is the idea that there is nothing quite like *doing* leadership for learning leadership. Through the many opportunities to provide leadership for children and youth, Bonhoeffer found his style of leadership. Closely related, only through his many reflections on both what he believed and how he behaved, came his integrated persona in leadership. Over time, as the experiences of leadership built upon one another, Bonhoeffer emerged as a truly influential leader. There may be no better formula for leadership development than to study, to act, to reflect, and then to repeat that process over time again and again.

Bonhoeffer's relational leadership is still influencing us today. Koehn, in her evaluation of Bonhoeffer's life, suggests that the magnitude of his life is "how he made his way through the world" with mission, purpose, courage, and respect.[62] His "living thoughtfully, living rightly are powerful acts of leadership unto themselves."[63] Bonhoeffer's life is a tremendous case study for how leaders develop, especially in a relational sense.

Endnotes

[1] Andrew Root, *Bonhoeffer as Youth Worker: A Theological Vision for Discipleship and Life Together* (Grand Rapids, MI: Baker Academic, 2014), 67.

[2] Ibid., 43.

[3] Eric Metaxas, *Bonhoeffer: Pastor, Martyr, Prophet, Spy* (Nashville, TN: Thomas Nelson, 2010), 63.

[4] Edwin Fleishman, "The Description of Supervisory Behavior," *Journal of Applied Psychology*, no. 37 (1953); Daniel Katz, Nathan Maccoby, & Nancy Morse, *Productivity, Supervision, and Morale in an Office Situation* (Ann Arbor, MI: Institute for Social Research, 1950).

[5] Robert R. Blake and Jane S. Mouton, *The Managerial Grid: The Key to Leadership Excellence* (Houston, TX: Gulf Publishing, 1974).

[6] Robert Greenleaf, *Servant Leadership: A Journey Into the Nature of Legitimate Power & Greatness* (New York, NY: Paulist Press, 1977).

[7] James Burns, *Transforming Leadership* (New York, NY: Grove Press, 2003), 9.

[8] Ibid., 25.

[9] Ibid., 27-29.

[10] Bernard M. Bass, *A New Paradigm of Leadership: An Inquiry Into Transformational Leadership* (Alexandria, VA: U.S. Army Research Institute, 1996).

[11] George Graen and Mary Uhl-Bien, "Relationship-Based Approach to Leadership: Development of Leader-Member Exchange (LMX) Theory of Leadership over 25 Years," *Leadership Quarterly* 6, no. 2 (1995): 219-247.

[12] Max Weber, *The Theory of Social and Economic Organizations,* ed. Talcott Parsons, trans. A.M. Henderson and Talcott Parsons (New York, NY: Free Press, 1947).

[13] Jay A. Conger and Rabindra N. Kanungo, *Charismatic Leadership in Organizations* (Thousand Oaks, CA: Sage Publications, 1998); Boas Shamir, Robert J. House, and Michael B. Arthur, "The Motivational Effects of Charismatic Leadership: A Self-Concept Based Theory," *Organization Science* 4, No. 4 (November 1993): 1-17.

[14] Daniel Goleman, *Emotional Intelligence: Why it Can Matter More Than IQ* (New York, NY: Bantam Books, 1995).

[15] Daniel Goleman, Richard Boyatzis, and Annie McGee, *Primal Leadership: Unleashing the Power of Emotional Intelligence* (Boston, MA: Harvard Business Press, 2013), 6.

[16] Ibid., 5, 30-31.

[17] Marcus Warner and Jim Wilder, *Rare Leadership: 4 Uncommon Habits for Increasing Trust, Joy, and Engagement in the People You Lead* (Chicago, IL: Moody Publishers, 2016).

[18] James M. Kouzes and Barry Z. Posner, *The Leadership Challenge: How to Make Extraordinary Things Happen in Organizations*, 3rd ed. (San Francisco, CA: Jossey-Bass, 2002), 20.

[19] Metaxas, *Bonhoeffer,* 65.

[20] Ibid., 61.

[21] Charles Marsh, *Strange Glory: A Life of Dietrich Bonhoeffer* (New York, NY: Vintage Books: a division of Penguin Random House LLC, 2015), 11.

[22] Ibid., 23.

[23] Susan R. Komives et al., "A Leadership Identity Development Model: Applications from a Grounded Theory," *Journal of College Student Development* 47, no. 4 (2006): 401-418.

[24] Marsh, *Strange Glory,* 16.

[25] Komives et al., "Leadership Identity," 409.

[26] Marsh, *Strange Glory,* 40.

[27] Komives et al., "Leadership Identity," 411.

[28] Dietrich Bonhoeffer, *Letters and Papers From Prison*, ed. Eberhard Bethge, Enlarged ed. (New York, NY: Simon and Shuster, 1971), 144-147.

[29] Metaxas, *Bonhoeffer,* 528.

[30] J. Robert Clinton, *The Making of a Leader: Recognizing the Lessons and Stages of Leadership Development* (Colorado Springs, CO: NavPress, 1998), 30-32.

[31] Marsh, *Strange Glory,* 17.

[32] Ibid., 16.

[33] Metaxas, *Bonhoeffer,* 11.

[34] Ibid., 39.

[35] Marsh, *Strange Glory,* 17.

[36] Metaxas, *Bonhoeffer,* 38.

[37] Ibid., 39.

[38] Dietrich Bonhoeffer, *The Communion of Saints: A Dogmatic Inquiry Into the Sociology of the Church,* trans. R. Gregor Smith (New York, NY: Harper and Row, 1963), 85, 143, 197, 203.

[39] Komives et al., "Leadership Identity," 407-408.

[40] Clinton, *The Making of a Leader,* 31.

[41] Geffrey B. Kelly, "Editor's Introduction to the Reader's Edition of Life Together," in *Life Together,* ed. Victoria J. Barnett, trans. Daniel W. Bloesch, Reader's ed. *Dietrich Bonhoeffer Works* (Minneapolis, MN: Fortress Press, 2015), 5, 3-23.

[42] Bonhoeffer, *The Communion of Saints,* 51.

[43] Ibid., 66-69.

[44] Root, *Bonhoeffer as Youth Worker,* 56.

[45] Dietrich Bonhoeffer, *Creation and Fall: A Theological Exposition of Genesis 1-3,* ed. John W. de Gruchy, trans. Douglas Bax, vol. 3, *Dietrich Bonhoeffer Works* (Minneapolis, MN: Fortress Press, 2004), 60-67.

[46] Metaxas, *Bonhoeffer,* 64-65.

[47] Root, *Bonhoeffer as Youth Worker,* 65.

[48] Ibid., 65.

[49] Ibid., 79.

[50] Marsh, *Strange Glory,* 115.

[51] Root, *Bonhoeffer as Youth Worker,* 82.

[52] Metaxas, *Bonhoeffer,* 109.

[53] Marsh, *Strange Glory,* 151.

[54] Metaxas, *Bonhoeffer,* 125.

[55] Marsh, *Strange Glory,* 152.

[56] Ibid., 153.

[57] Eberhard Bethge, *Dietrich Bonhoeffer: A Biography,* ed. Victoria J. Barnett, trans. Betty and Peter Ross, Frank Clarke, and William Glen-Doepel, and Eric Mosbacher, Rev. ed. (Minneapolis, MN: Fortress Press, 2000), 226.

[58] Root, *Bonhoeffer as Youth Worker,* 99.

[59] Ibid., 105.

[60] Root, *Bonhoeffer as Youth Worker,* 109.

[61] Dietrich Bonhoeffer, *Theological Education Underground: 1937-1940,* ed. Victoria J. Barnett, trans. Victoria J. Barnett et al., vol. 15, *Dietrich Bonhoeffer Works* (Minneapolis, MN: Fortress Press, 2012), 210.

[62] Nancy F. Koehn, *Forged in Crises: Leadership in Turbulent Times* (New York, NY: Scribner, 2017), 366.

[63] Ibid., 367.

Chapter 9

BONHOEFFER'S LEADERSHIP THROUGH PREACHING

Dr. Brent A. Thomason

*Now I rejoice in my sufferings for your sake,
and in my flesh I am filling up what is
lacking in Christ's afflictions
for the sake of his body, that is, the church.*[1]
—Paul, The Apostle

Dietrich Bonhoeffer's life was cut short at the age of 39 when on April 9, 1945, he was hung at dawn at the Flossenbürg concentration camp in the final weeks of Nazi-controlled Germany. In the short span of his life, Bonhoeffer preached to congregations in Barcelona (1928-1929), Berlin (1933), London (1933-1935), and Finkenwalde (1935-1937), not to mention the underground Confessing Church after the Gestapo had restricted Bonhoeffer (1937-1940). And even when his official capacity as vicar dissolved due to his censorship and incarceration, he preached to his inmates while in prison (1943-1945). Of his sermons, seventy-one have been preserved in *Dietrich Bonhoeffer Werke,* the majority of which have been translated into English and compiled thus far in two volumes, *The Collected Sermons of Dietrich Bonhoeffer.*[2]

Bonhoeffer's sermons reveal how passionate he was about communicating the gospel through his preaching in a way that gave hope to the people in search of a meaningful Christian life.[3] For Bonhoeffer, preaching was confessing the faith through "the proclamation of the word of God as revealed in Scripture" in a way that demonstrated both his theology and worship of God.[4] But the tone of his preaching shifted on January 30, 1933, when Adolf Hitler was sworn in as chancellor of Germany. From that point, preaching became a "prophetic means to call his church and his students to withstand the ideological spirit of the times."[5] A sermon on the lips of Bonhoeffer was like a sword in the hand of a warrior—he wielded its power to both convict the wayward heart of the parishioner and defend against Hitler's Nationalist Socialist takeover of the church. A prophet of his time, Bonhoeffer warned *das Deutsche Volk (the German People)* of the ills of the Nazi agenda—a stance that would cost him his life, nothing less than the *Cost of Discipleship* to Christ!

Bonhoeffer's life and expositions from the pulpit modeled that of the prophets in the Old Testament and the apostles in the New. With the same vigor and fervor, Bonhoeffer led his congregations through his exegesis of Holy Writ. This chapter will survey a selection of sermons and scenes from his life to show how Bonhoeffer followed the paradigm of gospel proclamation and prophetic speech laid out in Scripture, thereby leading Germany through his powerful preaching.

Models of Biblical Preaching and Prophetic Speech

From the time of the ark-building Noah until the revelator John, preaching and prophetic speech flow from the lips of professional priests and part-time prophets. Their content criticizes kings and convicts the congregation. It encourages the community and calls for celebration. Yet, their role and relation to king and country all depended on the occasion and call from God. In this section, we will identify several purposes of preaching and prophetic speech from prophets, priests, and pastors found in the Bible to illustrate how Bonhoeffer confronted his *Führer* and led his *Volk* (German for "people") through his preaching.

Throughout the Bible, preachers have served to lead their communities back to God. To this end, they have exegeted God's law in their sermons. They have beseeched God's throne in their prayers. They have illustrated God's character in their person. Consequently, they have been heard and heeded. They have been ignored and forgotten. They have been ridiculed and persecuted. Irrespective of deplorable fate or blessed fortune, one thing remained constant: they discerned their times and did not shrink back from speaking into it. Four categories of leading through their preaching ministry emerge as a result of surveying the biblical data: they shepherd the sheep, they serve the flock, they criticize the social constructs, and they model a sacrifice.

Leading by Shepherding

The pages of Scripture are replete with shepherding imagery. In the Old Testament God is described as a shepherd. He identifies Himself as a shepherd when employing the shepherd metaphor by claiming the people of Israel are "my sheep, human sheep of my pasture" (Ezekiel 34:31). Micah 7:14 beckons the Lord to exercise His oversight and care for Israel by "shepherd[ing] your people with your staff, the flock of your inheritance." In the famous twenty-third Psalm, David praises the Lord for being his personal shepherd (verse 1). Jacob, himself an adept shepherd (Genesis 30:43), lauds the Lord for being a shepherd to him (Genesis 48:15). Countless other psalms and prophetic oracles ascribe shepherd-like qualities to the Lord.

It is no wonder, then, that as God's representatives on earth and mediators of Israel, the Lord would extend that shepherding function to Israel's prophets and leaders. The prophets Jeremiah and Ezekiel have much to say about the shepherds of Israel. Whereas Ezekiel indicts the wicked leaders over Israel for looking to their own interests while oppressing the weak sheep of Israel (Ezekiel 34:1-4), Jeremiah pronounces a woe upon them for having scattered the sheep of Israel rather than ministering to them (Jeremiah 23:1). Yet amid these rebukes aimed at the incompetent shepherds, Jeremiah prophesies that God will send righteous shepherds to care for the flock, those who would follow "after my own heart" (Jeremiah 3:15). Truly, Israel had already witnessed such righteous shepherds among both kings and prophets. David was such a man who pursued God's heart (Acts 13:22) and was taken from the shepherd fields to rule over Israel (1 Samuel 16:11). Similarly, Amos was called to the vocation of prophet while he was shepherding flocks on the hillsides of Judea (Amos 7:14-15). Indeed, Israel's leaders were likened to shepherds, whether friend or foe.

Not only were the prophets described as shepherds over Israel, but such imagery is also modeled in their preaching ministries. When the children of Israel demand their first king, Samuel "solemnly warn[ed] them" of the dangers such a pseudo-shepherd would bring—one who would not look out for the best interest of the people but who would exploit the sheep for his own gain (1 Samuel 8:9). When Nathan rebukes King David, he illustrates David's actions with a parable of how a man stole a sheep from another's flock rather than taking a lamb from among his own sheepfold (2 Samuel 12:1-4). Thus, the king was to be a model shepherd and Nathan's sermonic parable undergirded this imagery. But not all sermons and prophetic speech were admonishing. Some employed shepherd-like metaphors for affirming. Ezekiel prophesies over Israel that God would redeem them out of captivity and restore them to the Promised Land, much like sheep who have gone astray are brought back to green pastures: "I will feed them with good pasture, and on the mountain heights of Israel shall be their grazing land. There they shall lie down in good grazing land, and on rich pasture they shall feed on the mountains of Israel" (Ezekiel 34:14).

Similar to God in the Old Testament, Jesus in the New Testament identifies himself as "the good shepherd" who "lays down his life for the sheep" (John 10:11). He is intimately acquainted with each sheep; he calls them by name; they hear his voice and follow him as he leads them out of the pen and into the pasture (John 10:3-4). Peter identifies Jesus as the "chief Shepherd" under whom pastors shepherd their individual congregations (1 Peter 5:1-4). Depending on the occasion, their shepherding role called them to redirect the wandering lamb and ward off the wolf. Jesus was known to welcome the toddler (Matthew 19:13-15) and drive away the abusers of Israel (John 2:15) as the situation warranted. Following the model of Jesus, the apostles too provided for the needs of the least in the kingdom (Acts 20:10-11) and safeguarded the flock against predators (Acts 13:9-11).

Like the Old Testament prophets, the New Testament apostles model the shepherding metaphors in their speeches and letters taking their cue from Jesus. Jesus's compassion for the congregation of Israel is on full display as He weeps on several occasions over the brokenness of the flock (Matthew 14:14; Luke 19:41; John 11:35). His shepherding actions are undergirded by his speeches and teaching on the Kingdom of Heaven. The quintessential example arrives when Jesus explains His relationship to the "tax collectors and sinners" as that of a shepherd who leaves the ninety-nine sheep in pursuit of the one lost sheep (Luke 15:1-7). Likewise, the disciples rebuke the wolves who threaten the safety of the flock as in the case of Ananias and Sapphira (Acts 5:1-11), and they speak tenderly to the wounded among Israel to restore health like that of the beggar sitting at the Beautiful Gate (Acts 3:6).

Throughout the Bible, the prophets and preachers are exercising leadership as shepherds over God's people. Their speeches don't need to appeal to the shepherding metaphor explicitly, though many times they do. But their references to the shepherding metaphor in their sermons exegete their actions toward the nation as that of shepherds over the flock of Israel. Thus, their prophetic speech and sermons "feed my lambs…[and] my sheep" (John 21:15, 17) which reinforces their ministries to "tend my lambs" (John 21:16).

Leading by Serving

God's appointed leaders in the Old Testament faithfully served the congregation of Israel. Many ministered to their communities until their death and often never saw the benefit nor the impact of their oversight. The leaders and prophets approached this lackluster and at times thankless job from a posture of humility and service to God through their ministry to the nation. Their model of servant leadership set a precedent for the apostles thereafter. For instance, we see Moses serving the congregation in the wilderness by providing water in the face of their grumbling and ungrateful hearts (Numbers 20:11). Even when Israel's malcontent drove them to challenge Moses and recall his appointment as leader over them, Moses served them faithfully and petitioned God on their behalf (Numbers 12:13). Similarly, the judges delivered Israel from her oppressors, and often at immense cost to the judge (e.g., Jephthah's vow), even though the nation "did not listen to their judges" and "soon turned aside from the way in which their fathers had walked, who had obeyed the commandments of the Lord" (Judges 2:17).

These Old Testament servant leaders reinforced their examples through their preaching to and prayers for the community. In his farewell address, after recounting all the ways that he had served Israel, Joshua challenged the people to serve the Lord as he had done (Joshua 24:15). And despite Joshua knowing that the nation would fail to keep their promise to the Lord after they had pledged to serve him, Joshua still led them faithfully until his death. Upon learning that the men of Israel had intermarried with the foreign women of post-exilic Judea, Ezra the scribe rent his clothes, prostrated himself, and voiced a first-person plural prayer incorporating himself in the confession of Israel's transgressions though he himself was blameless (Ezra 9:3-15). Consequently, his prayer drew the congregation near to join in their admission of guilt before God (Ezra 10:1).

The same servant leadership in the lives and liturgy of the Old Testament saints is found in the New Testament apostles and the model of Jesus. Though He intended to retreat from the masses and steal away with His disciples to a deserted place, Jesus reassigned His agenda and selflessly served the crowds, feeding 5,000 with two fish and five loaves after having spent the day healing their sick (Matthew 14:13-21). On numerous occasions, Jesus's servant heart drove Him to heal the sick and give sight to the blind, speech to the mute, and hearing to the deaf, though it often delayed His plans or detoured His path (e.g., the hemorrhaging woman). Learning from this selfless servant's heart, the apostles mirrored the model of Jesus and served their communities. The first deacons were appointed to better serve the needy widows in Jerusalem. Yet these deacons were identified by their character and the leadership that they had already demonstrated (Acts 6:1-6). So as not to be a financial burden on the church at Corinth, Paul served as a tentmaker to lead the blossoming congregation on the Peloponnese peninsula (Acts 18:3). And Timothy, whom Paul identified as a young church leader who is "genuinely concerned for your welfare" and not like others "who seek their own interests," labored tirelessly on behalf of the church at Philippi with a servant's heart (Philippians 2:20-21).

Jesus wove servant leadership ideology throughout the tapestry of his teaching. It was on his lips as he commissioned the disciples to go two miles when only one was required (Matthew 5:41) or to visit the "least of these my brothers" who sat persecuted in prison (Matthew 25:40) or not to exercise lordship over one another but rather to "let the greatest among you become as the youngest, and the leader as one who serves" (Luke 22:26). The disciples carried the baton of this teaching when they beseeched others to lead by serving. Paul charged Timothy to examine the candidate to test if he would serve the church well as a deacon (1 Timothy 3:10) and Peter calls the church to serve one another through the exercise of their spiritual gifts (1 Peter 4:10). These positions in the church required that the participants lead by serving, according to the apostles.

As we have seen, servant leadership is embedded in the fabric of both the Old and New Testaments. It is illustrated through the lives of leaders and preached through the sermons of servants. The biblical example shows the prophetic speech and preaching of the nation is nothing shy of a call to lead by serving, for even the "Son of Man came not to be served but to serve" (Mark 10:45).

Leading by Criticizing Society

In seasons when Israel was ruled by a ruthless leader or governed by a tyrannical king, the Old Testament prophets and New Testament apostles found their voice in a sea of silence. Theirs would be the contradictory word to that of a king's edict. Theirs would be a cautionary warning among a wave of yes-men. They would rebuff and chastise, rebuke and criticize when others only flattered and agreed. They were courageous and fearless—men who did not mind standing alone against the establishment. They led their congregations, cities, and commonwealth by criticizing the injustices of their society.

In the Old Testament, we see prophets rebuke kings who were habitually sinful (e.g., Zechariah and Joash) and kings who were occasionally sinners (e.g., Nathan and David). They stood against international rulers who temporarily occupied Israel (e.g., Moses and Pharaoh) and domestic leaders who illegitimately assumed Israel's throne (e.g., Jehoiada and Athaliah). They chastised the people for disobeying God's law (e.g., Nehemiah and Sabbath-breakers) and criticized the priests for despising God's name (e.g., Malachi and sacrifice-blemishers). No sector of society was exempt from the sharp tongue of the prophet speaking on behalf of the Lord.

They were committed to their cause and convinced they were right. This led them to stand up and speak out against those whom they perceived were in the wrong. Nothing deterred them from their conviction to preach against the ills of society. Money did not entice them to keep silent. Daniel still prophesied against Belshazzar, though he was enticed by riches, saying, "Let your gifts be for yourself, and give your rewards to another" (Daniel 5:17). Uneven odds did not persuade them to back down. While standing alone and outnumbered by the 450 prophets of Baal and the 400 prophets of Asherah, Elijah still indicted Israel saying, "How long will you go limping between two different opinions? If the LORD is God, follow him; but if Baal, then follow him" (1 Kings 18:21). Personal relationships did not interfere with the harsh content of their message. Samuel did not let his affection for his mentor halt him from proclaiming the word of the Lord against Eli's sons saying, "And I declare to him that

I am about to punish his house forever, for the iniquity that he knew" (1 Samuel 3:13a).

The prophets' examples from the Old Testament transcend the New Testament among the apostles. They too could not be bought off nor bullied out from preaching against injustices. John the Baptist did not shrink back from publicly criticizing the sexual sins of Herod Antipas and Herodias (Matthew 14:3-4), and even after he was unlawfully imprisoned for criticizing the law-breaking king, he continued speaking truth to the tetrarch (Mark 6:20). Many times, Jesus openly criticized the religious leaders of Israel, and, on at least one occasion, drove them out of the temple with a whip (John 2:15)! Similarly, the apostles criticized religious leaders (2 Timothy 3:1-9), public officials (Acts 4:19), the church (1 Corinthians 5:2), and the first-century pagan culture (1 Corinthians 10:20). Their task was to assess the setting and discharge rebukes wherever they saw society at odds with the gospel.

From their lips flowed uncensored chastisement in the harshest of words and sternest of tones. Writing to the churches of Galatia, Paul spares neither time nor pleasantry to criticize their abandonment of the real gospel asking, "O foolish Galatians! Who has bewitched you?" (Galatians 3:1), while simultaneously declaring damnation upon the perpetrators of such a pseudo-gospel: "Let him be accursed" (Galatians 1:8). While baptizing for repentance in the Jordan River, John exposed the deceitful motives of the charlatan spiritual leaders in front of the crowds saying, "You brood of vipers! Who warned you to flee from the wrath to come?" (Matthew 3:7). Even the monarchy was not exempt from the critical words of Jesus when He called Herod "that fox" (Luke 13:32) in reference to his worthlessness as a national leader.

No stratum of society escaped unscathed from the piercing words of the prophets and preachers in the Bible. They criticized and chastised any area they identified as aberrant behavior or beliefs from God's standard. And they did not do so behind closed doors but followed the decree of God to voice these concerns publicly so that the nation would hear and heed (Jonah 1:2). Consequently, often their life was forfeit.

Leading by Modeling Sacrifice

The prophetic speakers and preachers of the Bible understood the gravity of their calling and the risk of their task to call a wayward society back to alignment with God's decrees. Knowing that the nation and its leaders might resist and turn hostile toward the preachers of God did not derail their momentum. With great resolve, they remained committed to their mission even when faced with imminent death by execution. The New Testament apostles stood in a long line of Old Testament prophets who were killed by the very nation they were trying to save. Jesus confesses that He would join the ranks of such men by giving His life to the cause of pointing an errant society back to God: "Nevertheless, I must go on my way today and tomorrow and the day following, for it cannot be that a prophet should perish away from Jerusalem. O Jerusalem, Jerusalem, the city that kills the prophets and stones those who are sent to it!" (Luke 13:33-34).

Moses demonstrated his willingness to sacrifice himself for the nation of Israel when he led them out of Egypt. God had called him in Midian from the burning bush and it was clear from his several objections that he was reluctant to return to the land from which he fled as a fugitive (Exodus 3:11-4:17). Moses knew he returned to Egypt at his own peril since Pharaoh wanted to kill him (Exodus 2:15). Still, he resolved to obey the Lord and serve Israel in this way, come what may. The prophets Elijah and Elisha lived under constant threat of execution while they preached against King Ahab and the incorrigible nation of Israel (1 Kings 18:4). And in summary fashion, Hebrews testifies that the Old Testament prophets regularly "were tortured…suffered mocking and flogging, and even chains and imprisonment…were stoned, they were sawn in two, they were killed with the sword" for preaching against the ills of society (Hebrews 11:35-37).

Their prophetic speech and sermons indicted personages and peasants alike while confessing their willingness to suffer death for the sake of their sermon. Shadrach, Meshach, and Abednego rebuked King Nebuchadnezzar for instituting idol worship and retorted that they would not bow down to "serve your gods or worship the golden image that you have set up" even when that meant they must now submit their bodies to the flames of the fiery furnace (Daniel 3:17-18). Even as Micaiah received a death threat if he prophesied anything contrary to the four hundred false prophets of King Jehoshaphat, he declared, "As the LORD lives, what the LORD says to me, that I will speak" (1 Kings 22:14). Consequently, Micaiah was beaten, imprisoned, and starved when he alone indicted the prophets in the presence of the king saying, "Now therefore behold, the LORD has put a lying spirit in the mouth of all these your prophets; the LORD has declared disaster for you" (1 Kings 22:23). Along with Shadrach, Meshach, and Abednego, the prophet Micaiah willingly submitted his body as a sacrifice in order to lead the nation and her king back to God.

In the New Testament, Jesus warned His apostles that their preaching against society would result in the sacrifice of their own bodies. Jesus likened the danger of the task to that of "sheep in the midst of wolves" who upon hearing their preaching will "deliver you over to courts and flog you in their synagogues, and you will be dragged before governors and kings for my sake" (Matthew 10:16-18). There was no illusion of grandeur among the apostles concerning their task; they were "like men sentenced to death, because we have become a spectacle to the world, to angels, and to men" (1 Corinthians 4:9). Rather, they reveled in modeling the example of the suffering servant; they too were like lambs before the slaughter (Isaiah 53:7). For instance, Peter and John rejoiced after having been flogged for preaching against the Sanhedrin for they "counted [themselves] worthy to suffer dishonor for the name" (Acts 5:41). And Paul considered it a badge of honor that he was stricken much more than anyone on account of his preaching against a sin-sick society (2 Corinthians 11:23-29). In all this, they held fast to the promise of Christ that they would be blessed because they suffered like the prophets on behalf of Jesus and would therefore receive a great reward in Heaven (Matthew 5:12).

Not only did the apostles show their willingness to sacrifice their bodies for the preaching of the gospel, but they also exhorted that sacrifice to others too. Encouraging the Ephesian elders, Paul announced that he is "ready not only to be imprisoned but even to die in Jerusalem for the name of the Lord Jesus" (Acts 21:13). Similarly, John exhorted the brethren to "lay down our lives for the brothers" (1 John 3:16) because such a selfless sacrifice follows the gospel-shaped love of Jesus on the cross (Mark 10:45). Not only did the apostles show a willingness to sacrifice their physical bodies for the sake of the gospel, but they were also willing to swap places with the damned in order to allow one wayward soul entrance into Heaven. For instance, in writing to the Romans, the apostle Paul resolved that he would "wish that I myself were accursed and cut off from Christ for the sake of my brothers" (Romans 9:3). At times that same apostle called others to model his example (1 Corinthians 11:1).

Under threat of persecution or execution, neither prophets nor apostles waffled or wavered in their resolve to sacrifice themselves for the sake of the preached gospel. Their resolution to proclaim God's Word did not stop with the willingness to forfeit only their life but even their souls. The world was not worthy of such sacrificial lambs and consequently, through their death, they obtained a better resurrection (Hebrews 11:35-38).

Bonhoeffer's Prophetic Preaching and Biblical Leadership

For Bonhoeffer, preaching like the biblical saints and modeling the leadership of the Savior were so intertwined, it was impossible to unravel the one without simultaneously losing the other. In Bonhoeffer's view, the sermon must be expressed beyond the vacuum of the pulpit ensuring that both "teaching and the living [were] two parts of the same thing."[6] Consequently, the sermon was like the incarnation—the Word of God taking on flesh through the person of the preacher. This provided advantage both for the hearer and the speaker: for the congregant "it was an opportunity to hear from heaven, and for the preacher, it was a holy privilege to be the vessel through whom God would speak."[7]

In this light, when Bonhoeffer's sermons are situated against the backdrop of his life and changing the culture of Germany, the same four strands of preaching purposes found in the biblical narrative emerge among his homilies. Our objective then is to analyze sections from and selections of Bonhoeffer's sermons to see how he led both church and country through his preaching.

The Shepherding Pastor

Bonhoeffer modeled the qualities of a shepherd through his sermons as he bears his soul to the congregants, pouring out his heart and pleading with them to secure their eternal destiny. He knows the alternative to a life without Christ, and thus he begs them to be reconciled with God. He also understands how they are like scare-easy sheep, ready to scatter at the sight of a lurking predator, and therefore in need of great comfort and courage in the face of fear. It is Bonhoeffer's compassion for and comfort of his congregation that makes him resemble the leading shepherd of Psalm 23.

By the end of the year, serving the small parish in Barcelona, Bonhoeffer's popularity had surged to such an extent that his "senior pastor stopped announcing ahead of time which of them would be preaching."[8] Capitalizing on the advent hype, on December 2, 1928, Bonhoeffer used the season to preach about Christ standing at the door and knocking.[9] In his homily, Bonhoeffer plays on the theme of Christ's knocking from both Revelation 3:20, that Christ is desirous of dining in fellowship, and Matthew 25:35, that Christ is the "least of these" desirous of an invitation—an ominous reminder that our actions in this life have weighty consequences for the second advent. As Bonhoeffer explains, that invitation is "truly not merely a message of joy, but first of all horrifying news for every person with a conscience...[because] Jesus is coming in both judgment and grace."[10] Given that "one day, at the Last Judgment, he will separate the sheep from the goats," Bonhoeffer begs his congregation, "Christ is at the door; he lives in the form of those around us. Will you close the door or open it for him?"[11] The church in Barcelona had not previously seen such passionate preaching and impassioned pleas from the pulpit.[12] Yet it was precisely Bonhoeffer's compassion for the flock that swelled the numbers of the church during the summer—a season historically known in Spain for its declining numbers—and grew the children's ministry from one to well over thirty in attendance each Sunday during his tenure.[13]

Bonhoeffer's shepherding heart shines brightly through his comforting sermon on Remembrance Sunday, November 1933.[14] His sermon stemmed not only from the encouragement of the Scripture but from empathy, having experienced great loss when his brother Walter was killed in action during The Great War. Thus, Dietrich approached this "Day of the Dead" sensitively and slyly. For those wondering, "Where have our dead gone?" Bonhoeffer offers hope by repeating the phrase "but they are at peace" throughout the sermon signaling that those deceased are in the realm of God. Like a good shepherd, he picks up his staff and chases away the fear of death by exposing that predator for what it is: "Death is not wild and terrible if only we can be still and hold fast to God's Word. Death is not bitter if we have not become bitter ourselves. Death is grace, the greatest gift of grace that God gives to people who believe."[15] By redefining the experience of death—a gift from God to enter into his presence—Bonhoeffer then seizes upon the opportunity to address the spiritual state of his hearers as it pertains to their posthumous destination. "Yes, death is indeed frightening, bony old Death with his scythe...if a person does not have faith, if he or she is not among the righteous of whom our Scripture says: But they are at peace."[16] He then calls his hearers to reflect upon their destination after death and take courage by placing their faith in God. Thus, Bonhoeffer shepherded his flock by comforting them on this reflective Sunday insofar as he offered them peace when faced with the dread of death: "Those who believe in God will have peace, death will not frighten them; it can no longer touch them, for they are in the hand of God, and no torment will ever touch them."[17]

A year prior, Bonhoeffer led the students at the Technical College in Berlin as seen in his comforting and encouraging sermon "Courage in Uncertain Times" from December 1932.[18] Earlier that year Adolf Hitler gained German citizenship and the Nazi Party saw a surge in political seats as *das Vaterland* (the Fatherland) tried to forge a new government. With massive unemployment dealing a devastating blow to Germany's economy, the students feared the future and felt as if they were "in free fall," according to Bonhoeffer.[19] Against this backdrop of the "valley of the shadow of death," Bonhoeffer shepherded his students by offering both comfort and courage. Consequently, he exhorts them from the book of Daniel when the prophet himself saw terrifying visions of the future and was encouraged by a messenger from the Lord to "be strong and of good courage" (Daniel 10:19). In this rather short homily, Bonhoeffer identified straightaway with the angst of his students: "When we are disturbed by chaos in our personal lives, and we can't cope with it anymore; when we feel as though every support keeps crumbling away, leaving us in free fall…when some incomprehensible stroke of fate, great suffering or great passion, leaves us bewildered and feeling completely at the mercy of this fate…."[20] He then paralleled their situation in Germany with that of Daniel in Babylon stating, "And now this thing that happened to Daniel is taking place in a very particular case, which we today can understand as hardly anyone has before,"[21] and finally concluded by exhorting his students to "be of good courage. What for? So that we, as men and women who have received strength, may hear God's voice speaking to God's people and make a new start at obeying and believing in God."[22] By charging his students to take courage, Bonhoeffer trusted that the sheep would clearly "hear his voice" amidst the talk of the turbulent times and follow their shepherd Christ in faith because "they know his voice" (John 10:3-4).

Even from prison, Bonhoeffer did not cease to shepherd the flock and comfort them in despairing situations. The Gestapo imprisoned Bonhoeffer at Tegel for eighteen months after discovering his involvement within the *Abwehr* to help Jews escape Germany. Yet, despite the terror Hitler released on the world from 1943-1944, an endless source of comfort and calm from the Scriptures emerged from Bonhoeffer's 6 x 9-foot prison cell as seen in his *Letters and Papers From Prison*. While serving time at

Tegel, Bonhoeffer shepherded even his own family as he wrote sermonic meditations from prison to niece Renate and husband Eberhard.[23] Seamlessly, Bonhoeffer wove together the shepherding metaphor with Isaiah 57:18 by the way God leads the stray and comforts his wounded sheep: "But God has seen our ways—and saw us wounded, astray, and frightened. Now God is there to heal us. God touches the wounds that the past has inflicted on us," and "God wants to lead us."[24] But, Bonhoeffer explained, the leading of God is not to any destination, but only to himself for just as the shepherd leads the sheep to himself when he calls (John 10:3-4), so "when God leads our way, then it leads to him. God's ways lead to God."[25] Bonhoeffer concluded his meditation by quoting the Scripture, "I healed; I led; I comforted—because I have seen their ways," and then posited, "How does God heal, lead, comfort? Solely by putting a voice within us… That is the Holy Spirit."[26] Consequently, we see Bonhoeffer comforting his family while he is imprisoned by appealing to the Scriptures which testify of the comfort God provides via the Holy Spirit. Ergo, Bonhoeffer led by pointing the church to the Chief Shepherd (1 Peter 5:4).

From his first congregation in Barcelona to his prison epistles, we see Bonhoeffer lead the church like a shepherd. He embodies the qualities of a shepherd for his congregation. He draws out shepherding motifs from the Scriptures to encourage the despairing, console the afflicted, and calm the restless amidst Hitler's rage. By pointing the straying flock back to the Chief Shepherd, Bonhoeffer proves to be an adept under-shepherd leader himself.

The Servant Leader

No other season of life better exemplified Bonhoeffer's servant leadership than the two years he ran the underground seminary at Finkenwalde to train pastors of the Confessing Church. The spiritual and theological fruit of this communal life bore such great works as *Life Together* and *The Cost of Discipleship*. Not only did he model servant leadership for his fellow parishioners, but he also preached its tenets to these pulpiteers. Two homilies from 1935 illuminate Bonhoeffer's commitment to lead the congregation by serving.

The first short homily is a morning devotional meditating on the way pastors should prepare themselves to meet the day. Speaking from an amalgamation of biblical texts, Bonhoeffer exhorted these seminarians to begin each morning "not [with] our own plans and worries, nor even our eagerness to get to work…but rather God's liberating grace, God's blessed nearness."[27] That liberating grace from and blessed nearness to God comes from spending time in prayer: "Those who wish to fulfill an exhausting spiritual office without compromising both themselves and their work with frantic activity would do well to learn the spiritual discipline of the *servant* Jesus Christ."[28] In fact, Bonhoeffer recommends that the young ministers follow the example of Jesus who rose early before daybreak to pray (Mark 1:35) and similarly "put aside [one hour] each morning for quiet prayer and worship together."[29] It is through prayer, Bonhoeffer explained, that they will receive God's enabling power "to help bear one another's burdens" throughout the day.[30] He then proceeded to divvy up the prayer time into three recommended areas. The first is to pray the Word of God. Arguably so, Bonhoeffer spends much time on the importance of communing with God through His Word. But the second and third recommendations show Bonhoeffer's servant-heartedness. He gives a single fleeting sentence on the necessity to pray for oneself saying, "We should not forget to pray for ourselves," and then concludes with another long section on the need to intercede for others, from which this excerpt follows:

> There is also the broad field of intercession. Here our own gaze broadens; we see people both near and far whom we would commend to God's grace. No one who has requested such intercession from us should be neglected. Moreover, there are also many who have been commended to us in a special sense either personally or professionally. Finally, we all know of people for whom hardly anyone performs this *service.*[31]

A vital element to beginning the day as a minister of God, according to Bonhoeffer, is to spend the better part of an hour in prayer serving others through intercession, while allocating a mere fraction of that time to pray for one's own needs. In doing so, the ministers will bear the burdens of their congregants and secure for themselves "neither to become windbags nor to get into a [spiritual] rut."[32] Herewith, Bonhoeffer emphasizes service over selfishness. He admonishes the budding pastors the lead their congregations by serving them in prayer, taking their cue from the *par excellence* servant leader, Jesus.

As was his habit at Finkenwalde, Bonhoeffer preached at vespers and communion while leaving the Sunday morning services for the young preachers to test their new homiletical wings. But occasionally, Bonhoeffer broke from this routine to address the larger community with an urgent matter. Such was the occasion on Sunday morning November 17, 1935.[33] In this second homily, Bonhoeffer preached on the necessity to forgive lavishly and repeatedly according to Matthew 18:21-35. For Bonhoeffer, failing to forgive is first and foremost a sign of selfishness. At the beginning of the sermon, Bonhoeffer exhorted his congregation to consider anyone whom they have neglected to forgive. If perchance none came to mind, Bonhoeffer indicted such persons as "inattentive," "indifferent," even "hard and proud and cold as a stone."[34] Bonhoeffer did not mince words pointing out that likely everyone was withholding forgiveness from another in some way and that such bridled forgiveness forfeited the support and service due that person. Consequently, failing to forgive is secondly failing to serve:

> To forgive would mean having nothing but good thoughts about the person and *supporting* that person whenever we can...and yet the whole point is to *support* such persons— to *support* them in all situations, with all their difficult and unpleasant sides, including any injustice and sin they may commit even against me—to be silent, to *support*, and to love without ceasing.[35]

Even if one has wronged another, Bonhoeffer explains, it is paramount that the offended forgive the offender and serve him, especially when it is unpleasant to do so. Bonhoeffer envisioned such an offended to lead by example, showing others that offering forgiveness liberates the soul from selfishness and loves the neighbor through service:

> Forgiving has neither beginning nor end; it takes place daily, unceasingly, for ultimately it comes from God. This is what liberates us from forced relationships with others, for here we are liberated from ourselves; here we may surrender our own rights merely in order to help and *serve* others.[36]

Like the prophets and apostles, Bonhoeffer exhorted the church to follow the biblical model of servant leadership. He admonished both preacher and parishioner to lead by serving. As these two sermons have shown,
whether through intercessory prayer or offering forgiveness, Bonhoeffer
impressed upon the people that the person touched by God desires but one
thing: "to help bear the distress of others, to serve, to help, to forgive."[37]
And that precisely is the heart of the servant leader.

The Social Critic

There are seasons when the ills of society are so pungent, the righteous
cannot keep silent even when faced with governmental persecution. Such
was the case of Bonhoeffer who, through prophetic insight, assessed the
times and criticized the social injustices around him. Two social wrongdo-
ings that were the unfortunate recipients of Bonhoeffer's scrutinizing sermons were the political takeover of the church by the *Deutsche Christen*
and Hitler's mistreatment of the Jews.

In early 1933, Adolf Hitler became chancellor over Germany and within a few months had gained direct control over all branches of government. The *Deutsche Christen*, the pro-Nazi German Christian Faith Movement, was to be the religious arm which wielded Hitler's Aryan agenda
in the church by creating religious laws conforming to those of the Nazi
state racial laws.[38] Recognizing Hitler's takeover of the German church,
Bonhoeffer became a leading voice critical of the Nazi's distortion of the
Christian faith. So, dissenting from the *Deutsche Christen*, Bonhoeffer
took up spiritual arms in the *Kirchenkampf*. Within a year, the battle lines
were drawn, the Confessing Church was born, and Bonhoeffer struggled
for the soul of the church.

Prophetically, Bonhoeffer recognized in the first few months of Hitler's
rise to power that the trajectory of the *Deutsche Christen* would place
the church farther from God and firmly in idolatry. It would have all the
appearances of a religious institution but would lack the commitment to
Christ—its loyalty lay with the worldly agenda of the National Socialists.
Consequently, on May 28, 1933, Bonhoeffer preached a sermon titled "Of
Priests and Prophets in the New Germany" indicting the *Deutsche Christen* as an idolatrous "church of the world" instead of a "church of the
word."[39] Appealing to the Exodus episode of Aaron and the golden calf,
Bonhoeffer commenced his scathing sermon thus: "The priest against the

prophet, the church of the world against the church of faith, the church of Aaron against the church of Moses."[40] Bonhoeffer charged the *Deutsche Christen* church to be impatient just like the Israelites at the base of Mount Sinai who desired to worship a god whom they could see. Because they had not seen or heard recently from God, they instituted an idol so that they might worship whom they wished on their own terms. Bonhoeffer admitted their desire to be a church "with gods and priests and religion, but a church of Aaron—without God."[41] That heretical church spares no expense to make the idol more glorious so that it can "celebrate itself, to worship its own accomplishments."[42] But for such "a church that is ready to make any sacrifice for the sake of idolatry, the glorification of human ideas and values—as a church that presumes divine authority for itself through its priesthood," Bonhoeffer projected an ominous fate: such a church will one day lie "shattered to pieces on the floor, as a church that has to hear anew, 'I am the Lord your God'…as a church that is struck by this word and crumbles."[43] He then calls what would become known as the Confessing Church to depart from the *Deutsche Christen* saying, "It is as the church of Moses, the church of the Word, that we should depart from one another."[44] Consequently, Bonhoeffer separated from the Nazi-controlled church and established himself as a leading social critic since the genesis of Hitler's Germany.

Four years later, Bonhoeffer's prediction about the trajectory of the *Deutsche Christen* came true. By the summer of 1937, the Gestapo banned the Confessing Church from taking collections and arrested a few of its key leaders, including Martin Niemöller on July 1, 1937. Within a few months, Heinrich Himmler would force Finkenwalde and other "illegal" seminaries to close. Against the backdrop of this political climate, Bonhoeffer delivered a sermon on "Preaching the Gospel in an Evil Age" on July 11, 1937, in which he criticized the injustices done by the government and the state-run church:[45]

> It is an evil age when the world silently allows wrong to be done. When the poor and weak cry out to heaven in their oppression, and yet the judges and lords of the earth are silent. When the persecuted church-community cries out to God and human beings for help in its tribulation, and not a single mouth on earth speaks up to provide justice…whenever

the mouths of the lords of the world are silent in the face of wrong, their hands are quick to engage in violent deeds.[46]

From Psalm 58, Bonhoeffer incriminated both the leaders of the National Socialists and their state-church cronies. While they were in power, the times had borne only wrongdoing and there was none to vindicate the innocence of its victims. Yet Bonhoeffer offered hope through the sobering reality that God would act and take vengeance on the enemies of his church, the Confessing Church that is:

And if we are horrified at the sight of human fists, how much more will we be horrified at the sight of God's fists, which will strike down the wicked for the sake of his kingdom, his name, his glory. The Lord of the world establishes his kingdom. Vengeance is the Lord's over his enemies.[47]

When that day would come that the Lord would answer the cry of the oppressed and seek retribution for the injustices inflicted on the church by the Nazi party, Bonhoeffer did not know. However, until vengeance came, Bonhoeffer charged the seminarians at Finkenwalde to continue praying that even the enemies of the church would be brought to repentance and reconciliation with Christ.[48] We see, therefore, that Bonhoeffer's criticism of society was driven by his desire to lead people to Christ.

By September 1935, the anti-Semitic Nuremberg Laws were enacted to preserve the German bloodlines. These racial laws forbade the intermarriage relationships between Germans and Jews and further made any bloodline ineligible for *Reich* citizenship save German and German-related ancestry. This latter law targeted Jews but later included other groups such as gypsies and people of color. On November 14, supplementary laws were passed defining who a Jew was so that the Reich Citizenship Law could take full effect. Though Bonhoeffer stood against the anti-Semitic legislation, few among the Confessing Church were willing to follow suit. Ten days after the legislation took effect, Bonhoeffer preached against it in a sermon titled "Standing Strong in Babylon."[49] From Revelation 14, Bonhoeffer pointedly criticized the law of the Nazis saying, "God will not ask—whether we were Germans or Jews, whether we were National Socialists, or even whether we belonged to the Confessing Church."[50] Neither political ideology nor purity of bloodline will have any effect on one's status in the final judgment according to Bonhoeffer. Moreover, for Bonhoeffer, the arbitrating factor determining one's eternal destination will not be a bloodline test per the Reich Citizenship Law but the gospel: "God will one day ask all human beings whether they believe they can prove themselves before the gospel—and the gospel alone will be our judge. It is the gospel that will separate souls in eternity."[51] Thus, a person's value does not rest in his genealogy but in his belief in the gospel.

Sunday service was not the only occasion Bonhoeffer used to criticize society through his preaching. On January 15, 1936, he seized upon the opportunity of his grandmother's funeral to attack the mistreatment of the Jews by the National Socialists. Alluding to her defiance of the Nazi-backed boycott of Jewish businesses in 1933, Bonhoeffer simultaneously praised the ideals for which Julie Tafel Bonhoeffer stood and rebuked those who would try to marginalize members of society based on ethnicity:

> The uncompromising nature of justice, the free word of the free person, the integrity of a person's word once given, clarity and sobriety of speech, sincerity and simplicity in private and public life—to these things she was committed with all her heart. She lived with these goals. And during her life she found that realizing these goals in one's own life required effort and work. But she did not shy away from this effort and work. She could not bear to see these goals held in contempt or to see another person's rights violated. Hence her final years were clouded by a great suffering she endured because of the fate of the Jews among our people, which she bore and suffered in sympathy with them.[52]

Personal suffering for the cause of equity in the midst of an unjust society was for Bonhoeffer to be expected. Yet he did not desire to depart the funeral that day in sadness reflecting on the final years of Julie's sorrow for the Jews. Rather, he exhorted them, "Let us go away from her grave strengthened. Strengthened by her image, by her life and death, but strengthened even more by faith in the God who is both her and our own refuge forever, strengthened by Jesus Christ."[53] Once more, according to Bonhoeffer the simultaneous sin of society was the solution of the Savior.

As his sermons testify, Bonhoeffer was not one to shy away from using the platform of the pulpit to criticize society. Whether rebuking the

Deutsche Christen for hijacking the church or reproving the National So-cialists for their anti-Semitic laws, no sector of society was exempt from Bonhoeffer's stinging indictments. Yet his assailment of society's ills and its leaders never ended in condemnation alone. There was always the offer of restorative hope for both offender and offended. Thus, Bonhoeffer en-visioned an alternative Final Solution: the gospel for both Nazi and Jew.

The Sacrificial Lamb

Throughout his homilies, Bonhoeffer consistently preached that follow-ing Jesus meant certain suffering and sacrifice. A life devoted to Jesus was likely bound to end in death at the hands of oppressors, according to Bonhoeffer. And the political climate of Nazi-controlled Germany proved a fitting foe for those truly committed to Christ. Like the biblical prophets and apostles, Bonhoeffer modeled sacrificial leadership and preached it as well. Three homilies capture this message of sacrifice which Bonhoeffer delivered to parishioners, pastors, and personally applies it to his own life.

In a short sermon titled "Following Christ through the World to the Cross" delivered on the first Sunday of Lent, February 11, 1932, Bonhoef-fer exhorted the congregation to follow Jesus's example of sacrifice by enduring the suffering that comes with bearing the cross. In his address, Bonhoeffer explained that "Jesus could have been the ruler of the world… he could have liberated Israel and led it to glory and honor" if he would have accepted the offer of Satan and bowed down to him (Luke 4:7).[54] However, Bonhoeffer notes, Jesus would have forfeited obedience to God by way of the cross and so He responds, "Worship the Lord your God, and him only shall you serve" (Luke 4:8). Such sole allegiance to God, though, means "lowliness, scorn, persecution, means not being understood, means hatred, death, cross…for it is the path of God. And that is why it is also the path to love for human beings."[55] The worship of God alone meant death for Christ; so also, it means death for the follower of Jesus. That is, after all, "for whom the first martyrs died," reminds Bonhoeffer.[56] They forfeit-ed their lives for the cause of Christ on the cross. Therefore, Bonhoeffer concluded, "We walk with him, as individuals and also as the church. We are the church under the cross—that is, hidden from view. But even here we can do nothing else but know that our kingdom, too, is not of this world."[57] In other words, the consolation of the Christian is knowing the victory that follows the suffering of his own cross.

Suffering is not something to be feared, explained Bonhoeffer to fellow seminarians on November 24, 1935. "'Fear God'—instead of the things you normally fear—do not fear the coming day; do not fear other people; do not fear violence and power, not even if they can rob you of life and possessions...but fear God, and only God."[58] This was a timely word to the future pastors who already experienced pressure from the Nazi-appointed Consistory officials who were "offering 'legalization' to the Confessing Church seminaries" and financial support if they agreed to conform to the theological positions of the Hitler-backed *Deutsche Christen*.[59] Similarly, in a fitting sermon for Remembrance Sunday, Bonhoeffer encourages pastors to endure the hardship of persecution for their preaching the gospel even if it results in their death, for then they will be blessed of the Lord:

> But not all the dead are blessed—only those 'who die in the Lord'—those who at the proper time learned how to die, those who kept the faith, those who held fast to Jesus even into that final hour whether amid the sufferings of public martyrdom or of the martyrdom of a quiet solitude of enduring life.[60]

Martyrdom, then, is an honorable death according to Bonhoeffer if one's faithfulness to Jesus remains intact to the end. Thus, Bonhoeffer charged the preachers not to let the word *Christ* be far from their lips in that final hour:

> Whether old or young, whether quickly or after long suffering, whether seized and coerced by the lord of Babylon, or whether quietly and gently, may our final word be: Christ, that is our prayer today...then we will have rest from our work, that is, from the tribulations and sufferings and temptations amid which we stand today.[61]

Great is the eternal reward and spiritual rest for the one who remains faithful to Christ in the final moments of his sacrificial life.

Bonhoeffer's charge to these budding preachers was a conviction he had already resolved in his own life a year prior. With autobiographical undertones, Bonhoeffer preached on the plight of the prophet Jeremiah to his London congregation on January 21, 1934. In a sermon titled "God's

Call to Prophetic Witness," Bonhoeffer paralleled the unrelenting burning within Jeremiah to preach the word of the Lord at the great price of persecution and suffering with his own experience of God wooing him back to *das Vaterland* and to help fellow compatriots and churchmen alike. According to correspondence with friend and colleague Karl Barth, Bonhoeffer admitted that his flight to London was more of a retreat because of his feeling isolated from fellow pastors due to his stance against the *Deutsche Christen* and *Reichskirche.*[62] The sermon hints at Bonhoeffer's realization that fate was bidding him to return to Germany and suffer for the truth of the gospel:

> The person is now a captive and must simply follow the path ordained for him or her. It is the path of someone whom God will not let go anymore, who will never again be without God...this path will lead right down into the deepest situation of human powerlessness. The follower becomes a laughingstock, scorned and taken for a fool, but a fool who is extremely dangerous to people's peace and comfort, so that he or she must be beaten, locked up, tortured, if not put to death right away.[63]

Bonhoeffer then compared the sacrifice of the Confessing Church pastors with the suffering of Jeremiah: "[Jeremiah] felt the pain of being continually humiliated and mocked, of the violence and brutality others used against him...today in our home church, thousands of parishioners and pastors are facing the danger of oppression and persecution because of their witness for the truth."[64] For Bonhoeffer, the call to preach the glory of the gospel of God was a call to sacrifice self and suffer in Germany. Thus, he concluded:

> So why be concerned about ourselves, our life, our happiness, our peace, our weakness, our sins? If only the word and the will and the power of God can be glorified in our weak, mortal, sinful lives, if only our powerlessness can be a dwelling place for divine power. Prisoners do not wear fancy clothes; they wear chains. Yet with those chains we glorify the victorious one who is advancing through the world, through all humankind. With our chains and ragged clothes

and scars we must bear, we praise the one whose truth and love and grace are glorified in us...the triumphal procession of truth and justice, of God and the gospel, continues through this world, pulling its captives after it in the wake of the victory chariot. Oh, that God would bind us at the last to his victory chariot.[65]

With these words, Bonhoeffer projected that, like Jeremiah, he too would be incarcerated, adorned with tattered inmate's clothes, and brandishing chains for the sake of the gospel. A prophet of his own time, Bonhoeffer led the church by his example of steadfast sacrifice by returning to his country.

Bonhoeffer's persistent exhortation to suffer and sacrifice on behalf of Jesus were not empty words. They were words of conviction and resolve. And as the Lamb of God was "led to the slaughter, and like a sheep that before its shearers is silent, so he opened not his mouth" (Isaiah 53:7), so Bonhoeffer did not protest on April 9, 1945, but submitted himself to the authorities unto death. No words better capture Bonhoeffer's sacrificial leadership than the recounting of his final moments by H. Fischer-Hüllstrung, the doctor at Flossenbürg:

On the morning of that day between five and six o'clock... through the half-open door in one of the rooms of the huts I saw Pastor Bonhoeffer, before taking off his prison garb, kneeling on the floor praying fervently to his God. I was most deeply moved by the way this lovable man prayed, so devout and so certain that God heard his prayer. At the place of execution, he again said a short prayer and then climbed the steps to the gallows, brave and composed. His death ensued after a few seconds. In the almost fifty years that I worked as a doctor, I have hardly ever seen a man die so entirely submissive to the will of God.[66]

No longer appealing to the examples of the prophets and apostles by way of exhorting others to suffer for the Lord, Bonhoeffer made the ultimate sacrifice and led both church and country through offering his own life. Indeed the doctor was correct. God heard and answered that same prayer offered by Bonhoeffer many years prior: "May it be granted to us that we not be weak in our final hour—that we may die as those who confess Christ,"[67] and again "Lord, entice us ever anew and become even stronger in our lives, that we may believe in you alone, live and die in you alone, that we may taste your victory."[68] Through death, Bonhoeffer tasted the victory of life.

Endnotes

[1] Colossians 1:24. All quotations in this chapter are from the English Standard Version. Scripture quotations are from the ESV® Bible (The Holy Bible, English Standard Version®), copyright © 2001 by Crossway, a publishing ministry of Good News Publishers. Used by permission. All rights reserved.

[2] All quotations and excerpts of Bonhoeffer's sermons are taken from these works.

[3] Isabel Best, ed., *The Collected Sermons of Dietrich Bonhoeffer*, vol. 1, trans. by Isabel Best et al. (Minneapolis, MN: Fortress Press, 2012), xiii.

[4] Best, ix.

[5] Ibid., x.

[6] Eric Metaxas, *Bonhoeffer: Pastor, Martyr, Prophet, Spy* (Nashville, TN: Thomas Nelson, 2010), 272.

[7] Metaxas, 272.

[8] Best, 7.

[9] Ibid., 7-12.

[10] Best, 10-11.

[11] Ibid., 11.

[12] Metaxas, 69-87.

[13] Ibid., 77.

[14] Best, 101-107. The title of the sermon bears the mark of Isaiah 66:13 (As a Mother Comforts Her Child), a metaphor that Bonhoeffer weaves throughout the homily to encourage his congregation.

[15] Best, 106.

[16] Ibid., 107.

[17] Ibid.

[18] Victoria J. Barnett, ed., *The Collected Sermons of Dietrich Bonhoeffer*, vol. 2, translated by Isabel Best et al. (Minneapolis, MN: Fortress Press, 2017), 101-104.

[19] Ibid., 103.

[20] Barnett, 103.

[21] Ibid., 104.

[22] Ibid.

[23] Ibid., 209-217.

[24] Barnett, 210.

[25] Ibid.

[26] Ibid., 211.

[27] Barnett, 155.

[28] Ibid., 156; emphasis added.

[29] Ibid., 155.

[30] Ibid., 156.

[31] Barnett, 156; emphasis added.
[32] Ibid.
[33] Best, 177-183.
[34] Ibid., 178-179.
[35] Ibid., 179; emphasis added.
[36] Ibid., 181; emphasis added.
[37] Ibid., 183.
[38] Barnett, 105-106.
[39] Ibid., 105-113.
[40] Ibid., 108.
[41] Ibid., 110.
[42] Ibid., 111.
[43] Ibid., 113.
[44] Ibid.
[45] Ibid., 175-183.
[46] Ibid., 178.
[47] Ibid., 180.
[48] Ibid., 183.
[49] Ibid., 159-168.
[50] Ibid., 163.
[51] Ibid., 164.
[52] Ibid., 173.
[53] Ibid., 174.
[54] Ibid., 68.
[55] Ibid., 69.
[56] Ibid., 68.
[57] Ibid., 70.
[58] Ibid., 163.
[59] Ibid., 160.
[60] Ibid., 167.
[61] Ibid.
[62] Metaxas, 196-197.
[63] Barnett, 117.
[64] Ibid., 118.
[65] Ibid., 120.
[66] Metaxas, 532.
[67] Barnett, 167.
[68] Ibid., 120.

Chapter 10

BONHOEFFER AS A TEACHING LEADER

Dr. Mark Cook

In the April 2014 edition of *First Things*, Professor Elizabeth Corey argued that the contemporary educational environment does not need better methods of teaching as much as it needs more teachers who love their subjects and can pass that love on to their students. "We need," she implores, "a particular person to tell us about a particular book or author or field of study, to demonstrate its significance in practice, to act as a master to whom we can apprentice ourselves."[1] Measurable, achievable outcomes have become buzzwords at all levels of education, symbolizing the shift from teacher-centric education to methodology-centric education. As society continues to grapple with the speed and expansiveness of technological innovations in the 21st century, educational leaders have become distracted by the myriad challenges of educating in such an environment and have sought solace in technique. Jacques Ellul's penetrating analysis in *The Technological Society*, written decades ago but still remarkably prescient, offers a way of understanding why the rational, methodological system of education has become so popular. His work provides a philosophical account of what modern writers Wendell Berry and Parker Palmer have applied with more specificity. Berry, a former college professor, argues "The complexity of our present trouble suggests as never before that we need to change our present concept of education. Education is not properly an industry, and its proper use is not to serve industries… A proper education enables young people to put their lives in order, which means knowing what things are more important than other things; it means putting first things first." (Thoughts in the Presence of Fear) Berry's idea of education centers on the need for more than the transfer of pre-packaged information from teacher to student. Inherent in Berry is an appreciation for the relationships between students and teachers. Parker Palmer picks up this theme in his work *The Courage to Teach*, where he posits: "In our rush to reform education, we have forgotten a simple truth: reform will never be achieved by renewing appropriations, restructuring schools, rewriting curricula, and revising texts if we continue to demean and dishearten the human resource called the teacher."[2]

The point that these writers make is not that methodology is unimportant, but rather that it needs to be re-prioritized under the human aspects of teaching. Curriculum is substantially important, as is thinking about how to ensure that students are growing in their learning. However, they must be embedded in a deeper understanding of teaching as a relational endeavor, where a teacher's relationship to the subject, to themselves, and to their students converge. Dietrich Bonhoeffer has much to offer in this respect. His time spent leading underground seminaries in Germany during the Nazi regime provides a marvelous case study in teaching leadership. In a depersonalized culture, Bonhoeffer's greatest contribution to educational leaders is to remind them of the power of personal, incarnational teaching.

Background on Bonhoeffer as a Teacher

While Bonhoeffer was a student before he became a teacher, he never jettisoned the habits he learned as a young scholar and would draw from this early part of his life throughout his time as a teacher. The enduring works that most epitomize his time as a teacher, *Discipleship* and *Life Together*, are themselves extrapolations of the themes that he first developed as a student at the University of Berlin in his dissertation, *Sanctorum Communio*. Victoria Barnett has noted that studying Bonhoeffer's life reveals how "fragmentary and turbulent" it was, yet even with the great upheavals and constant movement, there is an uncommon congruence to his life that emerges as well.[3] Much of this congruence derives from Bonhoeffer's desire to not simply study theology but to live his theology in the community of the Church. What began as the topic of his dissertation would come to be the reigning focus of his life.

Bonhoeffer's educational journey began as a child, as his family had deep ties to German higher education. His father, Karl Bonhoeffer, was one of the leading psychiatrists at the University of Berlin, and his mother came from a family of theologians. Bonhoeffer's studies took him first to Tubingen in 1923, then to the University of Berlin (at that time referred to as Friedrich-Wilhelm University) for more training. In 1927, at the age of 21, Bonhoeffer earned the equivalent of a Ph.D. with the acceptance of his dissertation, *Sanctorum Communio.*

After completing his dissertation, Bonhoeffer qualified for a teaching position at the University of Berlin just a few years later in the summer of 1930. He would not immediately begin the new post, however. Instead, he took a year to travel to the United States and spend time doing postgraduate work at Union Theological Seminary in New York. While studying at Union, Bonhoeffer witnessed an America bludgeoned by the first blows of the Great Depression and plagued by the problem of racism. Bonhoeffer also encountered an American Christianity that struck him as distant from the revealed Word of God. In an anecdote found in Marsh's biography of Bonhoeffer, *Strange Glory*, Bonhoeffer is said to have remarked to a fellow student that his time at Abyssinian Baptist Church in Harlem was the only time he had "experienced true religion in the United States."[4] As other leaders who have appropriated the lessons of travel have done, Bonhoeffer used this time of exploration to engage deeply with the American culture of the time. His insights would continue to inform the rest of his life, including how he introduced his later seminary students to the African American spirituals he encountered at Abyssinian Baptist Church through the records he brought back from his trip.

The period of learning and engagement in America ended rather abruptly when he returned home to Germany. As Bethge notes, "The period of learning and roaming had come to an end. He now began to teach on a faculty whose theology he did not share, and to preach in a church whose self-confidence he regarded as unfounded. More aware than before, he now became part of a society that was moving toward political, social, and economic chaos."[5] His new teaching duties forced him to adapt to a role he had limited experience with. "Lecturers had to draw their audiences," Paul House remarks. "They could not depend on a curriculum that delivered students to their classes to do that for them."[6] Ferdinand Schlingensiepen provides an invaluable summary of this early period of Bonhoeffer's teaching career, noting how students were immediately drawn to his clear, logical, and passionate lectures.[7] This circle of students gave Bonhoeffer encouragement, largely because it was with them that he found common convictions rather than with his fellow faculty. The students hungered for a belief in the Bible that was not met by other faculty members. Schlingensiepen's portrayal of Bonhoeffer's teaching foreshadows the later developments that would be at the heart of his teaching in the underground seminaries:

> When Bonhoeffer had been teaching at the university for half a year, his salary had finally paid him retroactively. With the money he bought a wooden cabin and had it put up in Biesenthal, near a small lake on the northern outskirts of Berlin. These were Spartan weekend quarters indeed, a single room used in the daytime for meals and discussions and at night as a dormitory; but it was here that, in the spring of 1932, the 'Bonhoeffer circle' experienced for the first time their teacher's idea of community. The days included devotions, Bible studies and singing, besides discussions on political, social and church issues, and also sharing meals, sports and games.[8]

These early gatherings would be expanded upon and serve as the basic organization of the underground seminaries. Bonhoeffer's teaching philosophy grew organically from his theological study, his experience of true community, and his deepening conviction of the importance of a personal devotional life.

As Hitler became Chancellor in 1933 and began to systematically reshape all aspects of German life, Bonhoeffer would increasingly find himself at odds with the emerging Nazi movement. As the German Church splintered in 1934, leading to the establishment of the Confessing Church through the Barmen Declaration, Bonhoeffer knew that the situation needed a different educational approach than that offered by those sympathetic to the Nazi cause. The first preacher's seminary of the Confessing Church began in April 1935, and with it, Bonhoeffer sought to get back to the roots of true pastoral training. In a powerful letter to Karl Barth, Bonhoeffer lays out his educational philosophy in moving detail:

What I find is that on the whole the young theologians who enter the seminary are raising the same questions I have been dealing with recently; naturally enough, this creates a situation that strongly influences life together here. I am strongly persuaded that both with regard to what they bring with them in the way of university experience and with regard to the kind of independent work being asked of them in con-gregations—especially here in the east—these young theo-logians need a completely different kind of training, training that absolutely should include such communal seminary experiences. One simply cannot imagine how empty and indeed utterly burned out most of the brothers come to the seminary. Empty both with regard to theological knowledge and certainly with regard to familiarity with the Bible, as well as with regard to their personal lives.[9]

As Bonhoeffer watched the unfolding events around him, he knew that his role as an educational leader was paramount if the next generation of pastors were to be trained in the proper way. These students needed a teacher, one who could show them the way forward. They needed the leadership of a teacher who embodied what they wanted to become them-selves. "The questions young theologians are seriously asking us today are: How can I learn to pray? How can I learn to read Scripture? If we do not help them with these questions, we are not helping them at all."[10] In Bonhoeffer, they found a teacher who exhibited these things. But how exactly did he do so? We now turn to how Bonhoeffer taught these two important subjects to his students, and to the leadership lessons we can glean from his example.

Teaching Pastors How to Read Scripture

As Bonhoeffer surveyed the situation around him, he realized that Ger-man pastoral training needed an overhaul. The verve and passion of the Karl Barth letter from spring 1935 shows that Bonhoeffer was convinced of the need to change course. In an environment increasingly hostile to authentic pastoral formation, Bonhoeffer wanted to establish a commu-nity of brothers that was set apart so that they might better serve their congregations in the future. He knew from firsthand experience that pastoral work was tremendously isolating, so he wanted the new seminary to have communal living as a key focus. Together in community, the brothers would not only benefit spiritually and socially, but also in their intellectual growth. He knew that studying together would propel his students forward and would sharpen each other. Bonhoeffer's vision for the seminary was to provide deep spiritual, intellectual, and personal formation. Each aspect needed attention, so it is no surprise that Bonhoeffer's plans included each. What is surprising, however, is the extent to which Bonhoeffer committed himself to the task. As House notes, Bonhoeffer's underground seminaries were by no means the first of their kind to employ such training: "The schedule and conditions at Bonhoeffer's seminaries were not unique. Many of their practices of daily worship and devotion he saw also in Anglican seminaries he visited…the most impressive and most needed component of Bonhoeffer's seminaries is the dedication to sacrificial ministry to others exemplified by [them]."[11] While they might not have been new, the unique element in these seminaries was the personal dedication of Bonhoeffer.

The foundation of all pastoral formation is through deep familiarity with the Christian Scriptures. The group of leaders, including Bonhoeffer, who initially purposed to establish the Confessional Church's seminaries, underscored its centrality: "Examination of the Holy Scriptures of the Old and New Testaments constitutes the central focus of all work. The goal of a Protestant pastor is to come of age in dealing with Holy Scripture."[12] These words were not merely outward projections of an ideal. They flowed from Bonhoeffer's own heart and passion for the Word of God. He wanted his students to learn more about the Bible itself, but even more than that he wanted them to learn how to encounter Christ through daily time in it. He himself had been transformed by the power of daily devotions and wanted to pass this along to his students. In a letter to his parents later in his life while imprisoned, he spoke of the way the Scriptures anchored his life: "By the way, I am reading the Bible straight through from the beginning and am just coming to Job, whom I especially love. I am also still reading the Psalms daily as I have done for years. There is no other book that I know and love as much."[13] The Scriptures had become the foundation of his life, so the way he taught his students about how to read and interpret Scripture flowed out of his own experience. In a lecture entitled "The Pastor and the Bible," Bonhoeffer taught the students that "The pastor encounters the Bible in threefold usage: in the pulpit, at the study desk, and on the prayer kneeler. He must learn to use it correctly in all three spheres."[14] He knew that one of the major dangers in a more focused study of the Bible was spiritual pride. "Knowledge and study [of the Bible] should never lead to one's own glory," he warned.[15] He wanted the students to understand the importance of deep knowledge and familiarity with the Scriptures so that they could minister from it. He knew that the first step in learning how to properly study the Bible, though, was to learn how to listen to what God was saying. Thus, in his instructions for Biblical meditation, he wanted his students to understand the difference between meditation and study:

> Just as the words of someone dear to you can follow you around the entire day, so also should the word of Scripture resonate in your ears incessantly and work on you. Just as you do not analyze the words of someone dear to you and instead simply accept them as they are spoken to you, so also accept the word of Scripture, pondering it in your heart just as Mary did.[10] And that is all. That is meditation. Do not look for new ideas and connections in the text as for a sermon! Do not ask: How can I pass these words along? But rather: What are they saying to me![11] Then ponder these words for a long time in your own heart until they completely enter into you and take possession of you.[16]

He did not want his students to merely know the content of the Scriptures, but to have a relationship with God. He knew that ingraining this habit in the life of his students would bear fruit for the rest of their lives. All other tasks in the seminary were dependent upon a daily encounter with Scripture because it was the place where strength was found:

> What we want is to encounter Christ in his own word. We come to the text anxious to hear what Christ wants to say and give to us today through his word. Each day see to it that you meet Christ before you meet other people. Each morning, before additional burdens are laid upon you, lay onto Christ everything that is stirring you, concerning you, and oppressing you. Ask yourself what things still might be keeping you from following him completely and allow him to become Lord over such things before new obstacles appear.

The goal is Christ's community, Christ's help, and Christ's guidance for the day through his word. It is thus that you will begin the day strengthened anew in your faith.[17]

Robert Greenleaf, best known for his exploration of the concept of servant leadership, argued that a key mark of leaders is "that they are better than most at pointing the direction."[18] Leaders know the goal they are trying to achieve. As they articulate the goal, though, they must be aware that there are constant distractions that threaten its realization. The Kierkegaardian ideal of willing one thing gets lost in the daily demands of living. Kouzes and Posner, in *The Leadership Challenge*, contend that good leaders constantly remind themselves, and their followers, of what is most important: "When there are daily challenges that can throw you off course, it's crucial that you have some signposts that tell you where you are."[19] Bonhoeffer knew from personal experience that daily time with Scripture would be no easy task, so he set about in his teaching to offer help for this struggle:

Those who seriously engage in the daily practice of meditation will quickly encounter great difficulties. Meditation and prayer must be practiced long and with great earnestness. The first thing to remember is: Do not become impatient with yourself. Do not get tied up in despair about being distracted. Simply sit down again each day and wait patiently.[20]

One of the greatest gifts teachers can give their students is not just a love for a particular field of study, but practical help with learning to engage with it themselves. In teaching how to read the Scriptures, Bonhoeffer knew that the perils of detached study would constantly threaten the students. His teaching confronted this peril head-on. He knew the challenge it would be, but also knew that the reward would be life-long. Bonhoeffer's teaching on how to read Scripture exemplified true spiritual leadership:

Spiritual leaders are not haphazard people. They are intentional. Just as they plan thoroughly for important meetings in their work, they also plan carefully to allow substantial time for listening to their Creator...An unhurried time with God is invaluable. There is no substitute for it. It is well worth the effort involved in maintaining and protecting it as first priority.[21]

Instruction on Prayer

If teaching the students how to read Scripture was of foremost importance to Bonhoeffer, teaching them how to pray was a natural next step. In fact, in one of his early lectures at Finkenwalde, Bonhoeffer explicitly stated how interconnected Scripture and prayer are: "The daily word should come before one's daily bread. Only thus do we also receive our daily bread with thanksgiving. The morning prayer belongs before our daily work. Only thus do we perform that work in fulfillment of the divine commandment."[22] Great teachers help their students make sense of the world and what is important by showing them how things are connected. Subjects and topics are not isolated in individually contained beakers. History impacts science, literature shines a light on history, art and music speak not only to culture but also to the human condition. By highlighting interrelationships, teachers help students see the world holistically. Parker Palmer says that "Good teachers possess a capacity for connectedness. They are able to weave a complex web of connections among themselves, their subjects, and their students so that students can learn to weave a world for themselves."[23] Bonhoeffer did not want his students to see Scripture reading and prayer as isolated entities, but as deeply interwoven. He taught his students that praying the words of Scripture provides pastors

> with firm footing. It should guide him in prayer and give him assurance in praying insofar as he is praying on the ground of God's word. It should provide him with a refuge when he is at wit's end, troubled, or at odds with people, tempted, doubtful, is having trouble praying, and before every momentous decision in his life.[24]

In a letter the students sent out to their supporters, it is clear that Bonhoeffer was making great strides in this endeavor: "The Bible stands at the center of our work. It has once again become the point of departure and the center of our theological work and of all our Christian activity. Here we have learned once again how to read the Bible prayerfully."[25]

Beyond understanding the interconnectedness of prayer and Scripture reading, Bonhoeffer wanted to teach his students the importance of making prayer a daily habit. He knew that many of the students found it hard to discipline themselves in this way, so during common worship every day he would often lead prayers, and in this way, he not only was able to pray for his students, but also model true prayer for them. Bethge's description of Bonhoeffer's prayers reveals how seriously he took them:

> During seminary worship he spoke almost all the prayers himself. His prayers were long and usually extemporaneous; occasionally he also used liturgical prayers. He would begin with detailed thanks for the gift of faith, for the seminary's communal life, for the sun and the sea. Next he would ask for daily and mutual tolerance within the fellowship. Much time was devoted to prayer for the Confessing church, its leaders and synods, for those in prison, those who had fallen by the wayside, and for enemies. There was a confession of those sins peculiar to the theologians and clergy, and intercession for them. He devoted much time and trouble to the preparation of these prayers and their inner structure. His language was devoted wholly to the issue at hand and free of all self-portrayal. He put his will, understanding, and heart into these prayers; yet he also believed that the language of prayer should be modeled and in harmony with that of the Psalms."[26]

He could not understand why so many others in the Confessing Church had such little time for prayer. In a letter to Karl Barth, he remarked, "theological work as well as genuine pastoral community emerges only from within a life defined by morning and evening reflection on the word and by fixed times of prayer."[27] In that same letter, he recounted to Barth about how he had heard one leader tell him that they would do better to train the pastors simply in how to preach, arguing that there was simply not enough time to teach them how to pray and meditate. Bonhoeffer believed, however, that rushing out to do the work of ministry without having the foundation of prayer was sheer folly. In his instructions to his students on how they should start their days, he taught them that they would burn themselves out without daily attention to prayer:

Disorder undermines and shatters faith. Theologians must pay special attention to learning this, since they so easily confuse a lack of discipline with Protestant freedom. Those who wish to fulfill an exhausting spiritual office without compromising both themselves and their work with frantic activity would do well to learn the spiritual discipline of the servant Jesus Christ. Young theologians will find it enormously helpful to set aside fixed times for quiet prayer and worship and then to keep those times with great perseverance and patience.[28]

Bonhoeffer's teaching about prayer is still deeply relevant in the 21st century. His focus on instructing his students in the importance of daily prayer shows just how important he believed it was to impart to them, and he not only instructed them in how to do it but modeled it for them as well. Educational leaders at all levels can glean much from this simple lesson. Students need incarnational teachers who can teach from their own inner lives. Henry Blackaby highlights that leaders often neglect prayer because it can seem passive, but in so doing they misunderstand the centrality of prayer for leadership: "More than any other single thing leaders do, it is their prayer life that determines their effectiveness. If leaders spend adequate time communing with God, the people they encounter that day will notice the difference... When spiritual leaders take their task of leading people seriously, they will be driven to their knees in prayer."[29] The fruit of a life surrendered in prayer are courage and joy. Courage comes from accepting the gifts and power of what only God can provide through prayer, and joy comes from seeing circumstances in light of God's sovereignty:

In all facets of our ministry, he will grant us cheerfulness and the courage to become engaged without fear of people, without fear of death, without despondency, and without weariness. Hence let us accept this gift. The way this happens is to read Scripture daily, to pray daily without ceasing for the proper witness, for the coming of the kingdom, for our congregations, and for our brothers.[30]

After impressing upon his students the interconnection of prayer and Scripture reading and its importance as a daily habit, he also sought to teach them about the significance of prayer in ministry. He knew his students would not only need to know how to cultivate the habits of prayer on their own behalf but would need to be able to bear the responsibility of interceding for those they were tasked with pastoring. He knew other seminaries did not include prayer in their curriculum, and he knew that if it was as important as he believed it to be, there was no possibility of leaving it up to the students to figure out on their own. They needed basic instruction in how to pray for others:

> There is also the broad field of intercession. Here our own gaze broadens; we see people both near and far whom we would commend to God's grace. No one who has requested such intercession from us should be neglected. Moreover, there are also many who have been commended to us in a special sense either personally or professionally. Finally, we all know of people for whom hardly anyone performs this service. Nor do we want to forget to give thanks to God for those who help and strengthen us through their own intercessions.[31]

Why would Bonhoeffer take the time to specifically point out the need to pray for all those who request prayer, as well as those who have few people to pray for them, if he did not believe that it was a cornerstone of pastoral ministry? Bonhoeffer surely had Ephesians 6:12 in mind when he declared that "We can depend on only one thing, namely, on the word and the help of God, and our strongest weapon remains our daily prayer. Only a praying church can successfully endure *this* struggle."[32] The great challenges of ministry during the Nazi regime required that pastors know that their greatest weapon was prayer. "The forces threatening the church are enormous. Here we must learn again: It is prayer that accomplishes things."[33]

Summary of Bonhoeffer's Teaching Leadership

Bonhoeffer's leadership through teaching illustrates the importance of personal, incarnational teaching. His focus on teaching his students how to read Scripture and how to pray became chief concerns for him, but by no means were the only things he sought to impart to his students. Beyond these two points of emphasis, there are several other significant leadership lessons from Bonhoeffer's life as a teacher.

The first lesson that emerges is that Bonhoeffer took the responsibility of teaching as a high calling. In a letter to a friend from London, he spoke of teaching in terms of being entrusted with it: "I have been entrusted with one of the most wonderful and indeed responsible tasks in the Confessing Church, namely, with training the next theological generation in a preachers' seminary."[34] Very few leadership books focus on the importance of teaching because modern society over-values entrepreneurs and vision-casters as images of leadership. Peruse the current best seller lists in leadership, for instance, and you will rarely find a book that offers a philosophical or historical perspective on the subject. Instead, the shelves are littered with pragmatic books that offer readers practical tips and personal stories of success. Even when teaching is mentioned, it is often relegated as a side role that can be disregarded if it does not suit the temperament of the leader. The modern conception of leadership must be broadened to understand the vital component of teaching that lies at the center of leadership. As Pulitzer Prize winning author James MacGregor Burns has noted, the element of teaching is what differentiates transformational leadership from transactional leadership.[35] Even more, Christians must deeply consider where they are getting their models for leadership. Why is pragmatism such a potent philosophy in contemporary Christian leadership models, when the life and teachings of Jesus seem to utterly contradict so much of what it posits as truth? Jesus is the greatest leader of all time, and teaching was at the core of His life. Paul, too, who helped shape Christianity and wrote so much of the New Testament, was a committed teacher. Why do 21st-century conceptions of leadership so completely ignore the aspect of teaching? Could it be that we have an impoverished understanding of its significance and importance? Christians, and all other leaders, for that matter, would be wise to learn from the life of Bonhoeffer that teaching is a high calling and vital component of leadership.

A second lesson from Bonhoeffer's teaching leadership is the way he encouraged a love of learning that exhorted them to continue their learning for the rest of their lives. One of the ways he did this was by keeping up with his students through individual and circular letters. These circular letters would go out to all former students of the seminary and would include updates from Bonhoeffer as well as encouragements for daily Bible readings and prayer concerns. These letters were lifelines to pastors out in the field who felt isolated and alone. Consider one such example:

> May God build a wall around us that we may remain together. In such times, let no one believe he or she can still stand alone. We, all of us, stand together through the prayer we pray for one another. Though things may yet become even more obscure and impenetrable, it will not be long before everything will be utterly clear. Let us, however, be all the more faithful in our daily ministry; let us be disciplined and set all our hope in grace. The deeper we descend now, the more quickly will we make it through. Let us adhere to our daily meditation on the word, to our intercessions, and to our examination of Scripture. Let us remain steadfast in our service to one another in which each strengthens the other. Let no one be ashamed should temptation succeed in bringing one down. Instead, let each help the other to find the right path again. That we might become free from ourselves, let us remind ourselves daily that it is not at all a matter of us personally. May God be with all of you, my dear brothers, you who now stand alone in a congregation. The rest of us are thinking of you first and foremost.[36]

Bonhoeffer's words provided encouragement, admonition, and a sense of connection to the community that had shaped them so strongly. This lesson reminds teachers, and educational leaders at all levels, that while curriculum development and lesson planning are important tasks, nothing will ever replace the importance of the teacher. As C.S. Lewis once quipped to a correspondent, "a school with good teachers is a good school even if it meets in a tin shed, and a school with bad teachers is a bad one even if it meets in a palace."[37]

The third and final lesson from Bonhoeffer's teaching leadership is that he modeled what it meant to be a pastor for his students. Both in the classroom and out of the classroom he sought to live a congruent life of discipleship to Jesus, and it was his life as well as his ideas that taught the students so much about what it meant to be pastors. In August of 1935, just as Finkenwalde was getting underway, several students penned a letter to leaders of the Confessing Church to report on what they were learning:

The course that has probably made the strongest impression on us is Discipleship in the New Testament. Dr. Bonhoeffer presents an exegesis of the call stories, of Jesus's statements concerning discipleship, and currently also of the Sermon on the Mount. Probably no one is unaffected by the seriousness with which these New Testament findings have drawn our attention to the phenomenon of discipleship. Discipleship is the unconditional, sole commitment to Jesus Christ and thus to the cross, a commitment whose content cannot wholly be articulated. The place to which the church is called is the cross, and the only form in which the church can exist is discipleship.[38]

While the students were gaining a deeper understanding of what Bonhoeffer was trying to teach them about discipleship in the traditional classroom setting, his daily example was making an equally strong impression. Bethge shares about Bonhoeffer's modeling of discipleship:

All this was clearly part of the practice of communal living and the personal training of future preachers; it occurred more through indirect suggestions than explicit words. In England Bonhoeffer had been struck by the pledge given by Baptist students before entering seminary, in which they affirmed their intention to become a preacher and undertook to conduct themselves accordingly. On their second day in Zingst, the students received their first lesson in this. A request arrived from the kitchen for help with the washing up, but there were no immediate volunteers. Without saying a word Bonhoeffer rose from the table, disappeared into the kitchen, and refused to let in the others who hurried to follow him. Afterward he rejoined the students on the beach but made no comment. And in Finkenwalde many a student was to discover with shame that someone else had made his bed in the big dormitory.[39]

Perhaps more than any of the other lessons Bonhoeffer provides for teaching leaders, this one about modeling provides the richest source of application for contemporary teachers. As the birth and expansion of the internet has come about, it has completely transformed the way information is accessed. Students now have access to information that past students could only dream of. However, at the same time, while access has increased, wisdom has not. Students have struggled to understand what information they need to be studying and why they should be studying it in the first place. Teachers play a vital role in not just dispensing information, but in curating knowledge, wisdom, and sources for students. If what is missing is not bricks, but mortar, teachers' own lives become that much more important as opportunities to truly teach the wisdom and discernment that is lacking. Personal, incarnational teaching, along the lines of Bonhoeffer's example, is not just a lofty example, but an imperative for teachers if they are to bridge the gap for contemporary students. Students need more than just great teaching; they need teachers who will embody the very ideals and wisdom they are seeking so desperately for.

Conclusion

In the modern educational atmosphere, there is a belief among many that teachers need to instruct less and guide more. This philosophy is a reaction to top-down teaching, where students are blank slates waiting to be filled with information. As a result, many modern educators seek to get out of the way of students so that the students can be free to explore and learn on their own. While surely well-intentioned, this philosophy is ultimately misleading. Students need to learn *how* to learn, *how* to think, and *how* to approach subjects. They need someone, to return to the image that Elizabeth Corey suggests, to apprentice themselves to. Bonhoeffer's enduring legacy as a teacher is that he gave students more than just the fruits of his intellect. He shared with them his very life.[40]

Endnotes

1 Elizabeth Corey, "Learning in Love," in April 2014 *First Things*, 43.

2 Palmer, Parker, *The Courage to Teach: Exploring the Inner Landscape of a Teacher's Life* (San Francisco, CA: Jossey-Bass, 2017), 4.

3 Victoria J. Barnett, "The Bonhoeffer Legacy as Work-in-Progress: Reflections on a Fragmentary Series," in *Interpreting Bonhoeffer: Historical Perspectives, Emerging Issues*, ed. Clifford J. Green and Guy C. Carter (Minneapolis, MN: Fortress Press, 2013), 95.

4 Marsh, *Strange Glory*, chapter 6.

5 Eberhard Bethge, *Dietrich Bonhoeffer: A Biography*, ed. Victoria J. Barnett, trans. Betty Ross, Frank Clarke, and William Glen-Doepel with Eric Mosbacher, Peter, Revised edition (Minneapolis, MN: Fortress Press, 2000), 173.

6 Paul House, *Seminary Vision* (Wheaton, Illinois: Crossway Books, 2015), 31.

7 Ferdinand Schlingensiepen, *Dietrich Bonhoeffer 1906–1945: Martyr, Thinker, Man of Resistance*, trans. Isabel Best (London, England; New York, NY: T&T Clark, 2012), 97-100.

8 Ibid., 99-100.

9 Dietrich Bonhoeffer, *Theological Education at Finkenwalde: 1935–1937*, ed. Victoria J. Barnett and Barbara Wojhoski, trans. Douglas W. Stott, vol. 14, *Dietrich Bonhoeffer Works* (Minneapolis, MN: Fortress Press, 2013), 253.

10 Dietrich Bonhoeffer, *Theological Education at Finkenwalde,* 254.

11 House, 53.

12 Dietrich Bonhoeffer, *Theological Education at Finkenwalde: 1935–1937*, 174.

13 Dietrich Bonhoeffer, *Letters and Papers From Prison*, ed. Christian Gremmels et al., trans. Isabel Best et al., vol. 8, *Dietrich Bonhoeffer Works* (Minneapolis, MN: Fortress Press, 2010), 81.

14 Dietrich Bonhoeffer, *Theological Education at Finkenwalde: 1935–1937*, 516.

15 Ibid., 517.

16 Dietrich Bonhoeffer, *Theological Education at Finkenwalde: 1935–1937*, 933. [10 Luke 2:19. 11 Cf. in Bethge's insertion further below; see p. 934, ed. note 16: characterization of meditation as "this personal process, this calm lingering with a single passage."]

17 Ibid., 932-933.

18 Robert Greenleaf, *Servant Leadership: A Journey into the Nature of Legitimate Power & Greatness* (New York, NY: Paulist Press, 1977), 29.

19 James M. Kouzes and Barry Z. Posner, *The Leadership Challenge: How to Make Extraordinary Things Happen in Organizations*, 3rd ed. (San Francisco, CA: Jossey-Bass, 2002), 51.

20 Dietrich Bonhoeffer, *Theological Education at Finkenwalde: 1935–1937*, 935.

21 Henry Blackaby and Richard Blackaby, *Spiritual Leadership: Moving People on to God's Agenda* (Nashville, TN: B&H Publishing Group, 2001), 251.

22 Dietrich Bonhoeffer, *Theological Education at Finkenwalde: 1935–1937*, 865.

23 Parker Palmer, *The Courage to Teach: Exploring the Inner Landscape of a Teacher's Life* (San Francisco, CA: Jossey-Bass, 1997), 11.

24 Dietrich Bonhoeffer, *Theological Education at Finkenwalde: 1935–1937*, 519.

25 Ibid., 111.

26 Eberhard Bethge, *Dietrich Bonhoeffer: A Biography*, ed. Victoria J. Barnett, trans. Betty Ross, Frank Clarke, and William Glen-Doepel with Eric Mosbacher, Peter, Revised edition. (Minneapolis, MN: Fortress Press, 2000), 464.

[27] Dietrich Bonhoeffer, *Theological Education at Finkenwalde: 1935–1937*, 254.

[28] Ibid., 865-866.

[29] Blackaby and Blackaby, 151.

[30] Dietrich Bonhoeffer, *Theological Education at Finkenwalde: 1935–1937*, 304.

[31] Ibid., 867.

[32] Ibid., 258.

[33] Ibid., 716.

[34] Ibid., 91.

[35] James MacGregor Burns, *Leadership,* (New York, NY: Harper & Row, 1978), 425.

[36] Dietrich Bonhoeffer, *Theological Education at Finkenwalde: 1935–1937*, 219.

[37] C. S. Lewis, *The Collected Letters of C. S. Lewis*, ed. Walter Hooper, vol. 3 (New York, NY: HarperCollins e-books; HarperSanFrancisco, 2004–2007), 1058.

[38] Dietrich Bonhoeffer, *Theological Education at Finkenwalde: 1935–1937*, 89.

[39] Eberhard Bethge, *Dietrich Bonhoeffer: A Biography*, ed. Victoria J. Barnett, trans. Betty Ross, Frank Clarke, and William Glen-Doepel with Eric Mosbacher, Peter, Revised edition. (Minneapolis, MN: Fortress Press, 2000), 429.

[40] 1 Thessalonians 2:8.

Chapter 11

BONHOEFFER'S LITERARY LEADERSHIP

Dr. Mary Nelson

"I've again been doing a good deal of writing lately, and for the work that I have set myself to do, the day is often too short, so that sometimes, comically enough, I even feel that I have 'no time' for this or that less important matter!" Dietrich Bonhoeffer, October 1943[1]

Introduction

Dietrich Bonhoeffer is largely considered one of the great theological writers of the 20th century, so his preoccupation with writing is hardly surprising. The context, however, of the above passage is indeed remarkable. Bonhoeffer penned this reflection after already enduring several months in Tegel Military Prison during the waning years of World War II. He ultimately spent eighteen months incarcerated in a cell, principally confined to a space no larger than seven feet by ten.[2] His imprisonment at the hands of the Nazis came, predictably, without due process or justification. When he wrote the above reflection, Bonhoeffer did not know if or when he would be released, if or when he would be reunited with his fiancé, family, or best friend, if or when he would ever preach or teach again; and yet his tone indicates he was not merely idling away the hours of incarceration. Instead, he seized time, the very treasure the Nazis attempted to steal from him and reclaimed it. His letters, even from his early days in confinement, reveal a pragmatic determination to advance his understanding of the human condition: "Of course, people outside find it difficult to imagine what prison life is like…The great thing is to stick to what one still has and can do—there is still plenty left—and not to be dominated by the thought of what one cannot do."[3] He went on to say, "No doubt these experiences are good and necessary, as they teach one to understand human life better."[4] In pursuit of this "better understanding," Bonhoeffer spent hours experimenting with new literary forms, teasing out complex theological questions, and perhaps most significantly, penning letters to family and friends that would not only sustain loved ones during the terrifying final days of World War II, but also buoy generations of readers. Bonhoeffer, a life-long student of the Scriptures' linguistic power to captivate him, capitalized on the leadership potential uniquely available through writing. Though imprisoned, he demonstrated language's limitless potential to subtly subvert the Third Reich's cruel determination to diminish Christian intellectual engagement, thwart communal fellowship, and destabilize familial bonds.

Intellectual Engagement Within a Nazi Prison

Incarceration in Tegel was certainly not conducive to reflective contemplation; instead, the grim nature of Bonhoeffer's surroundings was amplified by the frequency of air bombings and Nazi interrogations. He was not immune to the traumas of such horrors; his letters to his best friend and confidante, Eberhard Bethge, reveal that Bonhoeffer even considered suicide early in his imprisonment. He contemplated "suicide, not from a sense of guilt, but because I am basically already dead."[5] Yet Bonhoeffer fought through such despair and ultimately proved to be a source of great solace for his fellow prisoners. Bonhoeffer was a "towering rock of faith; he became a shining example to his fellow prisoners…consoling those who had lost all hope and giving them fresh courage."[6] By 1945, his steely resolve amidst the bombings was noted by a fellow prisoner: "He did not move a muscle."[7] Adolf Hitler would have certainly been surprised by the German pastor's military-like resolve. Hitler frequently derided Christianity: "It's been our misfortunate to have the wrong religion. Why did it have to be Christianity with its meekness and flabbiness?"[8] Yet Bonhoeffer demonstrated enough mental toughness not only to withstand the horrors and deprivations of prison life, but also to engage in riveting intellectual contemplation.

Bonhoeffer's intellectual discipline included his devotion to voluminous reading. Despite his accomplishments as a scholar and theologian, he humbly expressed to Bethge in a prison letter, "I always have all sort of things to learn."[9] He continually requested his parents to locate extremely dense texts and bring them to the prison; the list of texts include diverse, challenging works that would have challenged the brightest scholar in the best of contemplative environments. As Charles Marsh comments, "Not since university days had he had so much time to read—forced to remain in his cell for 14 hours a day."[10] His quest to understand the "human condition better," involved the study of a variety of his texts: he read "books in philosophy, science, art, political theory, history and literature."[11] Bonhoeffer's engagement with such diverse texts might have, in fact, prompted his own literary experimentation.

Through writing poetry, in particular, he reflected on the fears and anxieties he confronted in prison; Bethge commented that poetry represented his "efforts to overcome his isolation."[12] Though he self-deprecatingly dismissed his efforts saying, "I'm certainly no poet!," generations of readers have disagreed.[13] He composed "From All Good Powers" for what would be his final Christmas gift to his parents; the poem has become a favorite in Germany, included in many children's textbooks. Penned by Bonhoeffer in the last months of his life when he was cognizant of likely execution, the poem is a moving reflection that articulates both his angst and his acceptance:

> And should you offer us the cup of suffering,
> though heavy, brimming full and bitter brand,
> we'll thankfully accept it, never flinching,
> from your good heart and your beloved hand.[14]

Bonhoeffer's staunch determination to "never flinch" in the face of the unknown contrasts the gentle image of the Lord's "beloved hand," to which Bonhoeffer wholeheartedly entrusted his, and his family's fate.

Such literary experimentation demonstrates that rather than blunting his mental acuity, the time in incarceration seems to have prompted a period of unparalleled productivity for Bonhoeffer. Theological reflections written in prison have become some of Bonhoeffer's best known texts, perhaps proving Bonhoeffer's suggestion that "a period of enforced silence may be a good thing."[15] From Tegel, he continued work on his opus *Ethics* and wrote more than 200 pages of letters to Bethge including ideas "that electrified the postwar world."[16] Within these letters, he revealed an "outline of a book" that he was planning which would, among other things, demand "the church must come out of its stagnation."[17] As Bonhoeffer insisted in the book outline he wrote from Tegel, "The church is the church only when it exists for others."[18]

Bonhoeffer's frustration with the state of the Christian church stemmed in part from his dismay that so many Christian leaders had embraced— even venerated—Hitler's ascent to power. Friedrich Werner, a leader of the German Evangelical Church, echoed others when he said that through Hitler "God has given the German people a real miracle worker."[19] Yet despite such support, and Hitler's frequent invocation of Christianity for political purposes, the Nazi regime intended, ultimately, to destroy Christianity. Hitler privately declared, "I'll have my reckoning with the church. I'll have it reeling on the ropes." [20] Bonhoeffer perceived the threat that Hitler and his followers posed to the Christian church; he saw Hitler as essentially "the Antichrist who enjoys destruction."[21] Bonhoeffer also personally felt the sting of rejection from his fellow clergy, who, for the most part, dismissed him as a "political agitator" and refused to pray on his behalf during his imprisonment.[22] Despite this lack of support, Bonhoeffer engaged in thoughtful analysis of what the church must do to recover from its devastation at the hands of the Nazi party. Though Hitler himself was "on the ropes" by the time of Bonhoeffer's imprisonment in 1943, the damage he had done to the Christian church was devastating. From his cell, therefore, Bonhoeffer contemplated the importance of a "religionless" God.[23] As Bonhoeffer explained, "To be a Christian does not mean to be religious in a particular way."[24] Instead, Bonhoeffer challenged fellow Christians, even in the darkness of Nazi Germany, that "only by living completely in this world that one learns to have faith."[25] As Geffrey Kelly observes, "Many passages (from his theological letters) underline his conviction that the task of Christians is not to stand on the sidelines."[26] Despite the price he had paid for his opposition to Hitler, he insisted that his fellow Christians be actively engaged in the world on behalf of Christ.

Ironically, the provocative theological reflections that Bonhoeffer produced within Tegel prison are the very type of writing that would have been censored outside its walls. Nazis were notoriously obsessed with the destruction of what they described to be "harmful and undesirable" writings.[27] Before his imprisonment, Bonhoeffer's works had been banned by the Gestapo, and such censorship was not unique. Book burnings occurred regularly as early as 1933; authors were fleeing Nazi Germany because of suppression by 1939.[28] As Guenter Lewy notes, "Books on religious themes received special scrutiny, for religious belief was a competitor for the total allegiance demanded by the Nazi regime. In the struggle for the minds of the German people, the National Socialists did not want rivals."[29] But as Bonhoeffer wrote from Tegel, "God is no stop-gap; he must be recognized as the center of life; not when we are at the end of our resources; it is his will to be recognized in life, and not only when death comes."[30] As many of the letters with these theological insights were smuggled past censors,[31] Nazi leaders could not have imagined that some of the most powerful theological writings penned in the 20th century were produced as a result of Dietrich Bonhoeffer's incarceration.

Bolstering Christian Community

Bonhoeffer once described the Christian church as "Christ existing as community."[32] The notion of community was so essential to Bonhoeffer's belief system that the prospect of enforced isolation might have seemed a debilitating blow. Yet Bonhoeffer continued to cultivate, even within the walls of Tegel, a sense of fellowship among believers. As he remarked to his parents early in his captivity, "Well, Whitsuntide (Pentecost) is here, and we are still separated; but it is in a special way a feast of fellowship. When the bells rang this morning, I longed to go to church, but instead I…had a splendid service of my own, that I did not feel lonely at all, for you were all with me, every one of you, and so were the congregations in whose company I have kept Whitsuntide."[33] As time passed, rather than feeling the bonds of fellowship weakening, he demonstrated, through his own thoughtfully composed letters, his belief that "times of separation are not a total loss or unprofitable for our companionship, or at any rate they need not be so. In spite of all the difficulties they bring, they can be the means of strengthening fellowship quite remarkably."[34] The Nazis, with their vast network of cruel oppressions, could not combat spiritual fellowship that transcended space, time, and even the walls of Tegel prison.

Even before his incarceration, Bonhoeffer felt a special kinship with those groups oppressed by the Nazi regime. In particular, he felt "deep empathy for a specific group of compatriots, church ministers with a Jewish origin. Their exclusion was for him simply intolerable. Once kindled in this context, his active compassion then extended itself to wider circles."[35] He cherished relationships with two Jewish brothers-in-law and fostered relationships with people of diverse faiths through his ecumenical endeavors. Such efforts strengthened Bonhoeffer's "solidarity with those oppressed under Nazi rule."[36] Bonhoeffer insisted that "the church should assist the victims of injustice 'even if they do not belong to the Christian community.'"[37] In keeping with that conviction, before his incarceration he actively engaged in assisting a group of German Jews in escaping from Berlin; his arrest came about, in part, because he participated in this action. His letters further testify to the fact that rather than feeling estranged from fellow sufferers, he felt increasingly connected to the oppressed from prison: "It's remarkable how we think at such times about…how closely our own lives are bound up with other people's, and in fact how the center of our own lives is outside ourselves, and how little we are separate entities."[38]

Instead of diminishing bonds of fellowship and community, Bonhoeffer's letters testify to the flourishing of such bonds in the extreme situation that he and others encountered. Bonhoeffer insisted his isolation amidst the war made him all the more invested in others' lives instead of being fixated on his survival in such a vulnerable state: "The 'as though it were a part of me' is perfectly true, as I have often felt after hearing that one of my colleagues or pupils had been killed."[39] Bonhoeffer's reflection echoes John Donne's legendary refrain that "no man is an island." Bonhoeffer's existence in jail—though seemingly removed from his family, friends, colleagues, pupils—did not mitigate his connection to these loved ones. In fact, he felt a metaphysical bond with those he held dear. His letters testify, "I feel myself so much a part of you all that I know that we live and bear everything in common, acting and thinking for one another, even though we have to be separated."[40]

Even during the Christmas season, an especially challenging time to endure forced separation from the Christian community, Bonhoeffer insisted that Tegel afforded new opportunities for fellowship: "From the Christian point of view there is no special problem about Christmas in a prison cell…there are things a prisoner can understand better than other people; for him they really are glad tidings, and that faith gives him a part in the communion of saints, a Christian fellowship breaking the bounds of time."[41] Bonhoeffer seized the opportunity to bond with prison guards through his Christmas "celebration." Other prisoners observed how Bonhoeffer had "won over his wardens…who were not always kindly disposed."[42] Bonhoeffer also capitalized on this opportunity to minister to those within the walls of Tegel, and he used the Psalms as a resource in composing special Christmas prayers for his fellow prisoners.[43]

The Psalms were, in fact, Bonhoeffer's "great comfort" both before and during his imprisonment.[44] Early in his confinement, he wrote, "I am reading the Bible straight through from cover and cover, and have just got as far as Job, which I am particularly fond. I read the Psalms every day, as I have done for years. I know them and love them more than any other book."[45] Bonhoeffer's letters revealed his discipline of daily engagement with the sacred Scriptures, which was a means of "grounding and continuity."[46] Bonhoeffer commented on how the Old Testament books, in particular, took on an even great significance for him than before. As Marsh comments, "His faith had grown more at home in the Old Testament as he reached the extraordinary conclusion that whoever wishes to be and perceive things too quickly and too directly in New Testament ways is to my mind no Christian.'"[47]

His passion for the Old Testament signified again his affinity and bond with the persecuted Jewish community. As early as 1938, the Third Reich routinely publicly burned the Hebrew Bible. As Alon Confino notes, "For Germans…the Bible represented the Jewish and Christian traditions."[48] In particularly cruel episodes, "Jews were forced to burn their own Bibles."[49] This disavowal of the Old Testament unfortunately even found approbation among some Christian scholars who advocated the removal of the Old Testament from the Christian Bible because it was a Jewish book.[50] Yet Bonhoeffer embraced the Old Testament and was "enthralled by … the sacred texts cherished by Jew and Christians believers."[51] Bonhoeffer's written reflections of the Old Testament in prison were subversive; for while the Nazis sought a new German Christianity that "owed nothing to the Jews,"[52] this devoted Lutheran pastor insisted that "I am thinking and perceiving things in line with the Old Testament."[53]

Memorializing the Christian Family

Some of the most poignant passages of Bonhoeffer's letters from prison are a lasting tribute to the enduring bonds that persevered even during the horrifying days of his imprisonment. He was not the only family member incarcerated during these dark days—the Nazis also imprisoned his brother and brother-in-law. The tight-knit Bonhoeffer family reeled as a result of these incarcerations, and yet, as Bonhoeffer commented from his prison cell, their familial bonds actually flourished: "What a blessing it is, in such distressing times, to belong to a large, closely-knit family, where each trusts the other and stands by him...in just such times of separation the feeling of belonging together through thick and thin actually grows stronger."[54] As Eric Metaxas observes, this remarkable family "turned even the prison visits into small celebrations."[55] Despite the Nazis' most pernicious efforts to devastate families who opposed them, Bonhoeffer's writing memorializes a family who lovingly cherished one another in the wake of brutal oppression.

The Nazis' practice of dismantling the family unit, even the German family unit, has been well documented, and yet, the Bonhoeffers in many ways represented the ideal German family that the Nazi regime venerated.[56] Physically active, intellectually brilliant, professionally successful—the Bonhoeffers had every reason to take pride in their children's diverse accomplishments. Yet their beliefs left them in staunch opposition to Nazi doctrine, and their family suffered greatly for their resistance. Still, Dietrich was able to nurture the loving bonds among family members—even from a secluded distance—through his gifts as a writer. He penned moving tributes on the marriage of his niece, Renate, to his dearest friend, Bethge, and also wrote a beautiful sermon on the occasion of the birth of their son, his godson, Dietrich Bethge. As he remarked so joyously following the birth of his godson, "You've pushed our family on by one generation—[his birth] has created great-grandparents, grandparents, great-uncles and great-aunts and young uncles and aunts! That's a fine achievement of yours; you've promoted me to the third generation!"[57]

Such a celebration of this flourishing Christian family would have drawn the ire of the Nazi regime. As part of Hitler's diabolical plans for his own Germany people, Hitler cruelly taunted "older generations" as seen in his remark from a 1933 speech: "Your child belongs to us already... What are you? You will pass on. Your descendants, however, now stand in the new camp. In a short time they will know nothing else but this new community."[58] Bonhoeffer's loving baptismal message celebrated not only the birth of a new "Dietrich," but hope for the future of the restored German family unit: "In the coming years of upheaval, it will be the greatest of gifts to know that you are safe in a good home. It will be a bulwark against all dangers from without and within. The time when children arrogantly broke away from their parents will be past. The home will draw children back to their parent's care; it will be their refuge."[59] Bonhoeffer's allusion to "arrogant children" may refer to the society that Hitler had so methodically cultivated. Nazi programs such as "Hitler Youth" actively sought to diminish the loyalty of children to their parents. Such groups exacerbated generational conflicts within the family and proved to be "a disruptive influence upon family life, as an atmosphere of suspicion and mistrust was introduced into the house."[60] Bonhoeffer's writing anticipates the days when such division within the home will be eradicated, and at the same time, celebrates the loving traditions of his own, beloved family.

Bonhoeffer's letters serve, among other functions, as a paean to the beauty and strength of parental devotion. In a particularly moving letter to his father, Bonhoeffer remarked, "You and mother have remained the unchanged centre of family. There can be no doubt of that and I'm particularly grateful."[61] His love for his parents is revealed repeatedly as a sustaining force. When he first arrived in Tegel prison he noted, "The mere fact that you have been near me, the tangible evidence that you are still thinking and caring about me (which of course I really know anyway!) is enough to keep me happy for the rest of the day."[62] His parents' love and devotion, coupled with the adoration of his other family members, serve as a sharp refutation of Hitler's empty determination for the older generations to "pass on." Instead, Bonhoeffer appreciated his family even more in captivity, and reminds his readers of the fragility of time with loved ones: "This time of separation first makes it clear that often we take too little trouble to get together in normal times. Precisely because we do not feel it necessary to 'cultivate' the obvious family relationships, many things are often neglected, and that is a pity."[63]

Perhaps it comes as no surprise that Bonhoeffer's devotion to all aspects of familial life manifested itself in a desire for children of his own: "There comes over me a longing to have a child and not to vanish without a trace—an Old Testament rather than a New Testament wish I suppose."[64] But of course, as with writers before him, literary productions serve as legacies that have assured he has not "vanished." In some of his last writings, he described his poetry as "these new children of mine."[65] And in addition to these cherished texts, he was delighted to learn in prison that his godson would also be his namesake: "I'm very pleased that you've called your boy Dietrich. Not many people in my position will have a similar experience. In the midst of all our hardships we keep experiencing an overwhelming kindness and friendship."[66] Just as his parents urged Dietrich to see goodness in a world filled with the cruelties of Nazism, Bonhoeffer dared to dream of a better world for little Dietrich. Writing to Bethge, he declared, "If one day your son sees more of righteousness and the power of God on earth than we do, one will be able to call him happy."[67]

Conclusion

Bonhoeffer's final letters in many ways serve as a microcosm of the bulk of his letters in that he continued to lead his family, in this case preparing them for his impending death. After the failed plot to kill Hitler, in which he was at least tangentially involved, the inevitability of his death becomes clear in his letters. His stirring goodbye to Bethge was remarkable for its lack of bitterness. He insisted he felt "gratitude and cheerfulness along the road where I'm being led… I am so sure of God's guiding hand that I hope I shall always be kept in that certainty."[68] To his mother, he expressed, "I am constantly thinking of you and father every day, and I thank God for all that you are to me and the whole family. I know you've always lived for us and haven't lived a life of your own."[69] Finally, in his last recorded comment (after telling his family to dispense with his belongings), he pleaded, "Please leave some writing paper with the Commissar!"[70] How fitting that the last request from Bonhoeffer was a cry for more writing material—the life-sustaining force of writing had enabled him not only to survive captivity, but also to thrive—spiritually, mentally, and emotionally.

Bonhoeffer's vibrant prison writings provide for the modern reader a stark contrast with the reflections penned by another German prisoner twenty years earlier. In 1925, Adolf Hitler wrote his infamous autobiography, *Mein Kampf,* as he served prison time following his failed Beer Hall Putsch. The work is brimming with such vitriol and hate speech that it continues to incite anti-Semitism nine decades after its composition. In addition to the cruelty of his warped content, Hitler shows an utter misapprehension of the power of the written word: "I know that fewer people are won over by the written word than by the spoken word and that every great movement on this earth owes its growth to great speakers and not to great writers."[71] Hitler grossly underestimated the significant power of writing—his text, for instance, is tragically still a source of venom and cruelty. Conversely, Bonhoeffer, all these years later, leads through his writing by stimulating the intellect, challenging the unjust, and comforting the bereft. Hitler and his Nazis, long defeated, were unable to silence Bonhoeffer, still vibrantly relevant--proving that intellectual engagement and spiritual reflection might subvert the very forces daring to thwart them.

Endnotes

[1] Dietrich Bonhoeffer, *Letters and Papers From Prison*, ed. Eberhard Bethge (New York, NY: Touchstone, 1997), 119.

[2] Eberhard Bethge, *Dietrich Bonhoeffer: A Biography*, ed. Victoria J. Barnett, trans. Betty and Peter Ross, Frank Clarke, William Glen-Doepel, and Eric Mosbacher, Rev. ed. (Minneapolis, MN: Fortress Press, 2000), 828.

[3] Bonhoeffer, *Letters and Papers,* ed. Eberhard Bethge, 38-39.

[4] Ibid., 39.

[5] Ibid., 35.

[6] Geffrey Kelly, "Prayer and Action for Justice: Bonhoeffer's Spirituality," in *The Cambridge Companion to Dietrich Bonhoeffer,* ed. John W. de Gruchy (Cambridge, MA: Cambridge University Press, 1999), 258.

[7] Eric Metaxas, *Bonhoeffer: Pastor, Martyr, Prophet, Spy* (Nashville, TN: Thomas Nelson, 2010), 500.

[8] Ibid., 165.

[9] Charles Marsh, *Strange Glory: A Life of Dietrich Bonhoeffer* (New York, NY: Alfred Knopf, 2014), 251.

[10] Ibid., 355.

[11] Ibid.

[12] Bethge, *Dietrich Bonhoeffer: A Biography,* 841.

[13] Bonhoeffer, *Letters and Papers*, ed. Eberhard Bethge, 372.

[14] Marsh, *Strange Glory*, 386.

[15] Bonhoeffer, *Letters and Papers*, ed. Eberhard Bethge, 40.

[16] Dietrich Bonhoeffer, *Letters and Papers From Prison*, ed. Victoria J. Barnett, trans. Isabel Best et al., Reader's ed. vol. 8, *Dietrich Bonhoeffer Works* (Minneapolis, MN: Fortress Press, 2015), back cover.

[17] Bonhoeffer, *Letters and Papers*, ed. Eberhard Bethge, 378.

[18] Ibid., 382.

[19] Dietrich Bonhoeffer and F. Burton Nelson, *A Testament to Freedom: The Essential Writings of Dietrich Bonhoeffer*, ed. Geffrey Kelly and F. Burton Nelson (New York, NY: Harpers Collins, 1995), 34.

[20] Metaxas, *Bonhoeffer: Pastor, Martyr, Prophet, Spy*, 167.

[21] Gerhard Leibholz, "Memoir," in *The Cost of Discipleship* (New York, NY: Touchstone, 1995), 29.

[22] Kelly, "Prayer and Action for Justice," 252.

[23] Bonhoeffer, *Letters and Papers*, ed. Eberhard Bethge, 279.

[24] Ibid., 361.

[25] Ibid., 369.

[26] Kelly, "Prayer and Action for Justice," 253.

[27] Guenter Lewy, *Harmful and Undesirable: Book Censorship in Nazi Germany* (New York, NY: Oxford University Press, 2016).

[28] Ibid., xi.

[29] Lewy, *Harmful and Undesirable*, 91.

[30] Bonhoeffer, *Letters and Papers*, ed. Eberhard Bethge, 311.

[31] Remarkably, Bonhoeffer cultivated relationships with some prison guards who smuggled letters past censors between Bethge and Bonhoeffer. This explains the remarkable candidness of many of Bonhoeffer's missives.

[32] Kelly and Nelson, *A Testament to Freedom*, 150.

[33] Bonhoeffer, *Letters and Papers*, ed. Eberhard Bethge, 53.

[34] Ibid., 177.

[35] Raymond Mengus, "Dietrich Bonhoeffer and the Decision to Resist," *The Journal of Modern History* 64 (December 1992): 141.

[36] Kelly and Nelson, *A Testament to Freedom*, 35.

[37] Marsh, *Strange Glory*, 165.

[38] Bonhoeffer, *Letters and Papers*, ed. Eberhard Bethge, 105.

[39] Ibid., 105.

[40] Ibid., 40.

[41] Ibid., 166.

[42] Metaxas, *Bonhoeffer: Pastor, Martyr, Prophet, Spy*, 499.

[43] Geffrey Kelly and F. Burton Nelson, *The Cost of Moral Leadership: The Spirituality of Dietrich Bonhoeffer* (Grand Rapids, MI: Eerdmans, 2003) 233.

[44] Ibid.

[45] Bonhoeffer, *Letters and Papers*, ed. Eberhard Bethge, 40.

[46] Metaxas, *Bonhoeffer: Pastor, Martyr, Prophet, Spy*, 438.

[47] Marsh, *Strange Glory*, 369.

[48] Alon Confino, "Why Did the Nazis Burn the Hebrew Bible? Nazi Germany, Representations of the Past, and the Holocaust," *The Journal of Modern History* 84, no. 2 (June 2012): 376.

[49] Ibid., 389.

[50] Ibid., 384.

[51] Marsh, *Strange Glory*, 369.

[52] Ibid., 395.

[53] Ibid., 368.

[54] Bonhoeffer, *Letters and Papers*, ed. Eberhard Bethge, 70.

[55] Metaxas, *Bonhoeffer: Pastor, Martyr, Prophet, Spy*, 473.

[56] Lisa Pine, *Nazi Family Policy, 1933-1945* (Oxford: Berg Publishers, 1997).

[57] Bonhoeffer, *Letters and Papers*, ed. Eberhard Bethge, 209.

[58] William L. Shirer, *The Rise and Fall of the Third Reich: A History of Nazi Germany* (New York, NY: Simon and Schuster, 1960), 249.

[59] Bonhoeffer, *Letters and Papers*, ed. Eberhard Bethge, 385.

[60] Pine, *Nazi Family Policy*, 57.

[61] Bonhoeffer, *Letters and Papers*, ed. Eberhard Bethge, 235.

[62] Ibid., 26.

[63] Ibid., 77.

[64] Ibid., 163. Michael Williams comments, "His engagement to Maria shortly before his imprisonment seems to suggest that he was already considering this form of eternity without knowing for certain that he would be imprisoned" (note to author).

[65] Ibid., 333.

[66] Ibid., 210.

[67] Bonhoeffer, *Letters and Papers*, ed. Eberhard Bethge, 210.

[68] Ibid., 511.

[69] Ibid., 510.

[70] Ibid., 521.

[71] Adolf Hitler, *Mein Kampf* (1924; repr., New York, NY; Houghton Mifflin, 1977).

Chapter 12

THE LEADERSHIP PATH TO FLOSSENBÜRG

Dr. Jay Harley

Tourists can visit 43 Marienburger Allee in the Charlottenburg area of Berlin and see where the Bonhoeffer family lived. As visitors exit the closest train stop and walk the nearly one-mile down quiet streets, they will see beautiful late 19th and early 20th century homes. As they arrive at the Bonhoeffer House, they will recognize that it was in this quiet, upper-class neighborhood where the Bonhoeffer family lived and Dietrich studied, wrote, and was arrested by the Nazis. His study and writing room was restored and is likely where he wrote much of his work, *Ethics*. A visitor can look out of the window onto the street below where the black Mercedes driven by Gestapo officers arrived on the evening of April 5, 1943, to arrest Dietrich Bonhoeffer, a man they considered to be guilty of the crimes of pacifism and being an enemy of the state. It was one of the leaders of the official German church, Bishop Theodor Heckel, who charged him with these horrible crimes in blatant contempt of the Third Reich.[1] Did Dietrich, the enemy, resist? Not this evening. All accounts indicate that he went peacefully and somberly into the custody of the agents of the Third Reich. Almost exactly two years after his arrest, he would be killed by his captors at the Flossenbürg Concentration Camp.

In the annals of World War II history, the individuals who became known as heroes were ones who carried rifles, stormed the beaches of Normandy, fought in the Battle of the Bulge, rescued persecuted Jews from the grips of the Gestapo, or courageously survived life in a concentration camp.

These men and women certainly deserved the commendation bestowed upon them; however, Bonhoeffer was a different type of hero during this tumultuous time in world history. He never fired a shot in the war and never seemed to intend to do so. As Kirkpatrick noted in a work designed to draw attention to Bonhoeffer's possible influence upon other 20th century theologians: "Bonhoeffer was an academic who thrived in discussing theology with his peers and the wider academic community."[2] While not the typical view of a World War II-era leader, Bonhoeffer influenced in different ways. It must not be forgotten that while on the night of April 5, 1943, he went peaceably, he did resist. He may not have directly resisted with a gun or warfare, but he resisted with spirituality, written words, ideas, thought, and discipleship. He was asked to pledge allegiance to the Führer, Adolf Hitler, but refused, continued writing, and continued speaking. Bonhoeffer, himself, expressed his feelings about how one should act:

> Who stands firm? Only the one whose ultimate standard is not his reason, his principles, conscience, freedom, or virtue; only the one who is prepared to sacrifice all of these when, in faith and in relationship to God alone, he is called to obedient and responsible action. Such a person is the responsible one whose life is to be nothing but a response to God's question and call.[3]

He was aware of the hazards of resisting the Nazi regime. In 1932, thirteen years before his death, Bonhoeffer said in a sermon in a Berlin church, "We must not be surprised if once again times return for our church when the blood of martyrs will be required."[4] His willingness to resist the ideals and values of the Nazi regime led him to a martyr's death. Wilkes emphasized this component of leadership: "Trusting that God controls your eternity gives you the confidence to risk everything earthly to achieve anything eternal."[5] During these circumstances, Bonhoeffer's faith in Christ enabled him to courageously speak and write in opposition to the powerful Nazi regime.

The stories of courageous individuals, and even martyrs, throughout Christian history, are often well-documented and well-known. Bonhoeffer joined this courageous line of Christian witnesses who risked personal safety and comfort. Like other Christian leaders that faced persecution and death, Bonhoeffer bravely faced death for his faith, and through execution, became part of this exceptional lineage of faith and courage. Bonhoeffer would likely caution those who would desire to canonize him to Christian lore and would not consider himself to be extraordinary. This attitude was not unfamiliar among persecuted Christian leaders. It was the well-known Jim Elliott who was quoted by his wife before his martyrdom in South America as saying in great humility without significant self-sumptuousness: "When it comes time to die, make sure that all you have to do is die."[6] Tucker echoed this general sentiment, commenting on Christian missionaries who faced persecution to extend the message of Jesus to other parts of the world: "Who were these missionaries who sacrificed so much to carry the gospel to the ends of the earth? Were they spiritual giants who gloriously overcame the obstacles they confronted? No. They were ordinary individuals, plagued by human frailties and failures. Super Saints they were not."[7] Therefore, Bonhoeffer's story of courageous leadership should not intimidate those exploring his story even more than seventy years later but should encourage Christian courageous leadership.

It must not be forgotten that while on the night of April 5, 1943, he went peaceably, he did resist. He may not have directly resisted with a gun or warfare, but he resisted with spirituality, written words, ideas, and discipleship. He was asked to pledge allegiance to the Führer, Adolf Hitler but refused, continued writing, and continued speaking. Ministers were explicitly warned by the Nazis that they should not speak against the regime, which included a prohibition of evangelistic activities and religious teaching that would have agitated the people against Hitler and the Third Reich. Kelly and Nelson expressed Bonhoeffer's attitude about this ban by asserting, "Despite the risks of defying Nazism's threats against dissenters, including clergy who dared criticize official government policies, Bonhoeffer never backed down from his demand that Christians and their churches step up their visibility in witnessing to Jesus Christ."[8] Bonhoeffer thought and acted in the same disposition as the earliest believers in Jesus, as they also resisted the elevation of an earthly leader to a divine status. The New Testament Book of Acts reported an account of the persecution of the early Christians targeted for their view of Caesar. Acts 17:5-9 recorded this account:

> But the Jews were jealous, and taking some wicked men of the rabble, they formed a mob, set the city in an uproar, and attacked the house of Jason, seeking to bring them out to

the crowd. And when they could not find them, they dragged Jason and some of the brothers before the city authorities, shouting, "These men who have turned the world upside down have come here also, and Jason has received them, and they are all acting against the decrees of Caesar, saying that there is another king, Jesus." And the people and the city authorities were disturbed when they heard these things. And when they had taken money as security from Jason and the rest, they let them go (ESV).

The account from Acts provided the viewpoint of the jealous Jews regarding the ministry success of Paul and Silas. Their accusation against Paul and Silas stated that "they are all acting against the decrees of Caesar, saying that there is another king, Jesus."[9] However, the Jews grasped only part of the viewpoint of Paul, Silas, and the other initial Christian evangelists. They did not just think there was an additional king along with the Roman Emperor, but they recognized that the Roman Emperor was not king at all. Instead, Jesus was the true and divine king. In later writings, Paul even affirmed when he wrote to the Philippian church that their citizenship was not in Rome, but in the Kingdom of God. He stated this in Philippians 3:20 (ESV): "But our citizenship is in heaven." Therefore, comparable to these early believers, Bonhoeffer courageously called the German church to singular kingly attention, Jesus Christ. In a 1933 letter, Bonhoeffer expressed that he felt they, as Germans, must choose Germanism or Christianity.[10] Being German became the influencing factor of Christian faith, rather than vice versa, where true faith in Christ impacts the way Germans live in relationship to their country and government. It was common practice by Nazi leaders to create the type of Christianity that supported positive living and support of the Nazi regime.[11] Unfortunately, stories of Christians living in the Third Reich who resisted courageously were too few. Many German Christians went along with the Nazi ideals out of fear in order to protect themselves, or because they shared the Nazi belief system.

Bonhoeffer's valor and firm voice in opposition to the Nazis led to his death. He was executed at the Flossenbürg Concentration camp on April 9, 1945. As is well accounted, the Flossenbürg camp would be liberated by the allies just two weeks later. Although he was only at Flossenbürg for less than twenty-four hours, this concentration camp is connected to him because of his death there. In his substantial biography on Bonhoeffer, Marsh commented, "Bonhoeffer had always lived with premonitions of an early death."[12] An exemplary academic and evident pacifist, Bonhoeffer may not be easily associated with the ideas of courage or bravery. However, there is no doubt that he was true to his beliefs and maintained clear Christian convictions amid great difficulty, imprisonment, and even death.

The German Christian Movement

Mary Solberg, a principal expert on the German Church during the Third Reich, defined German Christians as individuals who were "not German people who were Christians, but rather to members of the German Christian faith movement."[13] She continued this description by explaining that multiple groups did exist with the same objective of bringing Nazi ideology to the forefront of the expression of the German Church. Solberg shared her thoughts Discussing Christian Ethics, while Hays questioned the stance of the German Christian: "How is it possible that masses of Christians in Germany acquiesced in the terrible slaughter of Jewish people? Is there some sense in which Christian theology or even the New Testament itself underwrote the destructive anti-Jewish agenda of Nazism?"[14] The German Christian movement twisted the message of the New Testament and focus of the church: "We recognize in race, ethnic culture, and nation orders of life given and entrusted to us by God, who has commanded us to preserve them. For this reason, race-mixing must be opposed."[15] This type of racism became the official position of the German Christians who were aligned with and controlled by the government. For those with more sensibilities and less comfort with the beliefs and policies on race and those believed to be inferior, the stance of the German Christian movement was disguised and expressed less bluntly by stating: "We are conscious of Christian duty toward and love for the helpless, but we also demand that the people be protected from those who are inept and inferior."[16] In hindsight, the incompatibility of these statements with biblical Christianity is obvious, but amid the enthusiasm of much of German culture and society of the Nazis and their promises, most church members appeared to at least passively go along with this type of doctrine and policy within the church.

Costly Leadership

Bonhoeffer would not fit the stereotypes of the modern leader. He had little legitimate authority, especially as Nazi control over German life increased. Leadership theorist Heifetz believed that lack of authority provided the opportunity for significant influence. He explained his reasons for this leadership possibility: "Yet the constraints of authority suggest that there may also be advantages to leading without it. First, the absence of authoritative decision-making. Instead of providing answers that soothe, one can more readily raise questions that disturb."[17] Bonhoeffer influenced greatly without authority, but in different and unique ways. To understand Bonhoeffer's leadership effectiveness, he must be disconnected from the stereotypical leader mindset. He did not have the leadership position and authority of contemporaries like Churchill or Roosevelt, nor did he need to make decisions that would impact an entire nation. Instead, he led in classrooms, on pulpits, and with paper. He did not influence policy or military decisions, but his decisions about his convictions still resonate more than seventy years later.

Even without official titles and leading in ways that would not be often discussed, Bonhoeffer exerted influence over his country, and his influence has continued to grow after his death. He certainly recognized the costliness of his leadership as he attempted to influence against the norms of his own culture. Bonhoeffer attempted to impact a nation understanding that he was in direct opposition to the government and the prevailing societal thought. Leadership theorists recognized the difficulty of effective leadership when it went against the majority view. Northouse discussed the social identity theory of leadership:

> From this perspective, leadership emergence is the degree to which a person fits with the identity of the group as a whole. As groups develop over time, a group prototype also develops. Individuals emerge as leaders in the group when they become most like the group prototype. Being like the prototype makes leaders attractive to the group and gives them influence with the group.[18]

Barton also challenged the idea that leadership is always linked to societal norms and approval when she said, "Leadership involves a very peculiar kind of loneliness. It has to do with seeing something that others do not see, do not see clearly, or perhaps have lost sight of. It involves staying faithful to God and to the tasks and decisions that are consistent with the journey God is leading us on even in the face of criticism, disbelief and failure."[19] Therefore, Bonhoeffer influences in opposition to the predominant views of society and government, and his words and actions eventually cost him his freedom and his life.

For Bonhoeffer, costly leadership and risky action were deliberate and intentional choices. In this way, he was no different from many of the others who opposed Nazi policies and exploits. He understood the risks yet chose to speak and act boldly for his beliefs and principles. Bonhoeffer was an early opponent of Nazi ideals, and in many ways served as a prophetic voice within German society regarding Hitler. Bonhoeffer's deliberate costly leadership began in his younger years, evidenced in his sermons preached in the early years of the 1930s. He remained a stalwart opponent of Nazi ideology throughout his life. His firm commitment endured as a primary thought leader for the internal resistance against the Third Reich. Bonhoeffer persisted through his arrest, imprisonment, and execution by the Nazi regime. Courageous leadership is a hallmark of effective leaders who are required by circumstances to take risks and lead courageously. In his inspiring book entitled *Spiritual Leadership,* Sanders pronounced, "Leaders require courage of the highest order—always moral courage and often physical courage as well. Courage is that quality of mind that enables people to encounter danger or difficulty firmly, without fear of discouragement."[20]

Early Sermons

Dietrich Bonhoeffer was certainly an excellent academic scholar and writer. The strength of his faith and thoughts are demonstrated in his preaching. While other church leaders showed reticence in speaking or writing against Hitler, Bonhoeffer was willing and prepared to write and speak truth boldly and clearly. Bonhoeffer understood the risks of defying the Nazis, and most of the German church did not follow Bonhoeffer's example, but rather, acquiesced to Nazi ideology. Heifetz lauded risk-taking among leaders: "We take risks for good reason: We hope to make a difference in people's lives."[21] The nationalism and hope for security and stability won the day, and the German church either tolerated or actively supported the intrusion of Nazi belief into the Christian church. It is well documented that most Protestant church pastors and leaders did not speak against the Nazis. The silence of Christian leaders was evident at the instituting of the anti-Jewish laws of April 1933. During this time, many Church leaders advocated for the conjoining of the German Church and the Nazi government. However, Bonhoeffer was an exception, as he was immediately concerned about the anti-Jewish laws and their relation to the church. He penned a treatise entitled, "The Church and the Jewish Question," and in it, he outlined the proper response of the church to these laws. A summary of the contents of the essay demonstrates his clear opposition:

> First, there are legitimate reasons to challenge the state if it is not acting properly in its role as state…Second, the church has an unconditional obligation to aid victims of the state. And third, if the church observes that the state is careening in a fundamentally destructive direction, it may seize the wheel of the state itself. That is, it may engage in specific and direct political action. Bonhoeffer went on to say that if the state were to exclude baptized Jews from Christian congregations, then this would be extremely serious. In fact, the church would find itself in *statu confessionis,* that is, in a formal state of confessional protest, because the truth and freedom of the gospel are at stake.[22]

Students of Bonhoeffer owe a debt of gratitude to the late Isabel Best for her translation into English of some of Bonhoeffer's most memorable sermons. She crafted outstanding introductions to each of these sermons, and to understand Bonhoeffer's preaching in the early years of the Nazi regime requires great reliance upon her work with these sermons.

On February 26, 1933, Bonhoeffer preached in Berlin on the first Sunday of Lent. Best provided introductory comments to her English translation of this sermon: "In this sermon, the first that he preached after Hitler's takeover of power, Bonhoeffer was concerned to put things in place, to proclaim at this moment when even German cathedrals were hung with swastika flags that for Christians there is only one Lord."[23] In that sermon, Judges 6 was the text, and Bonhoeffer proclaimed:

> In the church we have only one altar –the altar of the Most High, the One and Only, the Almighty, the Lord, to whom alone be honor and praise, the Creator before whom all creation bows down, before whom even the most powerful are but dust. We don't have any side altars at which to worship human beings. The worship of God and not of humankind is what takes place at the altar of our church. Anyone who wants to do otherwise should stay away and cannot come with us into God's house. Anyone who wants to build an altar to himself or to any other human is mocking God, and God will not allow such mockery. To be in the church means to have the courage to be alone with God as Lord, to worship God and not any human person. And it does take courage. The thing that most hinder us from letting God be Lord, that is, from believing in God, is our cowardice.[24]

While readers do not know for certain, some of these early sermons seem to issue a clear warning to his hearers about the dangers of the newly minted Nazi regime. The previous sermon was delivered in Berlin with Nazi authoritarian power evident, and Bonhoeffer advocated for the prominent place of Jesus over Hitler, National Socialism, and the nation. Why does Bonhoeffer feel as though Christians would elevate someone to a status of worship in place of Christ? Cowardice. According to Bonhoeffer, Christians needed the courage to oppose Nazi ideology by worshiping Christ alone. He upheld this theme throughout much of his preaching and writing.

Still early in Hitler's time in power, Bonhoeffer preached another sermon in which he delivered in July 1933: "Bonhoeffer preached his last sermon in Berlin on a day of great tension in the Protestant church. On short notice and in defiance of German law, Hitler had called national church elections for that very day, to allow the German Christians to put in place church leaders more to his liking."[25] Hitler's influence had infiltrated the church, and Hitler's allies would win this election of church leaders. Best commented on Bonhoeffer's approach, "As always, Bonhoeffer refrained from making direct political statements in his sermon. Instead, he sought to let his hearers feel the very ground, the rock on which the church of Christ is built."[26] The text for his message was from Matthew 16, and the theme of the sermon centered on the foundation of the church. Bonhoeffer expounded on this theme:

> No human being builds the church, but Christ alone. Anyone who proposes to build the church is certainly already on the way to destroying it, because it will turn out to be a temple of idolatry, though the builder does not intend that or know it. We are to confess, while God builds. We are to preach, while God builds. We are to pray to God, while God builds.[27]

He preaches with clarity that the foundation and builder of the church is Christ. No person, regardless of the outcome of church elections, can become the focus of the true church. Bonhoeffer also understood the enduring victory of the true church:

> Don't look for anyone's opinion; don't ask them what they think. Don't keep calculating; don't look around for support from others. Not only must church remain church, but you my church, confess, confess, confess...Christ alone is your Lord; by his grace alone you live; just as you are, Christ is building.
>
> And the gates of hell shall not prevail against you. Death is the great inheritor of everything that exists. This is as far as death goes. Right by the abyss of the valley of death is the foundation of the church, the church that confesses Christ as its life. The church has eternal life precisely there where death is reaching out for it, and death is reaching out for it precisely because it has eternal life. The church that confesses is the eternal church, for Christ is its protector. Its eternity is not visible to this world. It is not subject to challenge by the world, though the waves wash up over it and sometimes it looks completely covered over and lost. But victory belongs to the church, because Christ its Lord is with it and has overcome the world of death. Don't ask whether you can see victory but believe in the victory, for it is yours.[28]

Seen through his sermons from the earliest days of Nazi power, Bonhoeffer challenged Christians to maintain focus on and worship of Jesus. These early sermons and others, even from his pastorate in London, demonstrate that Bonhoeffer was keenly aware of the political and cultural events occurring in Germany.[29] In these example sermons and as expressed by Best, Bonhoeffer desired the focus to be on Christ, not Hitler or the Nazis. However, he did at times directly criticize the powerful government itself:

> The eternal law of individuality before God is terrible vengeful when offended and perverted. Thus the leader points to the office; leader and office, however, to the ultimate authority itself, before which Reich and state are penultimate authorities. Leader and office that turn themselves into gods mock God and the solitary individual before him who is becoming the individual and must collapse. Only the leader who is in the service of the penultimate and ultimate authority merits loyalty.[30]

Bonhoeffer's critique centered on the cultural posture on leadership, government, and national identity. His focus was not dishonoring Hitler or government officials, but his appraisal of the average German who unapologetically accepted the worldview of the Nazis and its practical implications. Bonhoeffer was also aiming to correct the acceptance by the Christian church of the values of the Third Reich which, as seen in the words of his sermons, was antithetical to the Scriptural understanding of faith in Christ. Thus, Bonhoeffer desired to encourage and challenge the worship of Jesus as foremost among the churches, and while unafraid to criticize the Nazi regime, he desired to see the worship of Jesus correct the beliefs and practices of the German church. He believed that the German church was a willing or mollifying accomplice in supporting the tenets of the Third Reich and the atrocities committed by the government and its agents.[31] Koehn lauded Bonhoeffer as having early recognition of the evils of Nazi ideology and action, and she acknowledged his courage to take a stance against the Nazis without many defenders.[32]

Bonhoeffer's focus on a proper view of Christ and its theoretical and functional implications was not accepted by the Nazi regime, and he clearly was an ardent opponent of the government and its leaders. Marsh commented, "He prayed for the defeat of his country and the assassination of the Führer, and in praying *with* conspirators, he conferred God's blessings on tyrannicide."[33] Bonhoeffer's outspoken, Christ-centered preaching and writing placed him as a clear opponent of the Third Reich. One of Hitler's appointed leaders of the German church, Bishop Theodor Heckel, identified him as a pacifist and enemy of the German nation.[34] While difficult for a twenty-first-century reader to understand the depth of this critique, a pacifist was antithetical to Nazi belief and practice.

As a pacifist who was against war, violence, and revenge, Bonhoeffer wrestled with the idea of assassinating Hitler. As a dedicated academic theologian with the heart of a caring pastor, he would not be tasked with personally assassinating any of the Nazi leaders, but he agonized over the stance he should take about the use of force against the awful leaders of Germany. In his influential modern-day biography on Bonhoeffer, Marsh discussed Bonhoeffer's struggle with what to do with Hitler:

> Bonhoeffer moved within an inescapable paradox; he gave his blessings to those who conspired to murder the Führer while affirming the essential nonviolence of the gospel. Responsible action meant killing the madman, even though such action violated God's commandment not to kill. How could it be otherwise? In the face of Hitler's atrocities, the way of nonviolence would bring inevitable guilt- both for the "uncontested" injustices and for the innocent lives that might have been saved. To act responsibly in these circumstances meant killing the madman if one could, even though such action violated God's commandment not to kill.[35]

Bonhoeffer's courageous leadership necessitated that he struggled through his own beliefs related to extreme action. He developed a perspective that was not the easy route, and these views and his involvement with others that conspired against the German government led to his imprisonment and eventual death.

According to Bonhoeffer, the state is in submission to divine authority, and if leaders elevate themselves to a place of equality with God or superiority above God, then no submission, obedience, or loyalty is required by citizens. As seen in previously cited writings and sermons, Bonhoeffer asked for Christians to be loyal to Jesus above any human leader.

Bonhoeffer courageously attempted to lead the German church to oppose the Nazis while giving their commitment and allegiance to Christ. His attitude and practice were demonstrated in his opposition to the Nazi policies against the Jews. Nancy Koehn wrote on leadership in crisis moments, and she tracked Bonhoeffer's resistance to the Aryan paragraph, which was the Nazi ideological statement on race and ethnicity that gave rise to their extreme persecution and murder of the Jews. She affirmed that Bonhoeffer was a solitary Christian voice against the ideology of the Nazis, and she outlined his threefold method of correct action by Christians: (1) question the state's actions, (2) care for and advocate for victims of oppression even if they are not Christians, and (3) attack the source of the persecution which in this case was the nation itself.[36] His writing on the Aryan paragraph and its relationship to the practices of the church show his principal disagreement with the laws against the Jews and their effect on the church:

> If the church excludes the Jewish Christians, it is setting up a law with which one must comply in order to be a member of the church community, namely, the racial law. It means that Jews can be asked at the door, before they can enter Christ's church in Germany, "Are you Aryan?" Only when they have complied with this law can I go to church with them. But by putting up this racial law at the door to the church community, the church is doing exactly what the Jewish Christian church was doing until Paul came, and in defiance of him; it was requiring people to become Jews in order to join the church –community. A church today that excludes Jewish Christians has itself become a Jewish Christian church and has fallen away from the gospel, back to the law.[37]

As a courageous and unaccompanied leader, Bonhoeffer exhorted the German church to resist the position of the government and the culture regarding the Jews. Bonhoeffer was not just a preacher and writer, but he lived his verbal convictions. He applied his beliefs on the Jewish Question to his own life as well. His involvement in attempts to aid Jews in escaping Germany led to his arrest.

Imprisonment

Dietrich Bonhoeffer was first arrested by the Gestapo in April of 1943 and remained a highly valued prisoner until his death at the hands of the Nazis on April 9, 1945. While some eyewitness testimonies of his imprisonment exist, much of the information about his imprisonment is learned from his own correspondence and writing during this time. Marsh described his arrest:

> When the knock on the door came on the evening of April 4, 1943, Bonhoeffer was sitting at his desk in his upstairs room. Some of his writings, including parts of his unfinished *Ethics*, were hidden in the rafters. The fictitious diary he had kept to disguise his conspiratorial activities lay on his desk. He surrendered to Gestapo agents and was led out of the house in handcuffs into a black Mercedes waiting at the end of the walkway. He was thirty-seven years old.[38]

The details described by Marsh demonstrated that Bonhoeffer was aware his activities could lead to trouble with the government regime, but he continued to act despite his knowledge of the risk.

The reason for his arrest was his involvement in attempting to rescue Jews, specifically by utilizing his permission to travel and communicate internationally to assist him in these efforts. Later, deeper connections were discovered with his involvement in resistance to the regime, and the discovery of this further activity led to the Nazis moving him to more secure prisons with stricter treatment. He was relocated from Tegel prison to the Gestapo prison in Berlin, and then in the final months of the war, he was transferred to the Buchenwald concentration camp. One of his major concerns while in prison was to minister to those in need, and he excelled at bringing comfort and spiritual care to his fellow inmates.[39] March commented on Bonhoeffer's posture while in prison stating that "he resisted the notion that he suffered in prison."[40]

In February of 1945, the Gestapo prison was heavily damaged by an allied forces air raid, so Bonhoeffer and others were relocated to the Buchenwald Concentration Camp. He was moved for the final time to the Flossenbürg concentration camp where he was executed by hanging at the direct order of Nazi leader Heinrich Himmler.[41] Leibolhtz reported on Bonhoeffer's imprisonment.

> "He refused to recant, and defied the Gestapo machine by openly admitting that, as a Christian, he was an implacable enemy of National Socialism and its totalitarian demands towards the citizen- defied it, although he was continually threatened with torture and with the arrest of his parents, his sisters and his fiancée, who all had a helping hand in his activities."[42]

Death

As he considered his activities, his commitment to Christ and to Christ's way of life was greater than his personal comfort within the Third Reich, or worse, passively going along with the ways of the regime. Confidence in God and the desire to build the true church in his home country drove this theologian to choose risk, danger, imprisonment, and eventual death. In *Jesus on Leadership,* Wilkes commented, "Trusting that God controls your eternity gives you the confidence to risk everything earthly to achieve anything eternal."[43] Bonhoeffer demonstrated his incredible trust in God while in prison when he wrote to his family and said, "I'm so glad to let you know that even here I'm having a happy Easter. Good Friday and Easter free us to think about other things far beyond our own personal fate, about the ultimate meaning of all life, suffering, and events; and we lay hold of a great hope."[44]

Bonhoeffer spoke and led courageously, striving to lead the German church away from agreement with National Socialism. This leadership through preaching, writing, and action led to his death. Heifetz and Linsky observed this as a key component to effective courageous leadership: "But the freedom to take risks and make meaningful progress comes in part from the realization that death is inevitable."[45]

The description of Bonhoeffer's death on the morning of April 9, 1945, was provided by the Flossenbürg camp physician. This witness to the execution of Dietrich Bonhoeffer remarked that he was impacted by the prisoner's demeanor while facing death. Bonhoeffer did not go to the gallows with fear, but with composure. He recounted that Bonhoeffer knelt and prayed before undressing and leaving his cell to walk outside to the place of execution. The doctor reported that Bonhoeffer prayed again immediately before the hanging. Emotionally stirred, the camp physician remarked that in his time as a doctor, he had not witnessed someone so brave and composed.[46]

Liebholtz explained one of the opportunities provided to Bonhoeffer to escape Nazi Germany and live peacefully in the United States:

> When war seemed inevitable, Bonhoeffer's friends abroad wanted him to leave Germany to save his life, for he was unalterably opposed to serving in the Army in an aggressive war. When asked by a Swede at the Ecumenical Conference at Fano, Denmark, in 1934, "What will you do when war comes?" he answered: "I shall pray to Christ to give me the power not to take up arms." In June 1939, American friends got him out of Germany. But soon he felt that he could not stay there, but that he had to return to his country. When he came to England on his return from the United States, his friends quickly realized that Bonhoeffer's heart belonged to his oppressed and persecuted fellow Christians in Germany and that he would not desert them at a time when they needed him most.[47]

With the opportunity to escape difficulty, Bonhoeffer returned to Germany to risk his life to save his country and the German people. These decisions aligned with leadership theorists about effective leadership: "Courageous leaders face unpleasant and even devastating situations with equanimity, then act firmly to bring good from trouble, even if their action is unpopular. Leadership always faces natural human inertia and opposition. But courage follows through with a task until it is done."[48] Heifetz's treatment of effective leadership affirmed that "leadership is dangerous, with or without authority."[49]

Bonhoeffer had early opportunities to escape punishment and execution by the Nazis and was aware of the direction his words and actions might take him. While the Nazis were responsible for the death of Dietrich Bonhoeffer, his own personal and leadership choices steered him to the point of facing death. Sanders observed that leadership had a cost, "To aspire to leadership in God's kingdom requires us to be willing to pay a price higher than others are willing to pay. The toll of true leadership is heavy, and the more effective the leadership, the greater the cost."[50] For Bonhoeffer, the cost of his courageous leadership was his happiness, his future, and his life.

Endnotes

[1] Charles Marsh, *A Strange Glory* (New York, NY: Alfred A. Knopf, 2014), 345.

[2] Matthew D. Kirkpatrick, ed. *Engaging Bonhoeffer: The Impact and Influence of Bonhoeffer's Life and Thought* (Minneapolis, MN: Fortress Press, 2016), xii.

[3] Marsh, *A Strange Glory,* p. 341.

[4] Geffrey Kelly & F. Burton Nelson, *The Cost of Moral Leadership: The Spirituality of Dietrich Bonhoeffer* (Grand Rapids, MI: Fortress Press, 2002), 35.

[5] Gene Wilkes, *Jesus on Leadership: Timeless Wisdom on Servant Leadership* (Carol Stream, IL: Tyndale House Publishers, 1998), 149.

[6] Elisabeth Elliot, *Through Gates of Splendor* (New York, NY: Harper & Brothers Publishers, 1957), 253.

[7] Ruth A. Tucker, *From Jerusalem to Irian Jaya: A Biographical History of Christian Missions, 2nd ed.* (Grand Rapids, MI: Zondervan, 2004), 13.

[8] Kelly & Nelson, p. 142.

[9] Acts 17:9b.

[10] Mark Thiessen Nation, Anthony G. Siegrist, & Daniel P. Umbel, *Bonhoeffer the Assassin?: Challenging The Myth, Recovering His Call To Peacemaking* (Ada, MI: Baker Academic, 2013), 229.

[11] Ibid, 230.

[12] Marsh, *A Strange Glory,* p. 392

[13] Mary M. Solberg, *A Church Undone: Documents from the German Christian Faith Movement, 1932-1940* (Minneapolis, MN: Augsburg Fortress Publishers, 2015), 1

[14] Richard B. Hays, *The Moral Vision of the New Testament: Community, Cross, New Creation, A Contemporary Introduction to New Testament Ethics* (New York, NY: Harper One, 1996), 408.

[15] Solberg, 170.

[16] Ibid, 170.

[17] Heifetz, p. 188.

[18] Peter G. Northouse, *Leadership: Theory and Practice, 7th Edition* (Newbury Park, CA: Sage Publications, 2015), 6.

[19] Ruth Haley Barton, *Strengthening the Soul of Your Leadership: Seeking God in the Crucible of Ministry* (Downers Grove, IL: IVP Books, 2018), 155.

[20] J. Oswald Sanders, *Spiritual Leadership* (Chicago, IL: Moody Publishers, 2007), 71.

[21] Ronald Heifetz and Marty Linsky, *Leadership on the Line: Staying Alive Through the Dangers of Change* (Cambridge, MA: Harvard Business Review Press, 2017), 210.

[22] Nation, Siegrist, & Umbel, 37.

[23] Isabel Best, ed., *The Collected Sermons of Dietrich Bonhoeffer*, vol. 1, trans. by Isabel Best et al. (Minneapolis, MN: Fortress Press, 2012), 67.

[24] Ibid., 68-69

[25] Ibid., 81.

[26] Ibid.

[27] Ibid., 85.

[28] Ibid., 85-86.

[29] Nation, Siegrest & Umbel, p. 55.

[30] Dietrich Bonhoeffer in Clifford Green and Michael P Dejonge, *The Bonhoeffer* R*eader: The Fuhrer and the Individual in the Younger Generation* (Minneapolis, MN: Fortress Press, 2013), 369.

[31] Kelley & Nelson, 131.

[32] Nancy Koehn, *Forged in Crisis: Leadership in Turbulent Times* (New York, NY: Scribner, 2017), 367.

[33] Marsh, *A Strange Glory,* 345.

[34] Ibid.

[35] Ibid., 345.

[36] Koen, 367.

[37] Dietrich Bonhoeffer in *The Bonhoeffer Reader: The Aryan Paragraph in the Church,* 383.

[38] Marsh, *A Strange Glory,* 352.

[39] Gerhard Liebolhtz, "Memoir," in *The Cost of Discipleship* (New York, NY: Touchstone, 1995), 18.

[40] Marsh, *A Strange Glory*, 353.

[41] Leibolhtz, 22.

[42] Ibid., 26.

[43] Wilkes, 149.

[44] Dietrich Bonhoeffer, *Letters and Papers From Prison* ed. Eberhard Bethge (New York, NY: Touchstone, 1971), 25.

[45] Heifetz and Linsky, 208.

[46] Kelly and Nelson, 35.

[47] Liebholtz, 17.

[48] Sanders, 72.

[49] Heifetz, 235.

[50] Sanders, 139.

BIBLIOGRAPHY

Barker, H. *The Cross of Reality; Luther's Theologia Crucis and Bonhoeffer's Christology*. Minneapolis, MN: Fortress Press, 2015.

Barnett, Victoria J. ed., *The Collected Sermons of Dietrich Bonhoeffer*, vol. 2, translated by Isabel Best et al. Minneapolis, MN: Fortress Press, 2017.

Barnett, Victoria J. "The Bonhoeffer Legacy as Work-in-Progress: Reflections on a Fragmentary Series," in *Interpreting Bonhoeffer: Historical Perspectives, Emerging Issues*, ed. Clifford J. Green and Guy C. Carter. Minneapolis, MN: Fortress Press, 2013.

Barton, Ruth Haley. *Strengthening the Soul of Your Leadership: Seeking God in the Crucible of Ministry*. Downers Grove, IL: IVP Books, 2018.

Bass, Bernard M. *A New Paradigm of Leadership: An Inquiry Into Transformational Leadership*, Alexandria, VA: U.S. Army Research Institute, 1996.

Bassett, Richard. *Hitler's Spy Chief: The Wilhelm Canaris Mystery*. London: Weidenfeld & Nicolson, 2005.

Bernier A, Carlson SM, Whipple N. "From external regulation to self-regulation: early parenting precursors of young children's executive functioning." Child Dev. 2010 Jan-Feb;81(1):326-39.

Best, Isabel ed., *The Collected Sermons of Dietrich Bonhoeffer*, vol. 1, trans. by Isabel Best et al. Minneapolis, MN: Fortress Press, 2012.

Bethge, Eberhard. *Dietrich Bonhoeffer: A Biography*, ed. Victoria J. Barnett, trans. Betty and Peter Ross, Frank Clarke, and William Glen-Doepel, and Eric Mosbacher, Rev. ed. Minneapolis, MN: Fortress Press, 2000.

Bethge, Eberhard. Translated by Rosaleen Ockenden, *Costly Grace: An Illustrated Biography of Dietrich Bonhoeffer*. New York, NY: Harper & Row Publisher, 1979.

Bethge, Eberhard. Translated by Eric Mosbacher. *Dietrich Bonhoeffer: Man of Vision, Man of Courage*. New York, NY: Harper & Row, 1970.

Bethge, Renate. "Foreword." In *The Cost of Moral Leadership: The Spirituality of Dietrich Bonhoeffer*. Grand Rapids, MI: Eerdmans, 2002.

Blackaby, Henry and Blackaby, Richard. *Spiritual Leadership: Moving People on to God's Agenda*. Nashville, TN: B&H Publishing Group, 2001.

Blake Robert R. and Mouton, Jane S. *The Managerial Grid: The Key to Leadership Excellence*. Houston, TX: Gulf Publishing, 1974.

Bonhoeffer, Dietrich. *Berlin: 1932-1933*, ed. Carsten Nicolaisen, Ernest-Albert Scharffenorth and Larry L. Rasmussen, trans. Isabel Best, David Higgins, and Douglas W. Scott, vol. 12, *Dietrich Bonhoeffer Works.* Minneapolis, MN: Fortress Press, 2009.

Bonhoeffer, Dietrich and Nelson, F. Burton. *A Testament to Freedom: The Essential Writings of Dietrich Bonhoeffer*, ed. Geffrey Kelly and F. Burton Nelson. New York, NY: Harpers Collins, 1995.

Bonhoeffer, Dietrich. *Creation and Fall: A Theological Exposition of Genesis 1-3,* ed. John W. de Gruchy, trans. Douglas Bax, vol. 3, *Dietrich Bonhoeffer Works.* Minneapolis, MN: Fortress Press, 2004.

Bonhoeffer, Dietrich "Act and Being" in *The Bonhoeffer Reader* Edited by Green, Clifford J. and DeJonge, Michael P. Minneapolis, MN: Fortress Press, 2013.

Bonhoeffer, Dietrich. *Dietrich Bonhoeffer Reflections on the Bible*, edited by Weber and Manfred. Peabody, MA: Hendrickson Publishers, 2004.

Bonhoeffer, Dietrich. *Discipleship*, ed. Victoria J. Barnett, trans. Barbara Green and Reinhard Krauss, Reader's ed. vol. 4, *Dietrich Bonhoeffer Works.* Minneapolis, MN: Fortress Press, 2015.

Bonhoeffer, Dietrich, *Ethics,* ed. Victoria J. Barnett, trans. Reinhard Krauss and Charles C. West, Reader's Ed. vol 6, *Dietrich Bonhoeffer Works.* Minneapolis, MN: Fortress Press, 2015.

Bonhoeffer, Dietrich. *Ethics.* New York, NY: Touchstone Books, 1955.

Bonhoeffer, Dietrich. "Eulogy for Adolf von Harnack" in *The Bonhoeffer Reader* Edited by Green, Clifford J. and DeJonge, Michael P. Minneapolis, MN: Fortress Press, 2013.

Bonhoeffer, Dietrich. "History and Good" in *The Bonhoeffer Reader* Edited by Green, Clifford J. and DeJonge, Michael P. Minneapolis, MN: Fortress Press, 2013.

Bonhoeffer, Dietrich "Jesus Christ and the Essence of Christianity" in *The Bonhoeffer Reader* Edited by Green, Clifford J. and DeJonge, Michael P. Minneapolis, MN: Fortress Press, 2013.

Bonhoeffer, Dietrich. *Letters and Papers From Prison.* Edited by Eberhard Bethge. New York, NY: Touchstone, 1971.

Bonhoeffer, Dietrich. *Letters and Papers From Prison*, ed. Victoria J. Barnett, trans. Isabel Best et al., Reader's ed. vol. 8, *Dietrich Bonhoeffer Works.* Minneapolis, MN: Fortress Press, 2015.

Bonhoeffer, Dietrich "Sanctorum Communio" in *The Bonhoeffer Reader* Edited by Green, Clifford J. and DeJonge, Michael P. Minneapolis, MN: Fortress Press, 2013.

Bonhoeffer, Dietrich. *The Collected Sermons of Dietrich Bonhoeffer*, ed. Isabel Best, Minneapolis, MN: Fortress Press, 2012.

Bonhoeffer, Dietrich. *The Communion of Saints: A Dogmatic Inquiry Into the Sociology of the Church,* trans. R. Gregor Smith. New York, NY: Harper and Row, 1963.

Bonhoeffer, Dietrich. *The Cost of Discipleship.* New York, NY: Touchstone Books, 2005.

Bonhoeffer, Dietrich. *Life Together.* New York, NY: HarperCollins, 1954.

Bonhoeffer, Dietrich "The History of Twentieth Century Systematic Theology" in *The Bonhoeffer Reader* Edited by Green, Clifford J. and DeJonge, Michael P. Minneapolis, MN: Fortress Press, 2013.

Bonhoeffer, Dietrich. *Theological Education at Finkenwalde: 1935–1937*, ed. Victoria J. Barnett and Barbara Wojhoski, trans. Douglas W. Stott, vol. 14, *Dietrich Bonhoeffer Works*. Minneapolis, MN: Fortress Press, 2013.

Bonhoeffer, Dietrich. *Theological Education Underground: 1937-1940*, ed. Victoria J. Barnett, trans. Victoria J. Barnett et al., vol. 15, *Dietrich Bonhoeffer Works* (Minneapolis, MN: Fortress Press, 2012.

Bosanquet, Mary. *The Life and Death of Dietrich Bonhoeffer.* Hatchett, United Kingdom: Hodder & Stoughton, 1968.

Bowen, Murray. *Family Therapy in Clinical Practice.* New York, NY: Jason Aronson, 1978.

Brooks, David. "At the Edge of the Inside," *New York Times*, June 24, 2016.

Burns, James Macgregor. *Leadership.* New York, NY: Harper & Row, 1978.

Burns, James. *Transforming Leadership.* New York, NY: Grove Press, 2003.

Bush, George W, "Speech in Berlin on May 23, 2002," accessed November 8, 2020, www.theguardian.com/world/2002/may/23/usa.georgebush.

Burleigh, Michael. *The Third Reich: A New History.* New York, NY: Hill and Wang, 2000.

Clinton, J. Robert. *The Making of a Leader: Recognizing the Lessons and Stages of Leadership Development.* Colorado Springs, CO: NavPress, 1998, 30-32.

Cochrane, Arthur. *The Church's Confession under Hitler.* Philadelphia, PA: Westminster Press, 1962.

Confino, Alon. "Why Did the Nazis Burn the Hebrew Bible? Nazi Germany, Representations of the Past, and the Holocaust," *The Journal of Modern History* 84, no. 2, June 2012.

Conger Jay A. and Kanungo Rabindra N. *Charismatic Leadership in Organizations.* Thousand Oaks, CA: Sage Publications, 1998.

Corey, Elizabeth. "Learning in Love," in April 2014 *First Things.*

Devine, Mark. *Bonhoeffer Speaks Today: Following Jesus at All Costs.* Nashville, TN: Broadman & Holman Publishers, 2005.

Duckworth, Angela. *Grit: The Power of Passion and Perseverance.* New York, NY: Scribner, 2016.

Elliot, Elisabeth. *Through Gates of Splendor.* New York, NY: Harper & Brothers Publishers, 1957.

Elshtain, Jean Bethke. "Bonhoeffer on Modernity: 'Sic et Non," *The Journal of Religious Ethics 29*(2001).

Evans, Richard. *The Third Reich in Power.* New York, NY: The Penguin Press, 2005.

Fleishman, Edwin. "The Description of Supervisory Behavior," *Journal of Applied Psychology,* no. 37 (1953).

George Graen and Mary Uhl-Bien, "Relationship-Based Approach to Leadership: Development of Leader-Member Exchange (LMX) Theory of Leadership over 25 Years" in *Leadership Quarterly* 6, no. 2 *(*1995): 219-247.

Goleman, Daniel. *Emotional Intelligence: Why it Can Matter More Than IQ.* New York, NY: Bantam Books, 1995.

Goleman, Daniel, Boyatzis, Richard, and McGee, Annie. *Primal Leadership: Unleashing the Power of Emotional Intelligence.* Boston, MA: Harvard Business Press, 2013.

Greenleaf, Robert. *Servant Leadership: A Journey Into the Nature of Legitimate Power & Greatness.* New York, NY: Paulist Press, 1977.

Haein Park, "The Face of the Other: Suffering, *Kenosis*, and a Hermeneutics of Love in Dietrich Bonhoeffer's *Letters and Papers From Prison* and Marilynne Robinson's *Gilead,*" *Renascence* Vol. 66, Issue 2 (Spring 2014): 103-118.

Harley, Jay. "Luther as a Transformational Leader" in *Luther on Leadership: Leadership Insights From the Great Reformer* ed. by David Cook. Eugene, OR: Wipf and Stock, 2017.

Hays, Richard B. *The Moral Vision of the New Testament: Community, Cross, New Creation, A Contemporary Introduction to New Testament Ethics.* New York, NY: Harper One, 1996.

Heifetz, Ronald. *Leadership Without Easy Answers.* Cambridge, MA: Harvard University Press, 1998.

Heifetz, Ronald & Linsky, Marty. *Leadership on the Line: Staying Alive Through the Dangers of Change.* Cambridge, MA: Harvard Business Review Press, 2017.

Hitler, Adolf. *Mein Kampf.* New York, NY; Houghton Mifflin, Adolf Hitler, 1924; repr., 1977

House, Paul R. *Bonhoeffer's Seminary Vision: A Case for Costly Discipleship and Life Together.* Wheaton, IL: Crossway, 2015.

Katz, Daniel, Maccoby, Nathan & Morse, Nancy. *Productivity, Supervision, and Morale in an Office Situation.* Ann Arbor, MI: Institute for Social Research, 1950.

Kelly, Geffrey B. "Editor's Introduction to the Reader's Edition of Life Together," in *Life Together*, ed. Victoria J. Barnett, trans. Daniel W. Bloesch, Reader's ed. *Dietrich Bonhoeffer Works.* Minneapolis, MN: Fortress Press, 2015.

Kelly, Geffrey. "Prayer and Action for Justice: Bonhoeffer's Spirituality," in *The Cambridge Companion to Dietrich Bonhoeffer,* ed. John W. de Gruchy. Cambridge, MA: Cambridge University Press, 1999.

Kelly, Geffrey and Nelson, F. Burton. *The Cost of Moral Leadership: The Spirituality of Dietrich Bonhoeffer.* Grand Rapids, MI: Eerdmans, 2002.

Kelly, Geffrey. "The Life and Death of a Modern Martyr," in *Christian History*, X:32:10, 37.

Kelly, Robert. *The Power of Followership: How to Create Leaders People Want to Follow and Followers Who Lead Themselves.* New York, NY: Doubleday, 1992.

Kelly, Robert. *Luther's Works.* Edited by Jaroslav Pelikan and Helmut T. Lehman. Philadelphia, PA: Fortress, 1955-86.

Kirkpatrick, 2016. *Engaging Bonhoeffer: The Impact and Influence of Bonhoeffer's Life and Thought.* Minneapolis, MN: Fortress Press, 2016.

Koehn, Nancy F. *Forged in Crises: Leadership in Turbulent Times.* New York, NY: Scribner, 2017.

Kohlberg, Lawrence. *The Philosophy of Moral Development: Moral Stages and the Idea of Justice.* New York, NY: Harper & Row, 1981.

Komives, Susan R. et al. "A Leadership Identity Development Model: Applications from a Grounded Theory," *Journal of College Student Development* 47, no. 4 (2006): 401-418.

Kouzes, James M. and Posner, Barry Z. *The Leadership Challenge: How to Make Extraordinary Things Happen in Organizations*, 3rd ed. San Francisco, CA: Jossey-Bass, 2002.

Lawrence, Joel. *Bonhoeffer: A Guide for the Perplexed.* New York, NY: T&T Clark International, 2010.

Leibholz, Gerhard. "Memoir," in *The Cost of Discipleship.* New York, NY: Touchstone, 1995.

Lewis, C.S. *The Collected Letters of C. S. Lewis*, ed. Walter Hooper, vol. 3. New York, NY: HarperCollins e-books; HarperSanFrancisco, 2004–2007.

Lewy, Guenter. *Harmful and Undesirable: Book Censorship in Nazi Germany.* New York, NY: Oxford University Press, 2016.

Marsh, Charles. *A Strange Glory: A Life of Dietrich Bonhoeffer.* New York, NY: Alfred A. Knopf, 2014.

Marsh, Charles. *God's Long Summer: Stories of Faith and Civil Rights.* Princeton, NJ: Princeton University Press, 1997.

Marsh, Charles. "The Overabundant Self and the Transcendental Tradition: Dietrich Bonhoeffer on the Self-Reflective Subject," *Journal of the American Academy of Religion 60* (1992).

Mason, John Brown. "Christianity Faces Caesarism," *The Sewanee Review 47* (1939).

Mason, John Brown "The Judicial System of the Nazi Party," *The American Political Science Review 38* (1944).

"Memorial to the Murdered Members of the Reichstag," Information Portal to European Sites of Remembrance, accessed November 20, 2020, https://www.memorialmuseums. org/eng/denkmaeler/view/1421/Memorial-to-the-Murdered-Members-of-the-Reichstag.

Mengus, Raymond. "Dietrich Bonhoeffer and the Decision to Resist," *The Journal of Modern History 64* (1992).

Metaxas, Eric. *Bonhoeffer: Pastor, Martyr, Prophet, Spy.* Nashville, TN: Thomas Nelson Publishers, 2011.

Nation, Mark Thiessen, Siegrest, Anthony G., & Umbel, Daniel P. *Bonhoeffer the Assassin? Challenging the Myth, Recovering his Call to Peacemaking.* Ada, MI: Baker Academic, 2013.

Neibuhr, Reinhold. *The Nature and Destiny of Man: A Christian Interpretation.* Louisville, KY: Westminster John Knox Press, 1996.

Niebuhr, Reinhold. *Moral Man and Immoral Society: A Study in Ethics and Politics.* Louisville, KY: Westminster John Knox Press, 1932.

Nelson, F. Burton. "Friends He Met in America," in *Christian History*, X:32:10, 37.

Northouse, Peter G. *Leadership: Theory and Practice, 7th Edition.* Newbury Park, CA: Sage Publications, 2015.

Nullens, Patrick. "Towards a Spirituality of Public Leadership: Engaging Dietrich Bonhoeffer," *International Journal of Public Theology* 7(2013): 91-113.

O'Shaughnessy, Nicholas. "Selling Hitler: Propaganda and the Nazi Brand," *Journal of Public Affairs, 9*(2009).

Palmer, Parker J. *The Courage to Teach: Exploring the Inner Landscape of a Teacher's Life.* San Francisco, CA: Jossey-Bass, 1997.

Pasada, G. and Kaloustian, G. *Attachment in Infancy.* Malden, MA: Wiley-Blackwell, 2010.

Pasquarello, III Michael. *Dietrich Bonhoeffer and the Theology of a Preaching Life.* Waco, TX: Baylor University Press, 2017.

Pennington, Jonathan T. *The Sermon on the Mount and Human Flourishing: A Theological Commentary,* Grand Rapids, MI: Baker Academic, 2017.

Pettegree, Andrew. *Brand Luther: How an Unheralded Monk Turned His Small Town into a Center of Publishing, Made Himself the Most Famous Man in Europe, and Started the Protestant Reformation.* London: Penguin Books, 2015.

Phillips, Donald T. *Martin Luther King, Jr. on Leadership: Inspiration & Wisdom for Challenging Times.* New York, NY: Grand Central Publishing, 1998.

Pine, Lisa. *Nazi Family Policy, 1933-1945.* Oxford: Berg Publishers, 1997.

Racz SJ, McMahon RJ. The relationship between parental knowledge and monitoring and child and adolescent conduct problems: a 10-year update. Clin Child Fam Psychol Rev. 2011 Dec;14(4):377-98

Rankin, Alex. "Dietrich Bonhoeffer, A Modern Martyr: Taking a Stand Against the State Gone Mad," *The History Teacher 40* (2006).

Roark, Dallas. *Dietrich Bonhoeffer.* Waco, TX: Word Books, 1972.

Root, Andrew. *Bonhoeffer as Youth Worker: A Theological Vision for Discipleship and Life Together.* Grand Rapids, MI: Baker Academic, 2014.

Sanders, J. Oswald. *Spiritual Leadership.* Chicago, IL: Moody Publishers, 2007.

Schlingensiepen, Ferdinand. *Dietrich Bonhoeffer 1906–1945: Martyr, Thinker, Man of Resistance*, trans. Isabel Best. New York, NY: T&T Clark, 2012.

Schwartz PD, Maynard AM, Uzelac SM. Adolescent egocentrism: a contemporary view. Adolescence. 2008 Fall;43(171): 441-8

Shamir, Boas, House, Robert, J. and Arthur, Michael B. "The Motivational Effects of Charismatic Leadership: A Self-Concept Based Theory" in *Organization Science* 4, No. 4 (November 1993): 1-17.

Shirer, William L. *The Rise and Fall of the Third Reich: A History of Nazi Germany.* New York, NY: Simon and Schuster, 1960.

Slane, Craig. *Bonhoeffer as Martyr: Social Responsibility and Modern Christian Commitment* Ada, MI: Brazos Press, 2004.

Sockness, Brent W. "Luther's Two Kingdoms Revisited: A Response to Reinhold Niebuhr's Criticism of Luther." *The Journal of Religious Ethics 20,1*(1992): 93-110.

Solberg, Mary M. ed. & trans., *A Church Undone: Documents From the German Christian Faith Movement, 1932-1940.* Minneapolis, MN: Augsburg Fortress Publishers, 2015.

Stein, Henry. *Classical Adlerian Depth Psychotherapy Volume 1: Theory and Practice: A Socratic Approach to Democratic Living.* The Alfred Adler Institute of Northwestern Washington, 2013.

Stott, John. *The Message of Romans.* Downers Grove, IL: InterVarsity Press, 1994.

Stroup, J. "Political Theology and Secularization Theology in Germany, 1918-1939: Emanuel Hirsch as a Phenomenon of His Time," *The Harvard Theological Review* 80 (1987).

Taylor, Simon. "Symbol and Ritual under National Socialism," *The British Journal of Sociology* 32 (December), 1981.

"The Barmen Theological Declaration," accessed March 9, 2019, http://www.sacred-texts. com/chr/barmen.htm.

Tucker, Ruth A. *From Jerusalem to Irian Jaya: A Biographical History of Christian Missions, 2nd ed.* Grand Rapids, MI: Zondervan, 2004.

Van Dyke, Michael. *Radical Integrity: The Story of Dietrich Bonhoeffer.* Uhrichsville, OH: Barbour Publishing, Inc, 2001.

Walmer, George, J. "Hitler and the German Church," *The North American Review* 237 (1934).

Warner, Marcus and Wilder Jim. *Rare Leadership: 4 Uncommon Habits for Increasing Trust, Joy, and Engagement in the People You Lead.* Chicago, IL: Moody Publishers, 2016.

Weber, Max. *The Theory of Social and Economic Organizations,* ed. Talcott Parsons, trans. A.M. Henderson and Talcott Parsons. New York, NY: Free Press, 1947.

Weikart, R. "The Troubling Truth about Bonhoeffer's Theology." *Christian Research Journal*, 35(6), 2012.

Williams, Reggie. "Bonhoeffer and King: Christ the Moral Arc," *Black Theology 9.3*(2011): 356-369;

Williams, Reggie. *Bonhoeffer's Black Jesus: Harlem Renaissance Theology and the Ethic of Resistance*. Waco, TX: Baylor University Press, 2014.

Williams, Reggie. "Christ-Centered Concreteness: The Christian Activism of Dietrich Bonhoeffer and Martin Luther King, Jr.," *Dialog: A Journal of Theology*, Vol. 53, Issue 3 (Sep 2014): 185-194.

Woeffel, James. *Bonhoeffer's Theology: Classical and Revolutionary*. Nashville, TN: Abingdon Press, 1970.

Zimmerman, Wolf-Dieter and Smith, Ronald Gregor. *I Knew Dietrich Bonhoeffer,* trans. By Kathe Gregor Smith. New York, NY: Harper & Row, 1966.